P9-CSC-772

NASCAR WINSTON CUP 2002

2002 NASCAR WINSTON CUP SERIES
AWARDS CEREMONY

Manhattan Center, New York, NY
December 6, 2002

Acknowledgements 2002

It is with great pleasure that UMI Publications, Inc., presents NASCAR Winston Cup 2002, the season chronicle of stock car racing's top series. Perhaps no other season in recent memory has better illustrated the winds of change swirling within the sport, as a group of "young guns" came to the forefront time and again to do battle against the sport's longtime superstars.

In just his third full season of competition, Matt Kenseth topped the series' win column with five, followed closely by sophomore driver Kurt Busch, with four. First-year drivers Jimmie Johnson and Ryan Newman staged a torrid fight for rookie honors, with Johnson scoring three wins and Newman taking the checkers in The Winston and at New Hampshire. Newman also broke a rookie record by winning six poles and took the series' annual Bud Pole Award on the way to being named NASCAR Winston Cup Series Raybestos Rookie of the Year.

Not to be outdone by the so-called youth movement, a handful of longtime veterans showed they weren't ready to pass the torch just yet. Mark Martin, Rusty Wallace, Jeff Gordon, Dale Jarrett and Ricky Rudd all had solid seasons, and their names were scattered among those of the new young stars in the top 10 of the final point standings. Sterling Marlin became "Mr. Consistency" and topped the points for most of the season before being sidelined with an injury. And who could forget Bill Elliott's stirring win in the Brickyard 400, coming on the heels of victory at Pocono?

But when the final checkered flag fell at Homestead-Miami Speedway, fourth-year driver Tony Stewart claimed his first NASCAR Winston Cup Series championship. It was quite a year for Stewart, whose quest began with a last-place finish in the Daytona 500 after his engine failed just two laps into the event. From there, Tony's uphill battle became one of elation vs. frustration until, in mid-summer at Watkins Glen, Stewart grabbed his third win of the season in convincing fashion, making a statement that the Home Depot team was not about to fold up their tents. From there, Stewart and his Joe Gibbs Racing team, led by crew chief Greg Zipadelli, went on a tear, finishing no worse than eighth on nine occasions and climbing to the top rung of the point ladder, where Stewart stayed for the final seven races of the 2002 campaign.

This publication would not be possible without the help and guidance of many fine people. At NASCAR, we'd like to recognize the efforts of Bill France, Mike Helton, George Pyne, Paul Brooks, Jim Hunter, Jennifer White, Paul Schaefer and Ashley Costello. Working with them has, as always, been a pleasure for all of us.

Obviously, the NASCAR Winston Cup Series wouldn't be what it is today without the overwhelming support of the R.J. Reynolds Tobacco Company. We would also like to recognize and thank Rick Sanders, Greg Littell, Rich Habegger, Denny Darnell, Dennis Dawson, Rob Goodwin, Sean Kinder, Mark Clodfelter, Karen Davis, Mark Rogers, Guy Morgan and Chad Willis for their assistance in our efforts here.

UMI is thankful to have Bob Kelly, who, for the 12th consecutive year, expertly produced what you'll read on the following pages. We cannot thank him enough for his insight, his wonderful ability to tell the season's story and his longtime dedication to authoring this series of books.

The same thing goes when it comes to the efforts of our "shooters." The photographers for this year's edition of the NASCAR Winston Cup Series story are again Don Grassman, Ernie Masche and Gary Eller of CIA Stock Photography and veteran free-lancer David Chobat. We are most grateful for their efforts in bringing the 2002 season to life through their images.

We owe a special thanks also to Melissa Jones, our Senior Customer Service Representative at Quebecor World Kingsport Book Services, for her patience and care in the production of this book.

Most of all, we'd like to thank NASCAR's legions of fans and followers, without whom everything we do here would be for naught. Therefore, we dedicate this publication to you, the fans of the sport.

Please enjoy.

Preproduction work provided by ISCOA (International Scanning Corporation of America).

ISBN# 0-943860-27-X

umi staff

publisher
Ivan Mothershead

associate publisher
Charlie Keiger

vice president
Rick Peters

controller
Lewis Patton

chief operating officer & vice president and national advertising manager
Mark R. Cantey – 1-800-357-6584
mark@umipub.com

national advertising sales
Paul Kaperonis – 1-800-357-8535
paul@umipub.com

managing editor
Ward Woodbury

associate editor
Gary McCredie

senior editor
Bob Kelly

art director
Brett Shippy

senior designer
Paul Bond

information systems
Chris Devera

customer service representatives
Mary Flowe, Amy Makepeace, Renee Wedvick

"Our sport's veterans fared well, but the "young guns" clearly underscored their competitive nature and served notice they will be factors in upcoming battles for the NASCAR Winston Cup Series title."

Bill France

Foreword 2002

When the 2002 NASCAR Winston Cup Series season is compared with other great years in our sport's history, it takes its place as one of the most competitive in the record books.

It was a year in which we saw 18 different race winners go to victory lane to celebrate their good fortune resulting from great car preparation, strategic moves on pit road by hard-working crew members and some excellent examples of driving skill.

It was also a year in which 15 different drivers won Bud Pole qualifying awards, earning entry into February's under-the-lights running of the Bud Shootout at Daytona International Speedway.

The 2002 season marked a year in which drivers with less than five years of NASCAR Winston Cup Series experience won 19 races and The Winston, our sport's all-star event. Our sport's veterans fared well, but the "young guns" clearly underscored their competitive nature and served notice they will be factors in upcoming battles for the NASCAR Winston Cup Series title.

This was the year when two outstanding rookies squared off to battle for the Raybestos Rookie of the Year title and had an immense impact on the season and the year-end point standings. Jimmie Johnson and Ryan Newman captured the headlines and the hearts of tens of thousands of fans with their on-track performances throughout the season. Ryan emerged as the Raybestos Rookie of the Year.

We all celebrated Tony Stewart's championship-winning effort in the Home Depot Pontiac fielded by Joe Gibbs Racing. Tony and his team staged a gritty drive for the title, coming all the way from worst to first during the season. Who would have thought that the team would rebound with a championship-winning effort after Tony lost the engine in his Pontiac on the second lap of the season-opening Daytona 500 and ended up 43rd – last – in the first race of the season?

All of us at NASCAR congratulate Tony, Greg, Joe and all of the members of the team in their come-from-behind effort that resulted in the championship. We believe that Tony's fierce competitiveness on the track will keep him in contention for more NASCAR Winston Cup Series titles in the future.

Throughout its history, our sport has been blessed with extremely loyal fans and we continue to be grateful for your support. You are the backbone of our sport and we appreciate your dedication and helping our sport continue to grow.

I hope you will enjoy reliving the 2002 NASCAR Winston Cup Series season as you enjoy this book. All of us at NASCAR look forward to seeing you at the tracks on the tour during the 2003 season.

Sincerely,

Bill France
Chairman

Table of Contents

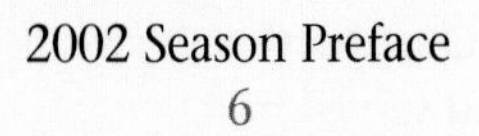

(Above) After two full seasons driving for Bill Davis Racing, Dave Blaney prepares to make the switch to the No. 77 Fords fielded by Jasper Motorsports, hoping to propel himself and the Jasper Engines team to the status of weekly contender.

(Right) One visible change for the 2002 NASCAR Winston Cup Series season results from the mandate that all personnel working on pit road – crew members as well as NASCAR officials – wear helmets in an effort to increase safety.

(Opposite Page) Three teams looking to establish themselves as weekly contenders in 2002 are the No. 97 Ford with sophomore driver Kurt Busch, one of four teams fielded by Roush Racing; the No. 30 AOL-sponsored team with former NASCAR Busch Series Champion Jeff Green, the second of three cars fielded by Richard Childress; and A.J. Foyt's No. 14 Conseco-sponsored Pontiac with Stacy Compton at the controls.

Preface 2002

The all-too-brief "off-season" between the 2001 finale at New Hampshire International Speedway and the 2002 lid-lifter at Daytona Beach, Fla., gave teams a short respite from the day-to-day and week-to-week grind. And as crew members prepared to head for the annual festival of speed called Speedweeks, many could not help but consider how much had changed since the season-opener last year at "The Beach."

The sport had lost icon Dale Earnhardt, a record number of drivers had emerged victorious during the ensuing season, and the nation had been shaken to its core by the vicious acts of September 11. The new television contracts between NASCAR and the networks had produced incredible numbers, but the country's economy was staggering and lurching, with several teams still searching for sponsorship as February approached. Other teams were on the brink of having sponsors pull back because of the state of the economy. Still, there was racing to be done and changes to be made within teams, as owners tried to find the right chemistry to enable them to move to the threshold of contending for the NASCAR Winston Cup Series championship.

Many expected defending champion Jeff Gordon to again lead the pack as he tried to defend his title. But the Dodge teams had shown considerable strength in 2001, their first season back in the fold in many years. With a year of on-track development by crews and engineers, no one would be surprised to see Sterling Marlin or Ward Burton emerge as a serious contender for the title.

At the same time, few expected Robert Yates Racing's Dale Jarrett and Ricky Rudd to have the same kind of inconsistent season they had in 2001. The same could be said for Bobby Labonte and Tony Stewart, as well as Mark Martin and Terry Labonte, among others. The lessons learned in 2001 by every team would be applied in 2002.

Few teams had remained intact during the

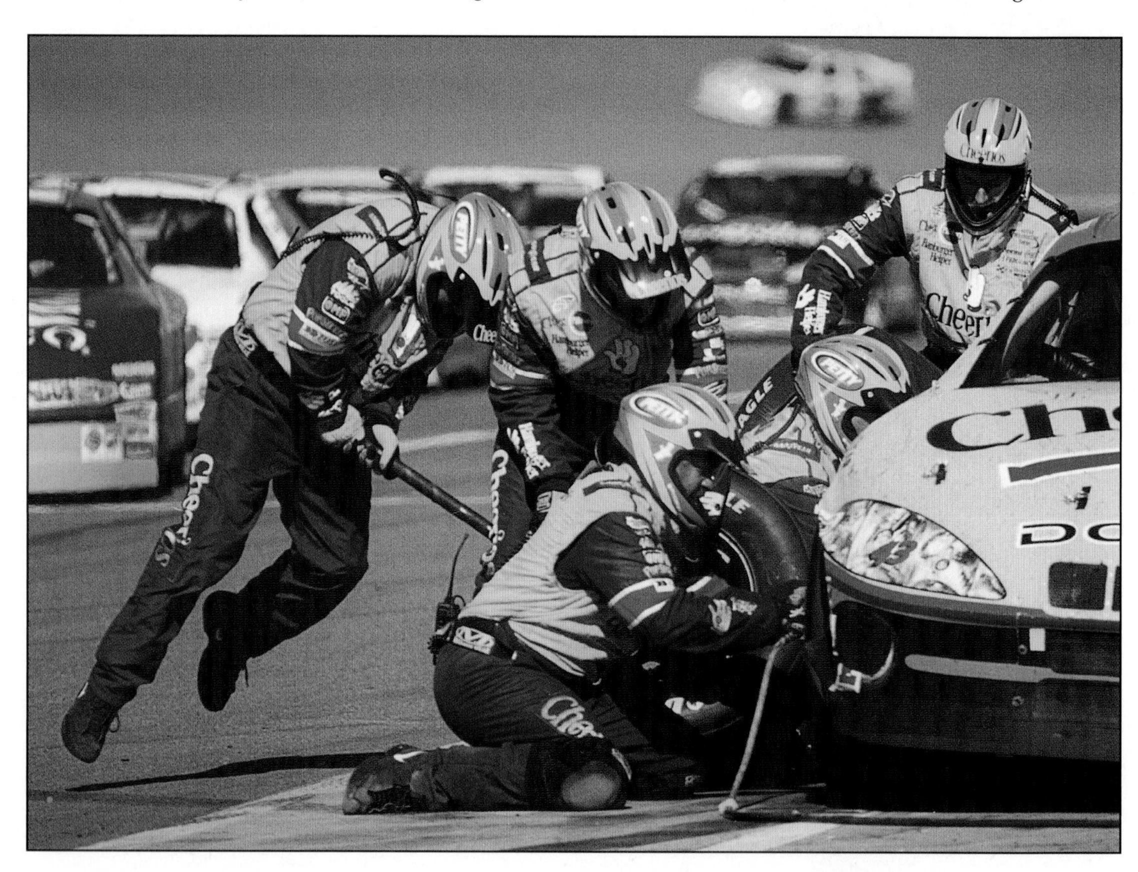

CONSECO
PONTIAC
GRAND PRIX
GOODYEAR
14
30
AOL
MONTE CARLO
GOODYEAR
Bud
CLEVITE
3M
INFOGRAMES
30
97
Rubbermaid
TAURUS
GOODYEAR
Holley
Bud
3M
OUTBACK
Bowman
INFOGRAMES
97

(Above) After four-plus years driving for Roger Penske, Jeremy Mayfield made the off-season switch to Ray Evernham's Dodge as teammate to Bill Elliott. That moved Casey Atwood, the 2001 pilot of the No. 19 Dodge, over to a joint effort with Evernham and Jim Smith.

(Above Right) Mike Skinner traded his blue Lowe's colors from Childress Racing for the Kodak yellow from the shops of Morgan-McClure. Now a veteran of five full seasons of NASCAR Winston Cup Series competition, Skinner hoped the change would propel him to his first big-league win.

(Right) Entering his sixth decade of fielding cars in the NASCAR Winston Cup Series, owner Junie Donlavey acquired sponsorship from Duke's Mayonnaise for his No. 90 Ford and installed veteran Rick Mast behind the wheel.

winter. Among drivers heading for Daytona with new crew chiefs were Rusty Wallace, with Billy Wilburn stepping into the lead role after Robin Pemberton made the decision to give up life on the road to spend more time with his family. Gary DeHart moved to a research and development role within Hendrick Motorsports, and Jim Long was named as Terry Labonte's new crew chief. Mark Martin prepared to partner with Ben Leslie, while Jimmy Fennig swapped teams within the Roush Racing organization to work with Kurt Busch.

Roger Penske folded the Mobil 1 team and prepared to field Ryan Newman's ALLTEL team with the number 12, allowing the car owner points to

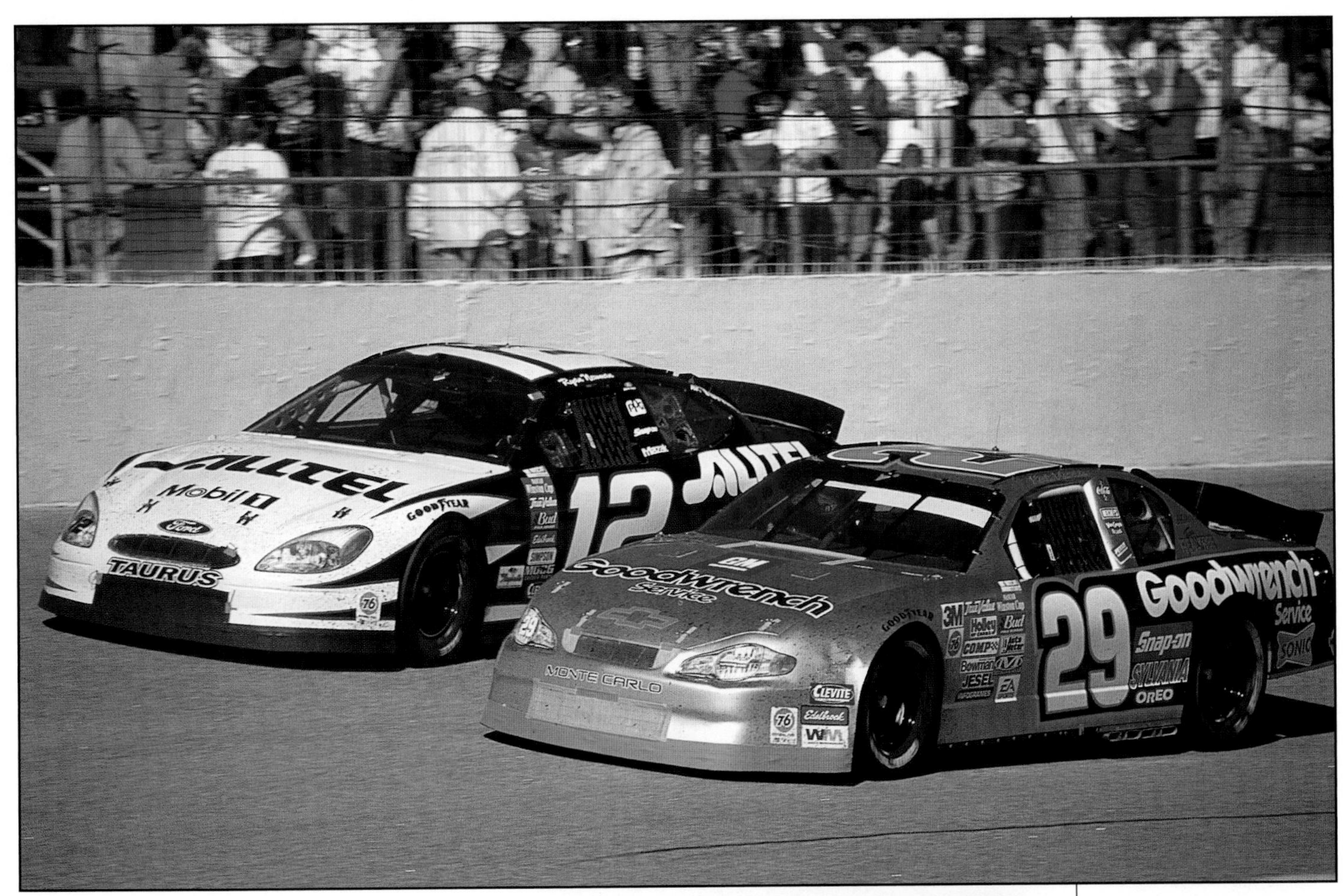

be transferred with the switch. Former No. 12 crew chief Peter Sospenzo and many of the team members were left out in the cold, with Matt Borlan named as Newman's head mechanic.

Hut Stricklin, Hills Brothers coffee and crew chief Philippe Lopez all joined Bill Davis Racing for the newly numbered "23" Dodge formerly driven by Dave Blaney and sponsored by Amoco. Chip Ganassi's second Dodge effort now carried Target Stores paint, a new number (41) and Jimmy Spencer behind the wheel, along with new crew chief Doug Randolph. At Hendrick Motorsports, a fourth team was created with the addition of Lowe's stores sponsorship, rookie driver Jimmie Johnson and crew chief Chad Knaus. Charlie Pressley moved to the Square D-sponsored team owned by Andy Petree with driver Bobby Hamilton. Pressley replaced Jimmy Elledge, who moved to the crew chief's role with Dale Jarrett's UPS Ford team at Robert Yates Racing. The opening was created when Todd Parrott was named Jarrett's team manager. By early April, though, Parrott reassumed his old role, leaving Elledge's future up in the air.

Kenny Wallace prepared to start the season behind the wheel of the Pennzoil Chevrolet fielded by Dale Earnhardt Inc., with Steve Park

(Above) NASCAR Winston Cup Series Rookie of the Year in 2001 and reigning NASCAR Busch Series Champion Kevin Harvick had a brief chance to take a breath during the off-season before embarking on his sophomore season behind the wheel of Richard Childress' GM Goodwrench Chevrolet. One preseason favorite for the 2002 rookie crown is Ryan Newman, installed full-time behind the wheel of Roger Penske's ALLTEL Ford.

(Left) Ryan Newman will surely be challenged for rookie honors by Jimmie Johnson, driving Chevrolets with joint ownership from Rick Hendrick and Jeff Gordon and sponsorship from Lowe's, which made the off-season move from Childress Racing to Hendrick Motorsports.

(Above) After finishing fifth in the 2000 point battle and fourth in 2001, driver Ricky Rudd prepares to compete in 2002 with every intention of challenging for his first NASCAR Winston Cup Series championship behind the wheel of the vaunted No. 28 Havoline Ford from Robert Yates Racing.

(Right) Driver Robby Gordon could only be optimistic entering 2002 after notching his first career win in the 2001 season finale at New Hampshire. With the departure of sponsor Lowe's, Cingular Wireless takes over on Richard Childress' No. 31 Chevrolet.

(Far Right) Shawna Robinson prepares to run a limited schedule of 24 events in 2002 driving for first-year team BAM Racing and owner Beth Ann Morgenthau.

still sidelined from his September NASCAR Busch Series accident at Darlington, S.C. After taking the latter part of the 2001 season off for knee surgery, Mike Skinner moved from Richard Childress Racing to the wheel of the Morgan-McClure Kodak Chevrolets, and Jim Smith put together a partnership with Ray Evernham that had Casey Atwood moving from Evernham's team to Smith's new Dodge Intrepids. That left the second seat open at Evernham's, with Jeremy Mayfield ready

to join the team after sitting out part of last year following his split with Penske Racing.

After claiming the NASCAR Busch Series title and the Raybestos NASCAR Rookie of the Year crown, Kevin Harvick prepared for the 2002 NASCAR Winston Cup Series wars with a new silver-and-black paint scheme on his Richard Childress-owned GM Goodwrench Chevrolet. Also at Childress' shop, crews were busily painting cars and equipment for the other two efforts to be fielded from Welcome, N.C. Jeff Green would pilot an America Online-sponsored Monte Carlo for the full season, while Cingular moved from Chip Ganassi's team to replace the departed

(Above) In the past, few rookies have come into the series driving for such well-funded and engineered teams as Jimmie Johnson enjoys in his Lowe's Chevrolet. Even better for Johnson, he will receive mentoring from four-time and reigning NASCAR Winston Cup Series Champion Jeff Gordon (24), who is also co-owner of the No. 48 team.

(Left) Entering the season, Tony Stewart simply has to be considered a threat to take it all in the championship chase. In three seasons of competition (104 starts), Stewart amassed 12 wins, 39 top fives and 66 top 10s, finishing fourth, sixth and second in the final point standings. With Home Depot on board for a fourth season and a solid crew backed by Joe Gibbs Racing, the orange-and-white Pontiac is ready to roll in 2002.

Lowe's stores sponsorship at Childress' shop. Robby Gordon was named to drive the black-and-orange "splotch" car.

The biggest question mark hung over Travis Carter's pair of entries for Joe Nemechek and Todd Bodine. With both cars sponsored by Kmart and with the company in serious financial difficulty, Carter was searching for replacement sponsorship. He planned to open the season with both cars but was unsure how long he could continue to field entries. Andy Petree and Brett Bodine were also in search of sponsorship. Petree had lost the Oakwood Homes colors and Bodine needed to replace the departed Ralph's grocery store chain.

As teams headed for The Beach, the split between manufacturers prepared to contest the season saw the Ford, Chevrolet and Dodge camps nearly equal. A total of 15 teams would field full-time Ford Taurus efforts, while 13 teams would chase the championship in Chevrolet Monte Carlos. Dodge efforts included 11 Intrepids. Just five teams would campaign the Pontiac Grand Prix model as development continued on the marque's new offering for the 2003 season.

Could Gordon successfully defend his title and claim a fifth NASCAR Winston Cup? Would Jarrett return to the front, or could Rudd win his first championship? Or would it finally be the year Mark Martin would claim the title he had chased for so long? Would youth be served in the shape of Kurt Busch, Kevin Harvick or Matt Kenseth in Jack Roush's fourth team Ford? And who would become this year's Raybestos Rookie of the Year? Both Ryan Newman and Jimmie Johnson were in well-funded teams with veteran crews behind them.

All these questions – and more – would be answered as teams began the season with the Daytona 500.

NASCAR Winston Cup Series Champion 2002

Tony Stewart

(Above) Tony Stewart gives a smile and a wave from the stage at Homestead-Miami Speedway as the newly crowned NASCAR Winston Cup Series champion.

(Right) After performing a celebratory burnout for the fans, Tony "Smoke" Stewart takes off on his victory lap with championship banner in hand, having just completed his quest to become the title holder.

(Opposite Page) After 140 starts over four seasons of working together, Tony Stewart and crew chief Greg Zipadelli have a chance to celebrate the pinnacle of their careers so far, the 2002 NASCAR Winston Cup Series championship.

After we finished second in last year's championship a lot of people said that it was just a matter of time before our Home Depot-sponsored team would win the NASCAR Winston Cup Series championship.

It all sounded good to us, after we had finished in the top six three times in the short history of this team owned by Joe Gibbs. So we headed for Daytona, and truly, we all thought we had a Pontiac capable of running at the front of the pack and winning the race. Well, that all came to an abrupt end after just two laps when the engine let go.

Instead of being around to challenge, and perhaps, win the Daytona 500, we were loading the car and heading home after being listed 43rd – last – on the results sheet. And that also meant we were last in the point standings after the first race of the season.

Certainly not the way we wanted to start the season, to say the least.

Each year we have tried to determine the weaknesses within our team, and then find the answers that would make us more competitive throughout the season, allowing us to mount a true challenge for the championship. That's where the leadership of Joe Gibbs and Greg Zipadelli has come into play.

Everyone knows about Joe and how he has always taken people and made them better with his ability to bring out the best in everyone. What a lot of people don't know is just how good Zippy is – not just as a crew chief, but also as a motivator, baby-sitter, coordinator, planner and all-around cheerleader. I am so fortunate to have him as my crew chief – and also as my friend.

Before Zippy joined Joe Gibbs Racing to be the crew chief on the Home Depot team, he won a pair of NASCAR Touring championships in the Featherlite Modified and Busch North series. He started working on Modifieds at the age of seven, and by the time he was 14, he was preparing race cars for his family-owned Sherwood Racing team. He wrenched Mike McLaughlin to the Modified title by the time he was 20. In 1997, he earned his second championship as a crew chief, steering Mike Stefanik to the Busch North Series crown.

After earning his second championship ring, Zippy headed south in 1998 to join Roush Racing as Jeff Burton's chassis specialist. After helping Jeff

NASCAR
Winston Cup
CHAMPION
2002
20 TONY STEWART
THE HOME DEPOT
PHILIPS
Coca-Cola
GOODYEAR
SIMPSON
NASCAR
Old Spice
NASCAR
Winston Cup
Series
MBNA
PONTIAC
CHAMPION
ConAgra
Foods
NASCAR
Winston Cup
Series

The Home Depot team is loaded with quality talent, including the pit crew, which kept their driver and car in the heat of battle throughout the year. Stewart is quick to give credit to his crew members, citing any NASCAR Winston Cup Series championship is truly an all-out team effort.

finish fifth in the point standings that year, he was Joe and Jimmy Makar's choice to become crew chief for the "20" team in 1999.

I tell you all this about Zippy because a lot of people don't know much about his background. A lot of people think he just arrived at the NASCAR Winston Cup Series level, but in truth, he's been around race cars and has been working on them for almost all his life. Along the way, he learned how to make a crew work, as well as make a car work. And more than anything else, perhaps, his talents in every aspect of the team made him the glue that held the team together this season and enabled us to mount the championship run that we did.

We knew we had to make ourselves better last winter if we were going to really be contenders, and we knew we had to do an even better job than the other leading teams because they also were concentrating on making themselves better. We knew we could win races – we proved that in each of the team's first three years – but we needed to improve our consistency and make ourselves better at some of the tracks where we had not been as competitive as we felt we should be.

And it was Zippy, working with Joe, who made it happen. I can't forget Home Depot here, either. Our partnership with Home Depot, which began with company founders Bernie Marcus and Arthur Blank and continues with current CEO Bob Nardelli, along with the ongoing support and cheerleading on the part of their more than 280,000 associates, meant we had the resources and encouragement to make the changes we needed to make.

We came back from Daytona with the Bud Shootout trophy and last place in the Daytona 500. How's that for both ends of the spectrum? At Rockingham we got back in our groove and finished fourth, and we followed that with a fifth place at Las Vegas. We had climbed back through the points in just two races, and our Atlanta win put us even closer to the front. That victory was a sweet one, coming in Home Depot's hometown in front of a huge crowd of orange-clad fans.

We hit a little inconsistent string, finishing 36th at Darlington and 15th at Bristol, fifth at Texas and third at Martinsville before we were 29th at Talladega and California. It seemed to all of us like we were just riding the roller coaster, and it continued with a win at Richmond, sixth at Charlotte, 11th at Dover, seventh at Pocono, 16th at Michigan, second at Sonoma. We went back to Daytona and finished 39th, and in the next race we were third at Chicagoland. At New Hampshire we finished 39th, and then we were seventh at

Pocono. It seemed every time we had a good run, we would have a problem in the next race. No one had any answers, and it was frustrating to all of us because we knew we were a good team, with good pit stops, good engines, good chassis setups and a good bunch of guys working their tails off. We just couldn't seem to get things sorted out.

At Indianapolis we won the pole and led a bunch of laps but finished 12th. Everyone knows what happened there, and my mistakes practically tore our team apart. I had made a real mess of things, and the reality of the situation was that Zippy was the guy who righted the ship and got us all pulling in the right direction. We came back the very next week at The Glen and won, and then went to Michigan and took second. Even a 24th at Bristol couldn't make us blink. Suddenly we were back together again, and after finishing eighth at Darlington and then 30th at Richmond, it all started clicking for us.

For the next seven races, we didn't finish lower than 11th. Along the way we finally broke through that fifth-place barrier in the standings, and we just kept chipping away from there on out. For a while we weren't thinking championship at all, we were just trying to go out every week and win races. We figured if we won races, the points would take care of themselves, and although we didn't win again after The Glen, we battled for every point and position in every race.

Finally we got to within 100 points of the lead, and at that point we sort of all looked at each other and said, "Hey, we've got a real chance to win the title." And just that quickly, we got our second wind. We took over the point lead at Talladega, and although we were a little nervous, because it seemed that every time someone got in the lead they'd lose it the next race, we just kept our focus and raced for wins.

We were third at Charlotte, 11th at Martinsville and then fourth at Atlanta. While we kept running well, all the other contenders were having a problem in one race or another. By the time we got to Rockingham and Phoenix, we knew that we were in position to win the championship if nothing happened to us. Even an ugly day at Rockingham where we finished 14th couldn't put us off-track. At Phoenix we finished eighth and then went to Homestead able to watch and see what we needed to do.

We tested at Homestead and had the fastest car, and I had the funniest feeling the night before the race. I was so calm and relaxed it was unreal. I guess knowing we had such a good history at the track – two wins in three tries – made me feel that way.

Then about 10 laps into the race, I realized we did not have the car to win the race like I thought we would have. In fact, what we had was handling like Santa's sleigh on gravel. I mean it was awful, and I thought to myself, "Whoa, we have issues here. This isn't like a normal Sunday at Homestead." It kept getting worse and I kept falling back and eventually lost a lap. At that point, I started getting nervous.

But it was also at that point that Zippy came on the radio and said, "Look, don't worry, we'll fix it and you'll get your lap back. Just believe." So I did, and they did, and we did, and then the changes they made got that Home Depot Pontiac racey again. And although we finished 18th, it was enough to ensure that we won the title.

None of us could have won the championship without the whole group. There's no question

At Watkins Glen, the 22nd race of the season, Stewart put on a brilliant driving display to notch his third win after a very difficult week following Indianapolis. From there, the Home Depot team began firing on all cylinders, fueling a rise to the top of the standings.

The clincher in Miami was not without a few tense moments, when the Home Depot Pontiac handled poorly and dropped Stewart into the pack where anything can happen – and often does. With moral support from Zipadelli and chassis adjustments by the crew, Stewart finished with a 38-point cushion over runner-up Mark Martin.

that it was a team effort this year. And I know that everyone always says that, but unless you have been in the chase for the title, you really don't know what all goes into winning the championship and how hard it is to do it. Zippy was so instrumental in helping the team keep its focus, even while all the stuff was happening to us this year.

There were times that people wanted to leave because they didn't want to work for me. I didn't blame them one bit. I wouldn't have worked for me, either. I've had heart-to-hearts with a lot of crew guys in Zippy's office and I've said, "I'm sorry for what I am doing to you guys. I'm not doing it because I want to hurt you; I'm doing it because I'm frustrated. If you bear with me, we'll make it right." Hopefully, winning the championship helped make some of the bad situations right. Regardless, these guys have stood behind me, through thick and thin, for four years. And the end result is that we're NASCAR Winston Cup Series champions.

Through it all, Zippy was the glue that held everyone together. He was the friend that got me back on track and got my mindset right to do what we did the rest of the year. He led the team, made the crew chemistry right, and I can't say enough about the way he made everything work.

In some ways, it was ironic that Mark Martin was the driver I had to beat for the championship in the final races. When I was a rookie driver in the NASCAR Busch Series, he was the one guy I went to for advice. And he always took time for me. I was a nobody running a part-time schedule and Mark always made time for me. He gave me plenty of good tips and answered questions that I had – and I had a lot of them.

When I was in the battle for the 1997 IRL title, it was with a buddy of mine, Davey Hamilton. Knowing that I was racing him for it, knowing that one of the two of us was going to win it was a good feeling. It was someone that I was a friend with, and I felt that way about racing Mark for this championship.

No matter what happened in that final race, and if we weren't fortunate enough to get the job done, the championship would then go to someone that I have a lot of respect and admiration for. Mark is very deserving of the championship. Some guys go their whole career and don't ever win a championship. I hope that doesn't happen to Mark. He is very deserving and I think that before it's all said and done, he'll get his.

One of the things that make this championship so special is the quality of the competition. We say it week in and week out, but it's the truth. Every week, 43 of the best stock car racers in the country are racing against each other in cars that are under such strict rules that they're very, very competitive with each other. It's hard to get a distinct advantage over anybody else. It's not like Formula One where one manufacturer finds something that helps them for the whole season, or the IRL where one team really gets on a roll and just wins three or four races in a row. It's very hard to do in this sport.

With the caliber of teams and car owners and crew chiefs and drivers that are out here, it really makes you respect the championship. This is one that, with all the pressures that go with it, the pressure itself is another obstacle that has to be overcome. You do a lot of work here and, for the amount of work that is required and asked of us, to be able to win the championship and accomplish this goal is what makes this championship such a special one to win.

A lot of people have asked if I will be able to represent the sport properly as its champion and as an ambassador for NASCAR Winston Cup Series racing. Honestly, I don't know how people will rank me with other champions from the past when this next year is over. I do understand that NASCAR is doing its very best to take care of everybody. Everyone is trying to do a job and the pressures get greater and greater. NASCAR is doing its best, and I can only try to do my best as well.

I'm just a race driver. I've never been one that

likes the limelight or has that bouncy television personality like some champions have had in the past. I'm just me. I'm the guy who has been racing since I started in go-karts when I was seven. I'm the guy who has raced all his life and done some nasty jobs along the way like sealing parking lots and driving a tow truck.

I'm the guy who was working at a machine shop for $5 an hour in Rush County, Indiana, having to bust my way through snow banks to get to and from work. I sat in a big barn on a metal stool on a concrete floor at a drill press, picking parts out of a cold, five-gallon bucket of solvent and de-burring the insides of the tubing. I'll never forget going to the Copper Classic in Phoenix, the first time I ever went out there in a Silver Crown car, and ran second to Mike Bliss. My share of the prize money was $3,500.

I went back to work at the drill press Monday and I found myself trying to figure out how many of the $5-an-hour hours I would have to work to make $3,500. And I quickly figured out that I like the racing hours a whole lot more than the drill press hours.

I haven't forgotten those days, and it's knowing where I've come from that has shaped who I am. I'm not a politician. I'm just a race driver who grew up in a small Indiana town. I hope I can be a good champion for the sport. I hope I can represent NASCAR, Joe Gibbs Racing and The Home Depot well. But I'm sure my idea of what a champion should or shouldn't be is different from other people's ideas.

I've always said that you never get an instructional video or a "freshman pamphlet" that tells you, "This is what your life is going to be like, this is how you do things, this is what is going to happen to you while you're in the garage area." It's trial and error, and Lord knows I've had enough trials and errors – and more errors than trials. But as you go on, you learn. You learn how to deal with things, and it's a continual learning process. I can only keep studying.

One thing I do know, however, is how great the NASCAR fans are. You may pull for me or you may not – everyone has his or her favorites. What I truly know is that you are the greatest fans of any sport in the world. You support the sport like no other group of fans has ever done and you are directly responsible for the growth of the sport. All of us at Joe Gibbs Racing and all the associates at The Home Depot salute you for your unwavering support of NASCAR Winston Cup Series racing.

Best regards,

#20

Tony Stewart
2002 NASCAR Winston Cup Series Champion

(Left) Joe Gibbs (left) joins Tony Stewart and Greg Zipadelli (right) to show off their new hardware. For Gibbs, who became a team owner 11 seasons ago, the championship trophy will make a perfect bookend to the one he got two years ago when Bobby Labonte took the title.

(Below) Although Stewart is somewhat known to have a fiery personality, he is, at heart, merely a "country boy" from central Indiana who's just a race driver. Not one to seek the limelight, Tony relishes his time behind the wheel where he can simply do what he loves most.

(Top Right) Veteran campaigner Dave Marcis celebrates gaining entry into his 33rd – and final – Daytona 500. Marcis, whose career began at Daytona 34 years ago, had announced that his driving days would end with this event.

(Middle Right) Dale Earnhardt Jr. celebrates his victory in the NASCAR Busch Series 300-mile race with Teresa Earnhardt. "Little E" continued to put the Earnhardt name in the record book for the event his dad won a record seven times, including five straight from 1990-94.

(Below Right) Tony Stewart hoists his second consecutive trophy for winning the Bud Shootout with crew chief Greg Zipadelli joining in the celebration. Stewart added an IROC win to his Speedweeks spoils but fell victim to engine failure in the opening laps of the Daytona 500.

(Below) Brothers Brett (left) and Geoffrey Bodine – two of three Bodines entered in the Daytona 500 – walk pit road as they've done many times before. Geoffrey, driving in a one-race deal for Phoenix Racing, had a fine performance in the "500," finishing third, while Brett took the 16th position after recovering from a spin at the 100-lap mark.

A year had passed since teams assembled at Daytona International Speedway for the 2001 running of the Daytona 500, but no one had forgotten what happened in the final lap of that event. The loss of Dale Earnhardt had hung over the sport throughout the 2001 season and there was no way to erase the memories.

Time had passed, the sport had moved on as it always does, and America was still smarting from the nightmarish events of September 11. The nation's economy appeared to be very slowly clawing its way out of recession, but when the economy struggles, one of the first budget categories to be chopped is advertising and marketing. Several teams arrived at Daytona still in search of sponsorship for the year, hoping a strong showing at the biggest race of the season would show those eyeing the sport there were still opportunities to sign on with competitive efforts.

One of the teams in the financial crunch was the Travis Carter/Carl Haas effort sponsored by the Kmart Corporation. Just a month before the season began, Carter was told that the national "department store" chain would continue to back his two Fords driven by Todd Bodine and Joe Nemechek. By the time the team arrived at Daytona, however, Kmart's bankruptcy filing had affected the sponsorship program. Carter would have financing from the company for the first two races of the season – Daytona and Rockingham, N.C. – but after that, things were exceedingly unclear. It didn't look good for the "Blue Light Specials."

Melling Racing fielded its Dodge for Robert Pressley with a one-race sponsorship from Brand Source, while Brett Bodine was still in search of a major sponsor for his Ford team. Shawna Robinson was also in search of money for her season effort, and Andy Petree was still hunting for dollars to replace the departed Oakwood Homes. Petree had entered the No. 33 in the Daytona 500 with Mike Wallace behind the wheel, but it was a one-race effort unless new funding could be found. Richmond, Va., car owner Junie Donlavey had a half-season deal with Duke's mayonnaise for Rick Mast, but he was searching for additional dollars to complete the schedule. Carl Long and the Mansion Motorsports team were also searching for sponsorship for the season.

While those teams were scrambling, Ricky Craven and the PPI team were quietly celebrating a two-year sponsorship extension by the folks at Tide. Casey Atwood, behind the wheel

of Jim Smith's Dodge, had found sponsorship with the new Sirius Satellite Radio effort. Target, ALLTEL and America Online had all stepped their programs up to full-time status from last year, with Jimmy Spencer, Ryan Newman and Jeff Green, respectively, wheeling mounts carrying the corporate colors.

(Left) Outside pole-winner Kevin Harvick (left) congratulates Jimmie Johnson on taking the Bud Pole for the Daytona 500. Johnson's Lowe's Chevrolet barely edged the GM Goodwrench Monte Carlo by a mere 16-thousandths of a second to make Johnson just the third rookie in history to capture the Daytona 500 pole.

Fans familiarized themselves with new teams, crew chiefs, sponsors and paint schemes, and they also found time to remember Earnhardt and his career. Tens of thousands passed over the new Dale Earnhardt (pedestrian) Bridge, spanning International Speedway Boulevard, and thousands of others paid a visit to the new (and exceptional) nine-foot-tall bronze statue of Earnhardt celebrating his 1998 Daytona 500 victory.

With 53 cars on hand, it was clear that qualifying times would be important, and as many as 10 drivers found themselves in the position of having to race their way into the field via strong finishes in the Gatorade Twins – the 125-mile qualifying races unique to Daytona that set the majority of the field behind the front row.

Jeff Gordon, obviously ready to begin pursuit of his fifth career NASCAR Winston Cup Series championship, just missed claiming a front-row

(Below) Kurt Busch (97) and Robby Gordon (31) race side by side in front of Mark Martin (6), with Michael Waltrip looking for room on the inside. Busch led 15 laps late in the race and stayed among the leaders to finish fourth, while Roush teammate Martin came all the way from the 39th starting spot to finish sixth.

DEI teammates Michael Waltrip (15) and Dale Earnhardt Jr. (8), who combined for a 1-2 finish in last year's Daytona 500, run together along the inside while John Andretti takes Richard Petty's Dodge up near the wall. After winning his Gatorade Twin, Waltrip stayed out of trouble and scored a top-five finish, while Earnhardt Jr., who started fifth, suffered tire problems that damaged his right-front fender and spoiled his run for the win.

position, and Pressley showed the Melling Racing Dodge's mettle by turning in the fourth-fastest lap of the Bud Pole qualifying session. The laps by Gordon and Pressley were laudable, but the heroes of the hour were Jimmie Johnson and Kevin Harvick.

Johnson, driving a Lowe's Monte Carlo for co-owners Rick Hendrick and Jeff Gordon, became the third rookie in history to claim the Daytona 500 pole, matching the feat accomplished by Loy Allen in 1994 and Mike Skinner in 1997. Harvick, the series' reigning Raybestos Rookie of the Year, was elated when he put Richard Childress' GM Goodwrench Chevrolet on the front row where it had been so many times in the past when driven by Earnhardt.

It was clear following qualifying that the Ford teams were struggling. The fastest Taurus in the field after the session was Dale Jarrett's UPS Ford, in 13th and nearly two miles per hour slower than Johnson's Chevrolet. NASCAR officials responded by allowing the Ford teams to trim a second quarter-inch off their rear spoilers.

The Budweiser Shootout gave drivers an indication of how their mounts would perform in traffic, and it appeared the Ford teams still had their troubles. Tony Stewart and teammate Bobby Labonte had their Joe Gibbs Pontiacs at the front of the field, and as the race drew to a close, Dale Earnhardt Jr. fought his way into contention.

After pit stops, a five-car pack broke away and there was not a Ford to be seen. Stewart, Gordon, Ken Schrader, "Little E" and Sterling Marlin were the contenders for the victory, and Tony's orange-and-black Home Depot Pontiac was the class of the field. Nothing Earnhardt Jr. did could change the course of the finish and Stewart rolled to his second straight Bud Shootout crown.

In the first of the Gatorade Twins, Jeff Gordon took the lead on the opening lap and rolled to an easy victory, beating "Little E" and Schrader. Michael Waltrip won the second 125-miler, keeping Stewart, Jerry Nadeau and Harvick behind his Chevrolet as he wove to the checkered flag.

Between the finishing order of the Gatorade Twins and the qualifying times posted, the field for the 2002 Daytona 500 was finalized. When the list was completed, several drivers found themselves on the outside looking in for the biggest race of the year. Hut Stricklin, Greg Biffle, Rick Mast, Buckshot Jones, Jimmy Spencer, Bobby Gerhart, Hermie Sadler, Kirk Shelmerdine, Carl Long and Norm Benning all failed to make the field, while Dave Marcis was in the lineup for the last race of his long and storied career.

The race, however, did include some long-shot entries, which had established their strength during practice and qualifying. Shawna Robinson was in the field, as was Geoffrey Bodine in a Phoenix Racing Chevrolet owned by James Finch.

Stewart added to his Daytona hardware by winning the IROC opener and Earnhardt Jr. returned a Chevrolet bearing Richard Childress' famed "3" to victory lane at Daytona by notching a solid triumph in the NASCAR Busch Series 300-mile race.

Finally, the time had arrived for the Daytona 500 field to take the green, ending long months of anticipation for millions of race fans. Few could imagine how bizarre this year's edition of the classic event would turn out.

Just two laps into the race, Tony Stewart lost the engine in his Home Depot Pontiac, and Earnhardt Jr.'s hopes for victory were quashed when a pair of cut tires ended his challenge. An 18-car accident on lap 149, triggered by a slight collision between Kevin Harvick and Jeff Gordon, ended the hopes of many others.

With the field shuffled after some lead-lap drivers chose to pit while others remained on the track during the seventh caution of the event, Kurt Busch became the leader. Jeff Gordon, running second on the restart, immediately mounted a challenge and held the point through the eighth caution period, brought out by Robby Gordon's second-turn spin with just over eight laps remaining.

If that wasn't enough excitement, when the field took the green flag on lap 195 – and before the pack could make it all the way around the

(Left) Kevin Harvick receives tires and fuel from his GM Goodwrench crew on pit road. Although fast on the track, Harvick could not avoid the multi-car accident on lap 148 that brought his race to a premature end.

(Below) The field of 43 cars, tightly bunched and three wide at nearly 200 miles per hour, streaks through Daytona's 31-degree banking to kick off the season in grand style.

(Right) Ward Burton hoists his trophy for all to see in what is easily the biggest win of his career. The victory was his fourth in NASCAR Winston Cup Series competition, all coming while driving for team owner Bill Davis.

(Far Right) Ward Burton (22) holds his own on the inside with Dale Jarrett (88), Jeff Green (30) and Bill Elliott (9) trailing in three-wide formation. Rookie Ryan Newman, driving the ALLTEL Ford for Penske Racing, stays low on the way to a strong seventh place in his NASCAR Winston Cup Series Daytona debut.

track – Michael Waltrip spun and several others followed suit. At the same time, Sterling Marlin made a bid for the lead, and when Gordon moved to block him the two collided, with Gordon spinning out.

The red flag came out to clean up the mess and the field was brought to a stop on the backstretch. Marlin climbed out of his car to assess the damage from his collision with Gordon and made the mistake of pulling out his car's crumpled fender. As no work on the cars is allowed under the red flag, NASCAR penalized Marlin by sending him to the back of the longest line on the restart. Marlin's miscue ended his hopes of victory. He, however, was not the only driver to feel the wrath of the pit-road police. Gordon, Rusty Wallace and Jeff Green also were penalized for heading onto pit road too soon.

With just three laps to go, Ward Burton found himself leading the Daytona 500 in his Caterpillar Dodge, while Geoffrey Bodine, Elliott Sadler, Dale Jarrett, Mark Martin and Ryan Newman were right behind him. Ward, who had led the most laps in last year's version of the event before being collected in a multicar accident, was not about to let this one get away.

Sadler immediately fought his way past Bodine, but he had nothing with which to challenge Burton. The soft-spoken Virginian eased his way to the checkered flag, bringing Dodge to Daytona's victory lane for the first time since 1977, and just one year since the Dodge Intrepids returned to NASCAR Winston Cup Series competition.

Sadler finished second ahead of the surprising Bodine, while Kurt Busch rallied to take fourth ahead of Michael Waltrip, Martin and Newman. The hapless Marlin, after pitting for four fresh tires, fought his way to an eighth-place finish ahead of Jeff Gordon and Johnny Benson.

Daytona 500 final race results

Fin. Pos.	Start Pos.	Car No.	Driver	Team
1	19	22	Ward Burton	Caterpillar Dodge
2	41	21	Elliott Sadler	Motorcraft Ford
3	35	09	Geoffrey Bodine	Miccosukee Indian Gaming Ford
4	15	97	Kurt Busch	Rubbermaid Ford
5	4	15	Michael Waltrip	NAPA Chevrolet
6	39	6	Mark Martin	Pfizer/Viagra Ford
7	23	12	Ryan Newman	ALLTEL Ford
8	13	40	Sterling Marlin	Coors Light Dodge
9	3	24	Jeff Gordon	DuPont Chevrolet
10	38	10	Johnny Benson	Valvoline Pontiac
11	29	9	Bill Elliott	Dodge Dealers/UAW Dodge
12	33	99	Jeff Burton	CITGO SUPERGARD Ford
13	12	31	Robby Gordon	Cingular Wireless Chevrolet
14	21	88	Dale Jarrett	UPS Ford
15	1	48	Jimmie Johnson	Lowe's Chevrolet
16	27	11	Brett Bodine	Wells Fargo Fin./Timberland Ford
17	43	32	Ricky Craven	Tide Ford
18	37	2	Rusty Wallace	Miller Lite Ford
19	30	30	Jeff Green	America Online Chevrolet
20	11	5	Terry Labonte	Kellogg's Chevrolet
21	17	33	Mike Wallace	Autoliv Chevrolet
22	31	92	Robert Pressley	Brand Source Dodge
23	20	4	Mike Skinner	Kodak Chevrolet
24	36	49	Shawna Robinson	BAM Racing Dodge
25	42	77	Dave Blaney	Jasper Engines & Transmissions Ford
26	7	36	Ken Schrader	M&M's Pontiac
27	24	14	Stacy Compton	Conseco Pontiac
28	8	25	Jerry Nadeau	UAW-Delphi Chevrolet
29	5	8	Dale Earnhardt Jr.	Budweiser Chevrolet
30	18	1	Kenny Wallace	Pennzoil Chevrolet
31	22	66	Todd Bodine	Kmart Ford
32	32	55	Bobby Hamilton	Schneider Electric Chevrolet
33	40	17	Matt Kenseth	DeWalt Power Tools Ford
34	10	18	Bobby Labonte	Interstate Batteries Pontiac
35	26	7	Casey Atwood	Sirius Satellite Radio Dodge
36	2	29	Kevin Harvick	GM Goodwrench Service Chevrolet
37	16	43	John Andretti	Cheerios Dodge
38	9	28	Ricky Rudd	Havoline Ford
39	28	19	Jeremy Mayfield	Dodge Dealers/UAW Dodge
40	25	26	Joe Nemechek	Kmart School Spirit Ford
41	34	45	Kyle Petty	Sprint Dodge
42	14	71	Dave Marcis	RealTree Chevrolet
43	6	20	Tony Stewart	Home Depot Pontiac

Subway 400

Jeff Gordon's DuPont crew scrambles to get their driver back in the fray. With their help, Gordon was able to fight through the field from his 33rd-place starting position to finish seventh and jump to fourth place in the early-season point standings.

Fritos
DUPONT
24
MOOG
CLEVITE
CAMS
3M
Bud
PEPSI
DUPONT
AUTOMOTIVE

(Above) The Havoline team pushes Ricky Rudd's Ford down pit road after it stalled during a stop under caution on lap 258. The miscue cost Rudd the lead in the race and a lap on the track, which he eventually made up on the way to a disappointing 18th-place finish.

(Right) Early-race action sees Jerry Nadeau (25) taking on Dale Jarrett (88), with Sterling Marlin (40) and Rusty Wallace (2) closing from behind after all four drivers started among the top 10. Jarrett lost the engine in his UPS Ford while leading on lap 145 and finished second from last, while Marlin took second from the top - good enough to seize first place in the point standings.

Daytona 500 winner Ward Burton had this bit of advice for his fellow drivers when he arrived at Rockingham, N.C., for the Subway 400: For those planning to win the season-opener in the future, Ward noted "they should plan accordingly" with their wardrobe.

Burton had embarked on a whirlwind two-day media tour following the victory and joked that he was so unprepared he had to wear his jacket continuously so no one would see his wrinkled shirt!

It wasn't really that bad, but it underscored the immediate fame a driver earns with a Daytona 500 victory. The days spent on the media tour helped him realize the enormity of his accomplishment. However, in the seeming blink of an eye, Burton was rejoining his Caterpillar Dodge teammates at "The Rock" for the season's second race. In reality, there had been little time to savor the important victory before it was time to resume "business as usual."

Daytona is a huge triumph, but it pays the same number of points toward the year-end championship as every other race. Burton and his Bill Davis Racing mates knew they needed another solid finish this weekend if they were to

remain atop the NASCAR Winston Cup Series point standings.

While Burton was accepting congratulations from rival drivers and teams, Tony Stewart and others who had struggled with disappointing Daytona finishes hoped to quickly get back into the hunt. Stewart's Speedweeks had been filled with outstanding performances, but the Home Depot Pontiac driver had seen his engine fail just two laps into the 500. As a result, Stewart – the Bud Shootout and IROC Daytona winner – gathered just 34 points toward the year-end NASCAR Winston Cup Series championship.

Others with poor Daytona results included Ricky Rudd (38th), Kevin Harvick (36th), Bobby Labonte (34th) and Matt Kenseth (33rd). Dale Earnhardt Jr. could only muster a 29th-place Daytona finish after a pair of cut tires and other problems, while Kenny Wallace, driving the Pennzoil Chevrolet for Dale Earnhardt Inc., was 30th at The Beach.

All aimed for better finishes at Rockingham to vault them back into the point battle before they were too far behind to mount a challenge.

Ricky Craven and his PPI teammates, still celebrating their two-year sponsorship extension with Tide, gave the Proctor & Gamble offices reason for an afternoon celebration when Craven rocketed his Ford around the 1.017-mile superspeedway to claim the Bud Pole for the Subway 400. His speed of 156.008 mph just nipped Ken Schrader's M&M's Pontiac for the No. 1 starting spot, while Johnny Benson and Dale Jarrett claimed the second-row starting positions. Jerry Nadeau and Sterling Marlin made up the third row ahead of Kurt Busch and Rusty Wallace, while Kenny Wallace and Bobby Hamilton grabbed the final top-10 starting positions.

(Below Left) Tony Stewart (20), Sterling Marlin (40) and Ricky Craven (32) receive service on pit road, which, with 10 cautions in the race, was a very busy place. All three drivers fared well, with Stewart rebounding from a last place at Daytona to finish fourth ahead of pole-winner Craven, while Marlin grabbed second place and the lead in the points.

(Bottom) Casey Atwood's Sirius Dodge gets some major repairs in Rockingham's garage after Atwood was bumped and spun along the backstretch on lap 157 in an accident that involved seven cars. The Ultra/Evernham Motorsports team was able to return the car to competition and Atwood finished the event under power in 29th place.

Bill Elliott gets underway after his Dodge receives new rubber and a full tank of fuel. Elliott's team adjusted his car continually during pit stops, finally hitting on a setup that allowed Bill to move up in the running order where he just missed a top-10 finish. His 11th place - matching his result at Daytona — was good enough to boost him into eighth place in the points after the race.

After finishing second the week before at Daytona, Elliott Sadler was forced to use a provisional to make the Rockingham field, as did Joe Nemechek, Hut Stricklin, Terry Labonte, Todd Bodine, Stacy Compton and Rick Mast. Dick Trickle, driving for Dave Marcis, failed to qualify fast enough to make the field, as did Randy Renfrow and Carl Long.

For nearly a year and a half, Matt Kenseth had sought to add a race-winner's trophy to the Coca-Cola 600 hardware he earned in his rookie NASCAR Winston Cup Series season. During the latter part of 2001, it appeared his DeWalt Tools team was getting into competitive shape, and Kenseth's confidence rose as his top-10 finishes increased in number. Perhaps, he had speculated, he and his Jack Roush-owned team would return to the winner's circle in 2002.

Just after the 100-lap mark, Kenseth emerged in the top 10 at Rockingham, and as the race wound on, he continued to move through the field. Buoyed by consistent 14-second pit stops by his crew, Kenseth took the point on lap 147 following a caution for Dale Jarrett's blown engine.

He went on to dominate the race, leading 152 laps, but in the closing miles, he felt his chance for victory would still have to wait for another day. During his final pit stop, under caution, for fuel and tires on lap 366, Ricky Craven made the decision to gamble that his tires would keep the Tide Ford in the lead for the final 23 laps. Kenseth was second and making a bid for the lead after the restart, but his Ford drifted high and Sterling Marlin, Rusty Wallace and Bobby Labonte swooped past him, leaving him in fifth place.

Craven fought desperately to keep Marlin at bay, and as he did, Kenseth was able to gather up his Ford and close the gap. Marlin finally forced his way past Craven with 18 laps to go. With Marlin and Labonte ready to battle for the victory, Kenseth got past the fading Craven, and with just eight laps remaining, Marlin, Labonte and Kenseth were running nose-to-tail in the battle for the win.

Then Robby Gordon spun in the second turn and Ken Schrader's Pontiac blew its engine right in front of the battle for the victory. Marlin and Labonte both slipped in Schrader's oil and gamely fought to keep their cars out of the wall. That opened the low lane for Kenseth, and he zipped

Matt Kenseth (17) takes the simultaneous yellow and checkered flags ahead of Sterling Marlin (40) and Bobby Labonte (18), with the battered machines of Mike Wallace (33) and Casey Atwood (7) to his left. The event marked the DeWalt driver's second career victory, ending a dry spell that dated back to his initial win at Charlotte in the 2000 Coca-Cola 600, 59 races ago.

past the leaders to take the point just before the yellow flag flew with five laps remaining in the race.

Kenseth circled around behind the pace car on the way to posting his second career victory. He became the eighth different winner in the last eight events at Rockingham.

Marlin recovered to finish second and take over the NASCAR Winston Cup Series point lead, while Bobby Labonte finished third ahead of teammate Stewart. Craven was fifth ahead of Jeff Burton, while Jeff Gordon was seventh. Rusty Wallace, Bobby Hamilton and Kenny Wallace filled out the top 10 finishers.

Subway 400 final race results

Fin. Pos.	Start Pos.	Car No.	Driver	Team
1	25	17	Matt Kenseth	DeWalt Power Tools Ford
2	6	40	Sterling Marlin	Coors Light Dodge
3	14	18	Bobby Labonte	Interstate Batteries Pontiac
4	19	20	Tony Stewart	Home Depot Pontiac
5	1	32	Ricky Craven	Tide Ford
6	22	99	Jeff Burton	CITGO SUPERGARD Ford
7	33	24	Jeff Gordon	DuPont Chevrolet
8	8	2	Rusty Wallace	Miller Lite Ford
9	10	55	Bobby Hamilton	Schneider Electric Chevrolet
10	9	1	Kenny Wallace	Pennzoil Chevrolet
11	28	9	Bill Elliott	Dodge Dealers/UAW Dodge
12	7	97	Kurt Busch	Rubbermaid Ford
13	18	22	Ward Burton	Caterpillar Dodge
14	23	12	Ryan Newman	ALLTEL Ford
15	35	43	John Andretti	Cheerios Dodge
16	40	5	Terry Labonte	Kellogg's Chevrolet
17	15	30	Jeff Green	America Online Chevrolet
18	27	28	Ricky Rudd	Havoline Ford
19	34	29	Kevin Harvick	GM Goodwrench Service Chevrolet
20	12	41	Jimmy Spencer	Target Dodge
21	17	6	Mark Martin	Pfizer/Viagra Ford
22	36	77	Dave Blaney	Jasper Engines & Transmissions Ford
23	3	10	Johnny Benson	Valvoline Pontiac
24	16	31	Robby Gordon	Cingular Wireless Chevrolet
25	5	25	Jerry Nadeau	UAW-Delphi Chevrolet
26	29	8	Dale Earnhardt Jr.	Budweiser Chevrolet
27	39	23	Hut Stricklin	Hills Bros Coffee Dodge
28	11	48	Jimmie Johnson	Lowe's Chevrolet
29	21	19	Jeremy Mayfield	Dodge Dealers/UAW Dodge
30	31	11	Brett Bodine	Dura Lube/W. Fargo Fin./Timberland Ford
31	38	21	Elliott Sadler	Motorcraft Ford
32	41	66	Todd Bodine	Kmart Ford
33	37	26	Joe Nemechek	Kmart School Spirit Ford
34	43	90	Rick Mast	Duke's Mayonnaise/Sauer's Ford
35	2	36	Ken Schrader	M&M's Pontiac
36	24	4	Mike Skinner	Kodak Chevrolet
37	32	45	Kyle Petty	Sprint Dodge
38	30	33	Mike Wallace	TBA Chevrolet
39	20	7	Casey Atwood	Sirius Satellite Radio Dodge
40	26	15	Michael Waltrip	NAPA Chevrolet
41	13	44	Buckshot Jones	Georgia Pacific Dodge
42	4	88	Dale Jarrett	UPS Ford
43	42	14	Stacy Compton	Conseco Pontiac

UAW-DaimlerChrysler 400

Rusty Wallace (2) contends for enough room to squeeze between Bill Elliott and Ken Schrader (36) during some rather fierce action on an otherwise roomy Las Vegas Motor Speedway.

ELVIS
LEGENDARY
© EPE
obil 1
Ford
URUS

(Above) Ryan Newman (left) and Todd Bodine congratulate each other on their superior qualifying efforts that put them together on the front row for the start of the race. For Bodine, winning the Bud Pole did more than put him first on the grid; it also secured a one-race sponsorship from Checker Auto Parts for the financially struggling team.

(Right, Above) Dale Earnhardt Jr. lights up the tires while leaving the pits after a stop. Timing of the six cautions required stops under both yellow and green and tested crews as they fought for track position for their drivers.

(Right) Todd Bodine (66) and Ryan Newman (12) lead the field into the first turn as the race gets underway. After fending off a side-by-side battle with Newman and a challenge from third-place starter Kurt Busch (97), Bodine came back to the start/finish line with the lead and took control of the early portion of the race.

At Rockingham, Michael Waltrip had seen his 500th career NASCAR Winston Cup Series start result in engine failure and a 40th-place finish. Richard Childress hoped the same fate would not befall one of his entries at Las Vegas Motor Speedway when he reached the milestone of having his Chevrolets make the 1,000th start of his long and storied career as a car owner.

Childress, who began his NASCAR Winston Cup Series career as a driver and car owner on Sept. 14, 1969, could merely marvel at the changes that had occurred during the more than three decades he had competed in the sport. His multimillion-dollar shops, motorhomes, planes, transporters and his far-flung business interests were a far cry from the driver who worked on his own cars, hauled them to the track on a flatbed trailer and whose "gourmet" track lunches for his pickup crew consisted of a loaf of bread and a jar of peanut butter.

Now, in the "City of Neon," Childress would see his mounts make their 1,000th start. He attributed his longevity in the sport to the effort and perseverance of all those who had worked with him over the years. Had Childress not listened to Junior Johnson's advice to step out of his car as a driver and install Dale Earnhardt in 1981, he likely would have eventually gone the same way as many other low-budget independent teams over the years. Instead of being at the front

of the NASCAR history and record books, he and his efforts would likely be listed as a footnote.

Sterling Marlin's solid finishes in his Coors Light Dodge in the first two races of the season vaulted him past Ward Burton into the point lead as teams arrived in "Glitter Gulch." Burton struggled to a 13th-place finish at Rockingham and now trailed his fellow Dodge driver by 18 points. Las Vegas native Kurt Busch, 12th at The Rock, was in third place, three points ahead of Jeff Gordon and 17 markers behind the Caterpillar Dodge driver.

Jeff Burton was off to a good start in the 2002 season as well. After finishing sixth at Rockingham, he was fifth in the standings, seven

points behind Gordon and 10 ahead of Ricky Craven. Craven's late-race tire gamble had dropped him to fifth in the final Rockingham rundown, but he was just 10 points behind the CITGO Ford driver.

Rookie Ryan Newman continued to impress. He finished 14th at Rockingham and was now seventh in the standings, just five points behind Craven. Bill Elliott was eighth, seven points behind Newman and six points ahead of Rockingham winner Matt Kenseth, while Rusty Wallace held 10th place in the early-season standings. Mark Martin dropped to 11th after finishing 21st at The Rock, but one driver who made up a lot of lost ground after Daytona was Tony Stewart. The Home Depot Pontiac driver had moved up to 22nd in the standings after his disastrous Daytona start by finishing fourth at Rockingham.

Team owner Travis Carter brought his two Fords to Vegas, and both looked strange after carrying the Kmart colors for so long. Because of the company's financial problems, the sponsorship deal had ended at Rockingham and Carter bleakly stared from the back of his transporter as his crew worked on the twin entries. He could only hope strong performances from Todd Bodine and Joe Nemechek would help find financial assistance for the team or, he feared, this would be the final event for the two cars. Bodine

(Above Left) Jackman Mike Scearce hustles around the front of the Cingular Wireless Chevrolet during a stop for driver Robby Gordon.

(Above) Pit road is jammed as all the lead-lap cars stop on lap 63 during a caution for debris. Ryan Newman, first in line, came out second behind Kurt Busch, who is seen leaving his stall halfway up pit road.

(Above) Rusty Wallace (2) and Elliott Sadler (21) duel on the frontstretch in the Ford Tauruses. Wallace spent the afternoon charging through the field, picking up 27 positions after needing a provisional to make the starting lineup.

(Right) Mark Martin puts his Viagra Ford into the wind with Roush teammate Matt Kenseth and Tony Stewart in tow. Although Martin did not lead a lap at Las Vegas, he stayed among the top 10 all day and grabbed third place at the finish, boosting himself into fourth place in the points, an improvement of seven positions.

held up his end of the bargain by turning the fastest lap during Bud Pole qualifying and claiming the inside of the front row for the financially strapped team. That earned a one-race sponsorship deal from Checker Auto Parts for the Vegas race.

Ryan Newman qualified for the other front-row starting position, beating Busch and Jimmy Spencer for the honors, while the third row was made up of Waltrip and Mark Martin. The seventh- and eighth-fastest qualifiers were Johnny Benson and Matt Kenseth, while Ricky Craven and Dave Blaney grabbed the fifth-row starting positions.

Using provisionals to start the race were Dale Jarrett, Rusty Wallace (with a fabulous Elvis paint scheme to honor Pressley's career as an entertainer at Las Vegas) and Jeff Burton. Others taking provisional starts were Bobby Hamilton, Terry Labonte, Casey Atwood and Rick Mast, leaving Derrike Cope unable to make the field in his CLR Ford.

The UAW-DaimlerChrysler 400 marked the first Winston No Bull 5 race of the season, and Tony Stewart, Jeff Burton, Dale Earnhardt Jr., Matt Kenseth and Bobby Hamilton all were eligible to cash in on Winston's $1 million bonus if they

could score a Vegas victory. That quintet had finished in the top five positions in the last Winston No Bull 5 race at Talladega (Ala.) Superspeedway last fall.

As it turned out, Stewart had the best chance of claiming Winston's bonus but plummeted from the lead to sixth place during his final pit stop. Stuck in traffic in the closing laps, the Home Depot-sponsored driver had no chance to challenge for the victory.

While Stewart was struggling, Sterling Marlin was on the way to his first win of the season. At Daytona, Marlin had lost a chance to claim victory when he popped out of his car to tug on a fender during a late-race red flag. At Rockingham, the field had finished under yellow, denying Marlin a chance to mount a challenge in the closing laps. Now, at Vegas, Marlin's silver Dodge was at the point after taking advantage of a break earlier in the race.

On lap 121 of the 267-lap race, Marlin spun off the fourth turn after being bumped by Jerry Nadeau, and he blasted down pit road at well over the 45-mile per hour speed limit. If you get caught speeding on pit road it's an automatic 15-second penalty, but during the work in the Coors Light pit area, NASCAR officials in the tower were unable to contact the inspector working in Marlin's stall to tell him to hold the car for the penalty. Ten laps after the restart, Marlin was back at the point and, in the closing laps, held off Jeremy Mayfield and Mark Martin to claim the victory.

After being in position to win at Daytona before a red-flag violation, and then finishing behind Kenseth under yellow at Rockingham, Marlin suddenly got lucky at Las Vegas and came away with the victory. An eighth place, a second place and win in the first three events of the year had him solidly atop the point standings, 75 markers in front of Ryan Newman.

Ryan Newman finished a solid fourth, with Stewart rallying to claim fifth place. Jimmie Johnson was sixth ahead of Dale Jarrett and Bill Elliott, while Jeff Burton added to his string of strong finishes with a ninth-place showing ahead of Jimmy Spencer.

Todd Bodine was not so fortunate. After starting from the pole, he was relegated to 29th place, while Nemechek was 19th in the sister (and former Kmart) entry.

UAW-DaimlerChrysler 400 final race results

Fin. Pos.	Start Pos.	Car No.	Driver	Team
1	24	40	Sterling Marlin	Coors Light Dodge
2	18	19	Jeremy Mayfield	Dodge Dealers/UAW Dodge
3	6	6	Mark Martin	Pfizer/Viagra Ford
4	2	12	Ryan Newman	ALLTEL Ford
5	15	20	Tony Stewart	Home Depot Pontiac
6	25	48	Jimmie Johnson	Lowe's Chevrolet
7	37	88	Dale Jarrett	UPS Ford
8	23	9	Bill Elliott	Dodge Dealers/UAW Dodge
9	39	99	Jeff Burton	CITGO SUPERGARD Ford
10	4	41	Jimmy Spencer	Target Dodge
11	38	2	Rusty Wallace	Miller Lite Ford
12	33	18	Bobby Labonte	Interstate Batteries Pontiac
13	27	28	Ricky Rudd	Havoline Ford
14	8	17	Matt Kenseth	DeWalt Power Tools Ford
15	16	25	Jerry Nadeau	UAW-Delphi Chevrolet
16	35	8	Dale Earnhardt, Jr.	Budweiser Chevrolet
17	13	24	Jeff Gordon	DuPont Chevrolet
18	10	77	Dave Blaney	Jasper Engines & Transmissions Ford
19	20	26	Joe Nemechek	TBA Ford
20	3	97	Kurt Busch	Rubbermaid Ford
21	32	22	Ward Burton	Caterpillar Dodge
22	5	15	Michael Waltrip	NAPA Chevrolet
23	19	44	Buckshot Jones	Georgia Pacific Dodge
24	21	23	Hut Stricklin	Hills Bros Coffee Dodge
25	28	29	Kevin Harvick	GM Goodwrench Service Chevrolet
26	29	36	Ken Schrader	M&M's Pontiac
27	17	1	Kenny Wallace	Pennzoil Chevrolet
28	34	21	Elliott Sadler	Motorcraft Ford
29	1	66	Todd Bodine	Haas Carter Motorsports Ford
30	11	45	Kyle Petty	Sprint Dodge
31	9	32	Ricky Craven	Tide Ford
32	7	10	Johnny Benson	Valvoline Pontiac
33	22	30	Jeff Green	America Online Chevrolet
34	31	4	Mike Skinner	Kodak Chevrolet
35	14	11	Brett Bodine	Dura Lube/W. Fargo Fin./Timberland Ford
36	26	43	John Andretti	Cheerios Dodge
37	12	31	Robby Gordon	Cingular Wireless Chevrolet
38	41	5	Terry Labonte	Kellogg's Chevrolet
39	30	14	Stacy Compton	Conseco Pontiac
40	43	90	Rick Mast	Duke's Mayonnaise/Sauer's Ford
41	42	7	Casey Atwood	Sirius Satellite Radio Dodge
42	36	49	Shawna Robinson	BAM Racing Dodge
43	40	55	Bobby Hamilton	Schneider Electric Chevrolet

MBNA America 500

After having what was clearly the fastest car at Las Vegas only to have his bid for victory foiled during a late-race pit stop, Tony Stewart came out charging at Atlanta, leading the most laps for the second straight week and notching the win over Dale Earnhardt Jr.

(Below) Point leader Sterling Marlin continues his consistent performances at Atlanta. Although Marlin did not lead in the race, he kept his Coors Dodge close enough to the front to score his fourth top-10 finish in as many races and maintain a comfortable margin in the points.

(Right, Above) After disappointing qualifying efforts at Rockingham and Las Vegas, Dale Earnhardt Jr. turned the third-fastest lap at Atlanta. He followed that with a strong performance in the race, finishing second to Stewart at the checkered flag.

(Right, Below) Rookie Ryan Newman, looking calm and collected from the cockpit of his ALLTEL Ford, grabbed the outside of the front row in qualifying for the second straight week and maintained his runner-up spot in the point standings by finishing one spot behind Marlin.

Sterling Marlin's Las Vegas victory came as no surprise to anyone in the NASCAR Winston Cup Series garage area. The Tennessean's ninth career win seemed merely to be a continuation of the string he began last year, when he emerged from the pack with a rock-solid third place in the final point standings.

That surge continued into 2002, and Marlin's chance to win the Daytona 500 a third time was derailed when he got out of his Coors Light Dodge under a red flag and laid his hands on the right-front fender of his silver Intrepid. That was a violation of the rule prohibiting work on a race car when a race is completely halted, and Marlin immediately went from contender to also-ran.

He had taken a continuous ribbing from other drivers and crew members about his "mechanical ineptitude" in the weeks that followed, but Marlin merely shrugged it off with his usual infectious grin and laugh. Now after his Vegas triumph, he had the last laugh, notching victory early in the season, giving Dodge its sixth win in the last 17 races and solidifying his hold on the top slot of the NASCAR Winston Cup Series point ladder.

Marlin did not have the fastest car at Las Vegas. The No. 20 Home Depot Pontiac driven by Tony Stewart clearly held that honor. But throughout NASCAR's history, the fastest car has not always been the one arriving in victory lane for the post-race celebration. When Stewart's pit road problems in the final Vegas stop dropped him from the point, Marlin was ready – and able – to take advantage.

Ryan Newman's outstanding efforts in the first three races of the season put him right behind Marlin in the point standings, with the ALLTEL Ford driver 75 markers behind. Newman may have been the surprise of the early season, but at the same time, Jack Roush had a little smile on his face as he walked into the Atlanta Motor Speedway garage area for the MBNA America 500.

Roush had plenty of reason to be pleased with the efforts of his four-pronged assault on the NASCAR Winston Cup Series championship. Jeff Burton stood third in the standings with his CITGO Ford, 12 points behind Newman. Just five points behind Burton, Mark Martin and his Viagra Ford were truly in the hunt for the title, while Kurt Busch was eighth in the standings, a single point behind Jeff Gordon. Matt Kenseth was 10th, just six points behind Rusty Wallace and trailing Marlin by only 132. All four Roush drivers were solidly in the top 10.

While Roush liked his championship chances with his quartet occupying top-10 slots, team owner Joe Gibbs was licking his chops when he arrived in Atlanta. Clearly, Gibbs' Interstate Batteries Pontiac was the pre-event favorite, with Bobby Labonte toting home the Atlanta hardware five times in the last 11 races. And Gibbs was quick to point out that Tony Stewart's Home Depot Pontiac was just as potent, based on his Vegas performance, and that Home Depot's executives would be at this event in their hometown. Every effort had been made to give the twin Ponchos everything they needed for the first Atlanta stop on the circuit.

(Above) Dale Jarrett's UPS crew provides tires, fuel and a left-rear chassis adjustment during a green-flag pit stop. Jarrett, winner of this event in 1997, never quite got the Taurus dialed-in, continuing an up-and-down start to his season.

(Left) Rookie Jimmie Johnson pulls his Lowe's Chevrolet alongside Ward Burton's Caterpillar Dodge on Atlanta's super-fast frontstretch. Johnson, in his second Atlanta appearance, had a strong, third-place showing at the end of the day.

(Above) Ricky Craven puts his Tide Ford through its paces in traffic. After his third straight top-10 qualifying effort, Craven fought to his second top-five finish in the season's first four events.

(Right) Penske teammates Rusty Wallace (2) and Ryan Newman work together on Atlanta's tri-oval. Rusty, apparently having problems with the new "single engine" rule, had to take his third provisional of the season, but once again sliced through the pack, picking up 32 positions to finish sixth.

If Atlanta Motor Speedway president Ed Clark needed any help selling the few remaining tickets for the MBNA America 500, he received it at the conclusion of Bud Pole qualifying. "Hometown" hero Bill Elliott stepped up to the challenge and rolled his red Dodge to the pole at a speed in excess of 191.5 miles per hour. The Redhead quashed Newman's hopes for the pole with his speedy trip around the 1.54-mile oval, and Raybestos Rookie of the Year contender Newman was left with the outside of the front row.

Dale Earnhardt Jr. qualified third fastest, just a tick faster than Kurt Busch, while Jimmy Spencer and Ricky Craven were forced to be content with the third row. Dale Jarrett, looking for his first victory of the season in the hometown of sponsor UPS, claimed the inside of the fourth row with defending race champion Kevin Harvick on his right. Stewart was the faster of Gibbs' two entries with the ninth-quickest lap, while Johnny Benson plunked the Valvoline Pontiac on the outside of the fifth row.

Ricky Rudd, Rusty Wallace, Mark Martin, Jeremy Mayfield, Casey Atwood and Dick Trickle, in Dave Marcis' Chevrolet, had to use provisional starts. Brett Bodine, carrying the Hooters colors in a one-race sponsorship deal, also had to use a provisional to make the field. Ron Hornaday and Carl Long were forced to miss the race.

After finishing 43rd in the season-opening Daytona 500, Tony Stewart had posted a fourth-place showing at Rockingham and the aforementioned fifth after contending for victory at Vegas. He had rocketed from last place in the point standings following the Daytona race to 11th entering Atlanta, and after having the dominant car at Vegas, Stewart was determined to show the Home Depot folks he had everything he needed to post the win at Atlanta.

Stewart simply dominated the event at the super-fast oval, leading 143 of 325 laps, and not even a two-tire gamble by Ward Burton in the waning laps could keep Tony from his first 500-mile win. "Little E" stepped up to challenge at the

(Left) Ward Burton (22) drifts to the outside with Jeremy Mayfield on his bumper, while Tony Stewart (20) and Dale Earnhardt Jr. surge past on the inside. Burton held the point on the final two restarts after a two-tire stop put him out front on lap 283, but he was no match for the dominant Stewart, who took the lead for the last time with 23 laps remaining.

(Left, Below) Tony Stewart couldn't be happier in victory lane as he celebrates the win with crew chief Greg Zipadelli and Miss Winston Cielo Garcia. After a disastrous last-place finish at Daytona, Stewart had vaulted 38 positions to fifth in points in just three events.

end, but there was no denying Stewart. After watching a chance for a Winston No Bull 5 million-dollar bonus disappear the previous week, Tony was not about to let Atlanta get away.

His margin over Little E wasn't a huge one at the end – about three car-lengths – but it was all Tony needed to post his first victory of the season and the 13th of his brief NASCAR Winston Cup Series career.

Rookie Jimmie Johnson finished third behind Little E, with Matt Kenseth fourth and Ricky Craven fifth. Rusty Wallace worked his way from his provisional starting position to claim sixth place in an outstanding performance, while Ward Burton faded to seventh. Like Rusty, Mark Martin fought his way through the field from his 39th starting position and grabbed eighth place ahead of Marlin and Newman.

MBNA America 500 final race results

Fin. Pos.	Start Pos.	Car No.	Driver	Team
1	9	20	Tony Stewart	Home Depot Pontiac
2	3	8	Dale Earnhardt Jr.	Budweiser Chevrolet
3	15	48	Jimmie Johnson	Lowe's Chevrolet
4	32	17	Matt Kenseth	DeWalt Power Tools Ford
5	6	32	Ricky Craven	Tide Ford
6	38	2	Rusty Wallace	Miller Lite Ford
7	28	22	Ward Burton	Caterpillar Dodge
8	39	6	Mark Martin	Pfizer/Viagra Ford
9	12	40	Sterling Marlin	Coors Light Dodge
10	2	12	Ryan Newman	ALLTEL Ford
11	4	97	Kurt Busch	Rubbermaid Ford
12	14	44	Buckshot Jones	Georgia Pacific Dodge
13	7	88	Dale Jarrett	UPS Ford
14	13	5	Terry Labonte	Kellogg's Chevrolet
15	34	45	Kyle Petty	Sprint Dodge
16	19	24	Jeff Gordon	DuPont Chevrolet
17	24	77	Dave Blaney	Jasper Engines & Transmissions Ford
18	23	31	Robby Gordon	Cingular Wireless Chevrolet
19	16	21	Elliott Sadler	Motorcraft Ford
20	37	28	Ricky Rudd	Havoline Ford
21	30	99	Jeff Burton	CITGO SUPERGARD Ford
22	11	1	Kenny Wallace	Pennzoil Chevrolet
23	40	19	Jeremy Mayfield	Dodge Dealers/UAW Dodge
24	25	36	Ken Schrader	Pedigree Pontiac
25	27	26	Joe Nemechek	Haas Carter Motorsports Ford
26	5	41	Jimmy Spencer	Target Dodge
27	10	10	Johnny Benson	Valvoline Pontiac
28	21	4	Mike Skinner	Kodak Chevrolet
29	22	55	Bobby Hamilton	Schneider Electric Chevrolet
30	26	25	Jerry Nadeau	UAW-Delphi Chevrolet
31	35	14	Stacy Compton	Conseco Pontiac
32	41	7	Casey Atwood	Sirius Satellite Radio Dodge
33	29	90	Rick Mast	Duke's Mayonnaise/Sauer's Ford
34	31	49	Shawna Robinson	BAM Racing Dodge
35	1	9	Bill Elliott	Dodge Dealers/UAW Dodge
36	20	43	John Andretti	Cheerios Dodge
37	18	18	Bobby Labonte	Interstate Batteries Pontiac
38	42	11	Brett Bodine	Hooters/W. Fargo Fin./Timberland Ford
39	8	29	Kevin Harvick	GM Goodwrench Service Chevrolet
40	17	15	Michael Waltrip	NAPA Chevrolet
41	36	30	Jeff Green	America Online Chevrolet
42	43	71	Dick Trickle	Warranty Gold Chevrolet
43	33	23	Hut Stricklin	Hills Bros Coffee Dodge

(Above) Steve Park was back in uniform and ready to race at Darlington after a 16-race layoff dating back to September 2001, when he sustained injuries in a NASCAR Busch Series race at this very track. Park served notice he was ready to go by posting the fourth-fastest lap in qualifying.

(Right, Above) Tide driver Ricky Craven points out his speed of 170.089, fastest in qualifying and good for his second Bud Pole Award of the year, the sixth of his NASCAR Winston Cup Series career, and his fourth consecutive top-10 starting spot.

(Right) Jeff Gordon (24) leads Jimmy Spencer (41) and Elliott Sadler, with Mike Skinner (4) and Kyle Petty (45) on the inside, for a restart on lap 95 after the second caution of the race. Gordon, who started second, led three times for 176 laps and took the lap-leader bonus in the race.

There were plenty of story lines for reporters when they arrived at venerable old Darlington (S.C.) Raceway for the running of the Carolina Dodge Dealers 400.

First of all, Sterling Marlin had maintained his lead in the NASCAR Winston Cup Series point standings with a solid top-10 finish at Atlanta, and rookie protagonists Ryan Newman and Jimmie Johnson were performing like veterans. Newman remained second in the point standings, and Johnson's third place at Atlanta had moved him into 10th place on the point ladder.

Behind Newman, there was a virtual dogfight for the remainder of the top 10 positions, with a total of just 48 points separating third through 10th. Jeff Gordon was 11th, just a single marker behind Johnson.

All four of Jack Roush's drivers remained within the top nine in the standings and in truth, Mark Martin appeared as though he and his Viagra team had regained the fighting edge they didn't have last year.

Tony Stewart had climbed another six places in the standings following his Atlanta victory and he now stood fifth, 13 points behind Martin. It was a heady climb for the youngster following his nightmarish last-place finish at Daytona.

And then there was Steve Park, ready to make a comeback to racing after his bizarre NASCAR Busch Series accident last September at the tricky Darlington oval. Park's return marked the end of Kenny Wallace's fill-in stint in the yellow-and-black Pennzoil Chevrolet, but everyone gave Wallace exceedingly high marks for both his overall performance behind the wheel of the Monte Carlo and for his gracious handling of Park's return to racing.

Let's not forget Brett Bodine, who ran the Atlanta event with Hooters colors on his Ford and had the restaurant chain's familiar orange, brown and white on his Taurus again at Darlington. "Bob Brooks (CEO of Hooters) loves underdogs," Brett reminded those who asked. "Remember he joined forces with Alan Kulwicki when Alan was struggling searching for a sponsor.

"We hope that Mr. Brooks and Hooters will remain with us for the remainder of the year and that we can have some good runs to reward his confidence."

So, there was plenty for reporters to write and talk about.

And then the bombshell hit: Brooke Gordon had asked for a divorce from four-time NASCAR Winston Cup Series champion Jeff Gordon. The former Miss Winston filed papers in Palm Beach County, Fla., and although the driver asked racing-beat scribes to respect his privacy in the matter, the news was so stunning it had to be reported.

Gordon was obviously trying to not let the situation affect his on-track performance, and when Bud Pole qualifying was over, he could point to

(Above) Tony Stewart receives service under caution, one of five yellow flags thrown during the 400-mile event. After two straight outstanding performances, Stewart and his Home Depot crew came to Darlington ready to roll and looked poised for another fine finish until a tangle with Buckshot Jones triggered a multi-car accident that ended his day.

(Left) Less than 40 laps into the event, leader Steve Park (1) spins after making contact with Stacy Compton (14) and collects Ricky Craven (32) in the process. Running third at the time, Jeff Gordon (24) ducks onto the apron to avoid the mess and assumes the lead for the first time in the race.

(Right) Kevin Harvick's crew swarms the GM Goodwrench Chevrolet, providing superb pit work that keeps their driver in the hunt. Harvick stayed out of trouble and brought his Monte Carlo home third, his first finish better than 19th this season.

(Below) In a last-minute decision, the Wood Brothers loaded up Elliott Sadler's favorite Motorcraft Ford and brought it to Darlington, and Sadler responded with his second runner-up finish of the young season.

his outside front-row starting position with pride. He had, he believed, a car capable of taking him to victory lane again at Darlington.

Gordon's fast lap wasn't quite enough to dislodge Ricky Craven from the pole. Craven whistled his Tide Ford around the egg-shaped oval at a speed in excess of 170 miles per hour and Gordon simply couldn't match it. For the second straight race, rookie Ryan Newman had an outstanding qualifying effort, claiming the third-fastest lap, and Park made his return to the wheel an outstanding one, grabbing the outside of the second row. Jimmie Johnson and Elliott Sadler continued the youth movement by claiming the third row, while veterans Jimmy Spencer and Ken Schrader made up the fourth row. Jeff Green and Bill Elliott completed the top 10, beating Sterling Marlin and Bobby Labonte for the honors.

With just 43 cars on hand (the maximum number for a race), no one was forced to go home. However, Terry Labonte, Buckshot Jones, Hut Stricklin, Casey Atwood, Rick Mast, Shawna Robinson and Andy Hillinburg, a late entry in Dave Marcis' Chevrolet, all used provisional starts.

With NASCAR's "run-what-you-brung" engine rule in effect this season, point-leader Sterling Marlin watched warily as his engine tuners shook their heads following the final practice session. The engine in his silver Coors Light Dodge had a valve problem that could not be remedied, and Sterling would be forced to start from the rear of the field with a backup engine in his Intrepid.

(Left) Sterling Marlin becomes the first two-time winner of the year, matching his victory at Las Vegas and extending his lead in the points to 99 over Ryan Newman. Marlin was forced to come from last place after his crew had to change engines before the start of the race, a situation that ultimately played into his hands.

(Above) Marlin chases Dale Earnhardt Jr. after Little E snatched the lead from him on a restart at lap 241. Marlin chased the Budweiser Chevrolet for 10 laps before retaking the point for good. Earnhardt was also challenged by Sadler and Harvick before settling for a fourth-place finish.

As the Carolina Dodge Dealers 400 turned out, Marlin probably had reason to believe the engine switch was providential. At the front of the pack on lap 226, Buckshot Jones slipped sideways in his Georgia Pacific Dodge and collected race leader Tony Stewart. A melee ensued, with many of the best cars in the field collected in the accident. Gordon almost missed the mess, but nicked Stewart's car and needed work on the front of the DuPont Monte Carlo. And right behind Gordon, in the right place at the right time, was Marlin, who had marched his way into contention.

When Gordon hit pit road, Marlin was suddenly the leader. Although he gave up the point briefly to Dale Earnhardt Jr., Marlin regained the lead and then whistled his way to his second victory of the season. It turned into an easy win, with Elliott Sadler bringing the Wood Brothers' Motorcraft Ford home more than 3.56 seconds behind in second place. "Little E" faded to fourth, with Kevin Harvick edging the Budweiser Chevrolet driver, while rookies Ryan Newman and Jimmie Johnson had their own battle, with Newman emerging ahead at the end in fifth place. Rusty Wallace was a solid seventh ahead of Matt Kenseth, while Jeff Gordon struggled to finish ninth ahead of Bill Elliott.

Carolina Dodge Dealers 400 final race results

Fin. Pos.	Start Pos.	Car No.	Driver	Team
1	11	40	Sterling Marlin	Coors Light Dodge
2	6	21	Elliott Sadler	Motorcraft Ford
3	16	29	Kevin Harvick	GM Goodwrench Service Chevrolet
4	23	8	Dale Earnhardt Jr.	Budweiser Chevrolet
5	3	12	Ryan Newman	ALLTEL Ford
6	5	48	Jimmie Johnson	Lowe's Chevrolet
7	18	2	Rusty Wallace	Miller Lite Ford
8	34	17	Matt Kenseth	DeWalt Power Tools Ford
9	2	24	Jeff Gordon	DuPont Chevrolet
10	10	9	Bill Elliott	Dodge Dealers/UAW Dodge
11	14	99	Jeff Burton	CITGO SUPERGARD Ford
12	21	28	Ricky Rudd	Havoline Ford
13	26	55	Bobby Hamilton	Schneider Electric Chevrolet
14	30	45	Kyle Petty	Sprint Dodge
15	17	15	Michael Waltrip	NAPA Chevrolet
16	19	19	Jeremy Mayfield	Dodge Dealers/UAW Dodge
17	27	26	Joe Nemechek	Haas Carter Motorsports Ford
18	20	25	Jerry Nadeau	UAW-Delphi Chevrolet
19	38	44	Buckshot Jones	Georgia Pacific Dodge
20	29	4	Mike Skinner	Kodak Film Chevrolet
21	12	18	Bobby Labonte	Interstate Batteries Pontiac
22	35	43	John Andretti	Cheerios Dodge
23	37	5	Terry Labonte	Kellogg's Chevrolet
24	41	90	Rick Mast	Duke's Mayonnaise/Sauer's Ford
25	9	30	Jeff Green	America Online Chevrolet
26	40	7	Casey Atwood	Sirius Satellite Radio Dodge
27	32	14	Stacy Compton	Conseco Pontiac
28	13	97	Kurt Busch	Rubbermaid Ford
29	31	6	Mark Martin	Pfizer/Viagra Ford
30	25	77	Dave Blaney	Jasper Engines Ford
31	15	22	Ward Burton	Caterpillar Dodge
32	39	23	Hut Stricklin	Hills Bros Coffee Dodge
33	24	10	Johnny Benson	Valvoline Pontiac
34	28	31	Robby Gordon	Cingular Wireless Chevrolet
35	8	36	Ken Schrader	M&M's Pontiac
36	36	20	Tony Stewart	Home Depot Pontiac
37	7	41	Jimmy Spencer	Target Dodge
38	33	11	Brett Bodine	Hooters/W. Fargo Fin./Timberland Ford
39	4	1	Steve Park	Pennzoil Chevrolet
40	22	88	Dale Jarrett	UPS Ford
41	1	32	Ricky Craven	Tide Ford
42	42	49	Shawna Robinson	BAM Racing Dodge
43	43	71	Andy Hillenburg	Warranty Gold/Pro Motorsports Chevrolet

Food City 500

A huge crowd of more than 160,000 packs the grandstands at Bristol Motor Speedway on a clear spring day in the Tennessee mountains for the first short-track race of the season, the Food City 500.

(Above) Kurt Busch grasps his first NASCAR Winston Cup Series trophy after driving to victory at Bristol. The win came in his 48th career start and moved him from 11th to fifth in the championship point standings

(Right) Jeff Gordon (24) looks for room inside Jimmy Spencer's Dodge (41). After Gordon led the first 31 laps from the pole, he and Spencer traded the point on four occasions before Gordon clipped the apron and spun in turn two on lap 159. Spencer remained in contention throughout the day.

Before the opening of the 2002 NASCAR Winston Cup Series season, few people on either side of the fence would have predicted that Sterling Marlin would be perched on the catbird seat atop the NASCAR Winston Cup Series point ladder after the first five races of the season. Most expected Jeff Gordon to be in that spot.

Even fewer would have thought the Chip Ganassi Racing Dodge driver would win a pair of races in the opening events of the year – and in truth, he had cost himself the chance to make it three victories in five events with his ill-advised attempt to play on-track mechanic during the redflag at Daytona.

And fewer still would have predicted rookie Ryan Newman would be in second place in the point standings after the first five races. Or that fellow rookie Jimmie Johnson would be fifth, or that Matt Kenseth would be third.

Yet, that's the way the standings lined up as teams arrived at Bristol Motor Speedway in northeastern Tennessee for the first short-track event of the season, the Food City 500.

The top 10 in the standings had been jumbled following the Darlington race, with Ward Burton, Tony Stewart, Mark Martin and Kurt Busch all falling down the chart after their involvement in a multi-car accident. Stewart was hospitalized after the wreck, but all the tests were negative and the feisty Indiana "pacer" was ready to compete at Bristol.

While Ward, Tony, Mark and Kurt were hoping to climb back into contention in the chase for the championship, there were some other, simpler goals at the top of the list for some drivers. For Rusty Wallace, Jeff Gordon, Jeff Burton, Bill Elliott, Dale Jarrett, Terry Labonte and Robby Gordon, the goal at Bristol was to score a top-five finish for the first time this season.

While those drivers were trying to find the right combination, team owner/driver Brett Bodine was delighted to announce that the Atlanta-based Hooters restaurant chain had signed on to sponsor his Fords for the remainder of the season. In addition to the Hooters backing, two of Eastern Foods' other products – Naturally Fresh salad dressings and Jackaroo barbeque sauce – would also sponsor journeyman driver Kirk Shelmerdine in five NASCAR Winston Cup Series races. Shelmerdine, who won four championships as the late Dale Earnhardt's crew chief before he decided to pursue a career as a driver, would field Fords from Bodine's shop. It was great news for Bodine, who was on the brink of closing his shop's doors before Brooks and Hooters came to the rescue.

(Above) While running third, Ryan Newman (12) fights for control after a bump from Tony Stewart. Unable to correct, Newman made contact with the first-turn wall and the resulting damage ultimately dropped him to 37th place, his first finish out of the top 14 so far this year.

The Food City 500 marked a milestone for Mark Martin. It was his 500th career start, and he remarked how much the sport had changed since he made his NASCAR Winston Cup Series debut April 5, 1981 at North Wilkesboro (N.C.) Speedway. Gone were the days when cars were towed to the track on either flatbed or tilt-bed haulers; when volunteer crew members slept six or eight in a motel room on the floor to save enough to buy another set of tires. The old one-handled tool boxes, the auto supply store jackstands and the days of a driver working on his car, ferrying it to the track, racing it and then driving it home were now history. Yet Martin, who had once carried the "Dennis The Menace" character on his short-track cars, had done it all.

At the completion of Bud Pole qualifying, Bristol boasted an all Gordon front row. Jeff Gordon claimed the pole with a speed of over 127.2 mph on the high-banked half mile, while Robby Gordon had his Cingular Monte Carlo right alongside. Jeremy Mayfield and Jimmy Spencer dialed up hot laps in their Dodges to grab the second-row starting positions, relegating Mike Skinner and Matt Kenseth to the third row. Jerry Nadeau and Ryan Newman were seventh and eighth fastest, ahead of Michael Waltrip and defending race champion Elliott Sadler.

For the second straight race, only 43 cars were in the garage area, ensuring everyone of a starting position. NASCAR made the decision that when

(Left) Johnny Benson loses traction after a nudge from Sterling Marlin in the first turn on lap 133. The Valvoline Pontiac wound up backing into the wall, ending Benson's shot at a competitive finish.

(Right) Jimmie Johnson (48) tries the low groove on outside pole-winner Robby Gordon (31). Johnson, who started mid-pack in 33rd, managed to avoid being involved in any major incidents on his way to a lead-lap, seventh-place finish. His fourth consecutive top 10 moved Johnson into fourth in the standings, 118 points behind Marlin.

(Below) Ricky Rudd (28) enters the turn with John Andretti (43) and Kevin Harvick (29) hot on his tail. Rudd drove like the pro he is, working into the top 10 by midway through the race and finishing a strong third, his first top-10 finish of the season.

43 cars or less were at the track, the provisionals for starting positions 37-43 would not count against the year-end total for provisionals. Instead, those positions would be filled in order of car owner points. At Bristol, those starters were Martin, Terry Labonte, Joe Nemechek, Hut Stricklin, Rick Mast, Dick Trickle and Hermie Sadler.

The high-banked oval is kind of a throwback to the bullrings where many a NASCAR Winston Cup Series driver got his start. Racing is tight and fast and there's little room for error. Throw in the fact that the Food City 500 is the first short-track race of the season, and it all adds up to making the events at "Thunder Valley" some of the best of the year from the standpoint of on-track action. This year's edition of the spring Bristol race would be no exception.

It didn't take long to get started – just one lap, in fact – when Robby Gordon headed for pit road for a pass-through penalty for jumping the start. The first yellow flew on the fifth lap after Buckshot Jones spun and hit the wall, and before the afternoon was over, nearly every car in the field carried a battle scar or two.

Ward Burton had ignition problems, John Andretti hit the wall, Steve Park spun and hit the wall, Johnny Benson collected a wall, and Jeff Gordon clipped the apron and became yet another wall-whacker. Sterling Marlin cut a tire and lost a pair of laps, Jeff Burton clipped Ryan Newman, and when Newman came off the wall, he collected Dale Jarrett. Tony Stewart spun and

(Above) Kurt Busch receives congratulations from NASCAR president Mike Helton following his initial NASCAR Winston Cup Series win.

(Left) Kurt Busch (97) stretches his advantage over Jimmy Spencer (41), Sterling Marlin (40) and Ricky Rudd (28). Busch drove into the lead for the first time on lap 411 during the 13th caution of the race and led all but one of the remaining 90 laps to score the win.

then turned his car over to Todd Bodine after suffering lower back pain as a result of his Darlington accident.

In the final stages of the race, Spencer appeared headed for victory until Kurt Busch nudged him. Jimmy had to fight to get the car under control, and Busch scooted into the lead. The final yellow flag flew with 20 laps remaining when Hermie Sadler hit the fourth-turn wall, and when the race restarted, Kurt Busch fought off the advances of Spencer and went on to record his initial NASCAR Winston Cup Series victory. At 23, he became the youngest winner since Jeff Gordon won the 1994 Coca-Cola 600 at the age of 22.

Spencer was not pleased with being bumped from the lead and was forced to settle for second. Ricky Rudd survived to claim third ahead of Dale Earnhardt Jr., and Bobby Labonte came home in fifth place. Matt Kenseth was sixth ahead of Jimmie Johnson, with Jerry Nadeau eighth. Rusty Wallace and Kevin Harvick were ninth and 10th ahead of Mark Martin and Kyle Petty.

Food City 500 final race results

Fin. Pos.	Start Pos.	Car No.	Driver	Team
1	27	97	Kurt Busch	Rubbermaid Ford
2	4	41	Jimmy Spencer	Target Dodge
3	20	28	Ricky Rudd	Havoline Ford
4	23	8	Dale Earnhardt Jr.	Budweiser Chevrolet
5	32	18	Bobby Labonte	Interstate Batteries Pontiac
6	6	17	Matt Kenseth	DeWalt Power Tools Ford
7	33	48	Jimmie Johnson	Lowe's Chevrolet
8	7	25	Jerry Nadeau	UAW-Delphi Chevrolet
9	15	2	Rusty Wallace	Miller Lite Ford
10	22	29	Kevin Harvick	GM Goodwrench Service Chevrolet
11	37	6	Mark Martin	Pfizer/Viagra Ford
12	35	45	Kyle Petty	Sprint Dodge
13	11	32	Ricky Craven	Tide Ford
14	3	19	Jeremy Mayfield	Dodge Dealers/UAW Dodge
15	13	20	Tony Stewart	Home Depot Pontiac
16	38	5	Terry Labonte	Kellogg's Chevrolet
17	17	77	Dave Blaney	Jasper Engines & Transmissions Ford
18	19	7	Casey Atwood	Sirius Satellite Radio Dodge
19	16	40	Sterling Marlin	Coors Light Dodge
20	2	31	Robby Gordon	Cingular Wireless Chevrolet
21	30	9	Bill Elliott	Dodge Dealers/UAW Dodge
22	18	36	Ken Schrader	M&M's Pontiac
23	5	4	Mike Skinner	Kodak Chevrolet
24	34	1	Steve Park	Pennzoil Chevrolet
25	29	22	Ward Burton	Caterpillar Dodge
26	26	99	Jeff Burton	CITGO SUPERGARD Ford
27	24	30	Jeff Green	America Online Chevrolet
28	12	55	Bobby Hamilton	Schneider Electric Chevrolet
29	25	88	Dale Jarrett	UPS Ford
30	9	15	Michael Waltrip	NAPA Chevrolet
31	1	24	Jeff Gordon	DuPont Chevrolet
32	43	02	Hermie Sadler	Little Trees Chevrolet
33	41	90	Rick Mast	Duke's Mayonnaise/Sauer's Ford
34	21	43	John Andretti	Cheerios Dodge
35	40	23	Hut Stricklin	Hills Bros Coffee Dodge
36	31	11	Brett Bodine	Hooters/Wells Fargo Financial Ford
37	8	12	Ryan Newman	ALLTEL Ford
38	14	14	Stacy Compton	Conseco Pontiac
39	28	10	Johnny Benson	Valvoline Pontiac
40	36	44	Buckshot Jones	Georgia Pacific Dodge
41	10	21	Elliott Sadler	Motorcraft Ford
42	42	71	Dick Trickle	Warranty Gold/Pro Motorsports Chevrolet
43	39	26	Joe Nemechek	Haas Carter Motorsports Ford

Samsung/RadioShack 500

Duct tape peels back under force on Stacy Compton's Conseco Pontiac at super-fast Texas Motor Speedway. Newly repaved, Texas became one of the fastest venues on the tour when Bill Elliott clicked off a qualifying lap at 194.224 miles per hour to capture the Bud Pole for the race. Compton started sixth in his best qualifying effort so far this season.

(Right) The silver machines of Kevin Harvick (29) and Sterling Marlin (40) race together along Texas' frontstretch. After a temporary "setback" at Bristol, where Marlin finished out of the top 10 for the first time this season, the point leader was back on form with a seventh-place finish.

(Below) Matt Kenseth hoists the hardware after giving his competition the boot at Texas. The second two-time winner this season, Kenseth solidified his hold on second in the points.

(Bottom Right) Bobby Labonte, typically strong on the 1.5-mile quad-ovals including here in his native state where he sports three top threes and an eighth place in his last four appearances, stands ready prior to the Samsung/RadioShack 500. Unfortunately, his string of top 10s at Texas would end with a disappointing 30th place.

Unlike the winners of the first five races of the season, Kurt Busch had plenty of time to savor his first career NASCAR Winston Cup Series victory. Instead of heading for a test session or the next event on the schedule, Busch used the Easter weekend break to enjoy friends and family on a brief vacation to the Bahamas.

Other drivers and crew members also used the holiday respite to recharge their batteries and get acquainted with their families again, and by the time the NASCAR Winston Cup Series tour reassembled at Texas Motor Speedway for the Samsung/RadioShack 500, crew members were ready to rock and roll.

The Easter break also allowed frazzled tempers to cool down after doing the "Bristol stomp," although Kevin Harvick, Dale Earnhardt Jr. and Robby Gordon each found their wallets lighter after NASCAR fined the trio for their antics at "Thunder Valley."

Harvick's $15,000 fine came after his altercation with Greg Biffle following the NASCAR Busch Series event the day before the main event, and the GM Goodwrench Chevrolet driver also found himself on probation until the end of August. The punishment encompassed all NASCAR events, not just NBS races, and Harvick suddenly found he would have to think more than twice about how he reacted at the race track.

Gordon and Earnhardt's fines resulted from the "cool-off" lap altercation between the two following some race-time scuffles. "Little E," upset with what had happened during the race, whacked his Budweiser Chevrolet into the side of Gordon's Cingular Chevrolet on the cool-off lap and Gordon paid him back by belting the Budweiser Monte Carlo in the rear and triggering a pit-road spin as the two finished the event. Little E forked over $5,000 to NASCAR and Gordon was $10,000 lighter in his hip pocket.

expected at the repaved Texas track, Chevrolet's forces hoped they would return to the hunt for victory lane.

While the Chevrolet teams were reconfiguring the snouts of their mounts, Dale Jarrett anticipated the return of Todd Parrott as his crew chief. "D.J." had struggled through the first six races of the season in the "Big Brown Truck." It had become apparent to car owner Robert Yates that things weren't working the way he had hoped when Parrott became team manager and stepped away from the crew chief's role at the start of the season to be replaced by Jimmy Elledge. The two mechanical wizards never meshed the way Yates had hoped they would, and Elledge made the decision to step aside and relinquish his crew chief role. Jarrett was mired in 24th place in the standings and hoped to make advances beginning at Texas.

Despite that, the Chevrolet teams had high hopes heading to the 1.5-mile Fort Worth area oval, with NASCAR approving a 1.25-inch addition to the front of the Monte Carlos. The "Bowtie Brigade" had failed to win in the first six races of the season, and with high speeds

(Left) Robby Gordon oversees preparation of a backup Cingular Wireless Chevrolet after a brush with the wall in qualifying damaged his primary mount. Gordon's luck at Texas didn't get much better; he cut a tire and smacked the fourth turn wall, bringing out the fifth of seven cautions in the race.

(Below) Jimmie Johnson (48) is followed by fellow rookie Ryan Newman (12) and Dale Jarrett (88), with Mark Martin (6), Jeff Gordon (24) and Matt Kenseth on the outside. Kenseth, Gordon and Martin finished 1-2-3, while Johnson put on another impressive performance, posting his fifth straight finish of seventh or better.

(Above) Third-place starter Ricky Rudd (28) edges Elliott Sadler (21), who drove his Wood Brothers Ford to the outside pole in qualifying. Rudd, hitting his stride in the Havoline Ford after a shaky start to the season, stayed among the leaders throughout the race and posted his second straight top-five finish.

Despite finishing out of the top 10 for the first time in 2002, Sterling Marlin continued to lead the NASCAR Winston Cup Series point standings after Bristol. He had managed to make up one of the two laps lost when he cut a tire and finish 19th in the Food City 500.

Ryan Newman's 37th place at Bristol sent him plunging from second to seventh in the point standings, and that moved Matt Kenseth up into the runner-up slot on the point ladder.

Rusty Wallace also moved up, into third place, while Jimmie Johnson continued to impress by finishing seventh and advancing to fourth place in the standings. Kurt Busch's victory jumped his No. 97 Roush Racing/Rubbermaid/Sharpie Ford all the way to fifth place, three points ahead of Earnhardt Jr., while Mark Martin found himself eighth in points, 10 behind Newman. Jeff Burton was ninth, a single point ahead of Jeff Gordon, while Ward Burton fell out of the top 10.

Every team expected the new, smoother pavement at Texas would add to the pole speed, and after test sessions, some drivers acknowledged the speeds would be "extra fast." When Bud Pole qualifying was completed, Bill Elliott was the driver who held his breath the longest, bringing back memories of his "fighter pilot" approach to Talladega (Ala.) Superspeedway in the 1980s.

Elliott simply blistered the Texas oval, rocketing his No. 9 Evernham Dodge to a speed of more than 194.2 miles per hour and leaving the garage area residents shaking their heads at his accomplishment. Elliott Sadler put his Motorcraft Ford on the outside of the front row, to the delight of the Wood Brothers.

Ricky Rudd and Michael Waltrip made up the second row ahead of Dale Jarrett and Stacy Compton, while Jeremy Mayfield and Mark Martin claimed the fourth-row starting positions. Little E and Ricky Craven claimed the final top-10 starting positions. Ron Hornaday was the only driver not to make the field, with Jeff Burton, Jerry Nadeau, Dave Blaney, Bobby Hamilton,

(Below) Crews spring into action along pit road during green-flag pit stops. Although there were seven caution flags, the race saw three full rounds of stops under green.

Mike Skinner, Buckshot Jones and Brett Bodine using provisionals to make the field.

Two days of heavy rain and a tornado watch following qualifying meant the Samsung/RadioShack 500 would be held on Monday morning. For the first two-thirds of the race, it appeared Jarrett was on his way to notching his first victory of the season. He dominated the early going but ran out of fuel while running a tight second to Rusty Wallace. At the finish, Jarrett, in the No. 88 UPS Ford, could do no better than finish 24th, three laps down.

Matt Kenseth started 31st because of an engine problem that forced a motor change prior to qualifying; by lap 37 he had fought his way into the top 15. A pair of caution flags on laps 241 and 255 put the DeWalt Ford driver at the point when leader Tony Stewart pitted under the second yellow flag for tires, and from that point on, Kenseth had the horse for the course and took his nag to the flag.

Out in clean air, Kenseth had every answer for every challenge and rolled to his second victory of the season and the third of his career, giving Jack Roush's outfit two successive wins. Kenseth's convincing victory from the rear of the field underscored the competitiveness of his team and signaled his second place in the point standings was not a fluke.

Jeff Gordon fought to second place, beating Mark Martin for the position, while Ricky Rudd claimed fourth place. Stewart fought back to fifth in his Home Depot Pontiac, while Jimmie Johnson continued his impressive performances by grabbing sixth place from point-leader Sterling Marlin. Jimmy Spencer was eighth ahead of pole-winner Elliott, and Terry Labonte scored his first top-10 finish of the season.

(Above) Team owner Jack Roush (left) was more than happy to trade his usual Fedora for a more appropriate hat in Texas Motor Speedway's victory lane. Kenseth's second trip to the winner's circle this season was his car owner's second straight after teammate Kurt Busch posted the win at Bristol.

(Left) Jeff Gordon (24) tries to close the gap on Matt Kenseth with the laps winding down, but to no avail. Kenseth, after staring last due to an engine change, took the lead for the first time on lap 242, then set sail on the field, leading 85 of the final 93 laps in a convincing win.

Samsung/RadioShack 500 final race results

Fin. Pos.	Start Pos.	Car No.	Driver	Team
1	31	17	Matt Kenseth	DeWalt Power Tools Ford
2	26	24	Jeff Gordon	DuPont Chevrolet
3	8	6	Mark Martin	Pfizer/Viagra Ford
4	3	28	Ricky Rudd	Havoline Ford
5	29	20	Tony Stewart	Home Depot Pontiac
6	13	48	Jimmie Johnson	Lowe's Chevrolet
7	20	40	Sterling Marlin	Coors Light Dodge
8	21	41	Jimmy Spencer	Target Dodge
9	1	9	Bill Elliott	Dodge Dealers/UAW Dodge
10	27	5	Terry Labonte	Kellogg's Chevrolet
11	28	2	Rusty Wallace	Miller Lite Ford
12	41	4	Mike Skinner	Kodak Film Chevrolet
13	33	10	Johnny Benson	RadioShack/MLB Pontiac
14	10	32	Ricky Craven	Tide Ford
15	39	77	Dave Blaney	Jasper Engines Ford
16	17	30	Jeff Green	America Online Chevrolet
17	2	21	Elliott Sadler	Motorcraft Ford
18	7	19	Jeremy Mayfield	Dodge Dealers/UAW Dodge
19	6	14	Stacy Compton	Conseco Pontiac
20	11	1	Steve Park	Pennzoil Chevrolet
21	14	45	Kyle Petty	Sprint Dodge
22	18	43	John Andretti	Cheerios Dodge
23	19	97	Kurt Busch	Sharpie/Rubbermaid Ford
24	5	88	Dale Jarrett	UPS Ford
25	25	29	Kevin Harvick	GM Goodwrench Service Chevrolet
26	42	44	Buckshot Jones	Georgia Pacific Dodge
27	30	23	Hut Stricklin	Hills Bros Coffee Dodge
28	4	15	Michael Waltrip	NAPA Chevrolet
29	34	90	Rick Mast	Duke's Mayonnaise/Sauer's Ford
30	15	18	Bobby Labonte	Interstate Batteries Pontiac
31	40	55	Bobby Hamilton	Schneider Electric Chevrolet
32	38	25	Jerry Nadeau	UAW-Delphi Chevrolet
33	32	26	Frank Kimmel	Advanced Auto Parts Ford
34	12	36	Ken Schrader	Combos/Snickers Pontiac
35	23	7	Casey Atwood	Sirius Satellite Radio Dodge
36	16	49	Shawna Robinson	BAM Racing Dodge
37	35	71	Jay Sauter	Warranty Gold Chevrolet
38	43	11	Brett Bodine	Hooters Restaurants Ford
39	37	99	Jeff Burton	CITGO SUPERGARD Ford
40	36	12	Ryan Newman	ALLTEL Ford
41	24	31	Robby Gordon	Cingular Wireless Chevrolet
42	9	8	Dale Earnhardt Jr.	Budweiser Chevrolet
43	22	22	Ward Burton	Caterpillar Dodge

Virginia 500

Bobby Labonte salutes his team, already celebrating on pit road, after taking the checkers for his first win of the 2002 season.

2805
VIRGINIA
500
VIRGINIA
500

(Above) Bobby Hamilton (55) leads Jeff Gordon (24), Dale Earnhardt Jr. (8), Terry Labonte (5) and Rusty Wallace (2) into turn one in the opening laps. Hamilton, who turned the second-fastest lap in qualifying, led on three occasions and stayed among the leaders throughout most of the race.

(Right, Above) Six-time Martinsville winner Rusty Wallace (right) discusses matters with Jeff Burton, who won at the Virginia half mile in 1997. Wallace stayed near the front for most of the day until Mike Skinner clipped his car on pit road, resulting in an extra stop that dropped Rusty from winning contention.

(Right) Tony Stewart brings the Home Depot Pontiac down pit road while Ricky Rudd (28), Bill Elliott (9) and Ricky Craven (32) complete their stops under caution. Stewart's car was very strong and led the most laps in the event, but a late-race call for tires foiled his bid for the win.

Matt Kenseth's second victory of the young season did more than just allow him to close the margin on point leader Sterling Marlin. It was a huge confidence booster for his Roush Racing/DeWalt Tools team, and each of his yellow-and-black-clad crew members had a little extra spring in his step upon arrival at Martinsville Speedway for the Virginia 500.

It's hard enough to win a race on the NASCAR Winston Cup Series tour. So many teams are competitive and so many have the opportunity to accomplish the goal every week. Yet racing luck plays a huge role, and the right call at the right time on pit road by a crew chief can spell the difference between winning and losing. A fumbled lug nut on a pit stop, a set of mismatched tires, stalling the car on pit road and being mired in the middle of the pack for a late restart, being collected in someone else's mess – any one of these reasons and a hundred others can keep a driver and team from winning even when they have the fastest car in the field.

Winning one race is tough. Snaring a pair in the first seven races of the season is even more difficult. But when you do, and when your team has clearly established itself as a bona fide contender – well, that explains the attitude of the DeWalt team at Martinsville.

After chopping 29 points from Marlin's lead, Kenseth now trailed the Coors Light Dodge driver by just 70 markers. Jimmy Johnson continued his climb and moved to third place in the standings, trailing Kenseth by 49 points, while Rusty Wallace slipped from third to fourth following his 11th place at Texas.

Mark Martin's fighting third place moved him from eighth to fifth, just 12 points behind Rusty, and Jeff Gordon's second-place finish vaulted him from 10th to sixth, just 29 points behind Martin. Bristol winner Kurt Busch finished 23rd at Texas and slipped from fifth to seventh place in the standings, while Tony Stewart's fifth place moved him from 12th to eighth, six points behind Busch. Ricky Rudd's fourth place at Texas helped propel him into the top 10 in the point standings for the first time this season, while Bill Elliott's ninth place allowed him to ease past Dale Earnhardt Jr. for the final slot in the top 10.

"Little E" trailed Elliott by four points, and Ryan Newman's second straight poor finish dropped him from seventh to 12th on the point ladder.

The Martinsville paper clip-shaped half mile, nestled in the blooming azaleas and dogwoods, is one of the most beautiful sights and sites on the spring NASCAR Winston Cup Series tour. Whitewashed and sparkling under the leadership of Clay Campbell, millions of fans over the years have exulted in the spectacular beauty of the tiny track. Just as Bristol and its high banks provide action for the fans, the flat Martinsville layout promises plenty of bump-and-grind action every lap.

Jeff Gordon's second place at Texas was a major boost to his Hendrick Motorsports team. It was his first top-five finish of the season, and Gordon hoped it presaged good things to come for the DuPont team. He served notice to the field that he was back on form by turning the fastest lap in Bud Pole qualifying, rocking around the half mile with a lap at 94.181 mph. His speed just nipped the lap turned by Bobby Hamilton in Andy Petree's Square D Chevrolet, and forced Dale Earnhardt Jr. and Terry Labonte to settle for the second-row starting slots.

After the Chevrolets wrapped up the first two rows, Rusty Wallace found himself in the fastest Ford, with Bill Elliott's Dodge on his right in the third row. Kevin Harvick claimed the seventh-fastest time with Richard Childress' GM

(Above) Bobby Labonte holds his own in a crowd while taking the Interstate Batteries Pontiac (18) into the first turn with Jimmie Johnson (48) and Ryan Newman (12) on his right. Johnson and Newman, both making their first career starts at Martinsville, suffered mechanical woes resulting in their worst finishes of the year so far.

(Left) Jeff Burton (99) looks for room to squeeze under Jeremy Mayfield (19) with Hut Stricklin (23) closing from behind. Burton managed a ninth-place finish for the day, his first top 10 since Las Vegas, five races ago. Like Burton, Mayfield hadn't scored in the top 10 since his second place at Vegas, and he just missed at Martinsville, finishing 11th.

(Right) Rusty Wallace hangs on to his Miller Lite Ford after a little nudge from behind by Tony Stewart. Wallace gathered it in without further incident and both drivers continued on their way.

(Below) Michael Waltrip (15) and Dale Jarrett (88) charge into the turn inches apart. Jarrett worked through traffic after starting near the back of the field and put together a solid finish in fourth to post his first top five of the season.

Goodwrench Chevrolet, while Tony Stewart, Jimmy Spencer and Ryan Newman completed the top 10.

By the time the Virginia 500 took the green flag, however, Kenny Wallace had replaced Harvick in the silver-and-black Chevrolet. Harvick, competing in the Saturday NASCAR Craftsman Truck Series event, was penalized for rough driving. He spun Coy Gibbs during the event, and NASCAR took the step to sit Harvick out. Already on probation until the end of August, NASCAR officials yanked Harvick from the truck race and forced him to sit out Sunday's NASCAR Winston Cup Series event. A none-too-happy Richard Childress had to put Kenny Wallace in the No. 29 GM Goodwrench Chevrolet for the Virginia 500.

From the drop of the green flag, the 500-lap event looked like a runaway for Tony Stewart. Nearly recovered from the battering his body took in the Darlington accident, Stewart was on form early and often, leading 152 laps of the event and at times pulling away from the field to build leads in excess of two seconds.

But The Home Depot driver's hopes for victory came to an abrupt end on lap 446 when he and crew chief Greg Zipadelli made the decision to head for pit road under yellow and get new tires. Bobby Hamilton, running in second place, followed Stewart to pit road. That gave the lead to Bobby Labonte, who had no plans to pit with just over 50 laps left in the race. When the green flew, Labonte was at the point and not about to let anyone take the first short-track victory of his successful NASCAR Winston Cup Series career from him.

Two more cautions on laps 476 and 487 bunched the field and gave the likes of Matt Kenseth, Stewart and Dale Jarrett chances to make runs at the Interstate Batteries Pontiac driver, but Labonte kept everything in hand and fought back the challengers.

Kenseth, Stewart and Jarrett got into their own battle for second place, leaving Labonte alone at the point, and the Texan began to cruise away from the competition. With one lap remaining, Hamilton and Kyle Petty spun exiting the fourth turn, and when Labonte arrived at the start/finish line, he was given the yellow and white flags.

He settled back in his seat and completed the

final half mile, taking the checkered flag for the first time in 2002. The victory made him the 10th different winner in the last 10 events at Martinsville.

Kenseth won the battle for second place, with Stewart third and Jarrett fourth. Little E was fifth, with Terry Labonte, who led a green-flag lap for the first time since 2000, in sixth place. Ricky Rudd and Mark Martin were seventh and eighth, ahead of Jeff Burton and Kurt Busch, putting all four Jack Roush-owned cars in the top 10 at the checkered flag.

(Above) Joe Gibbs Racing was well represented at Martinsville with the Pontiacs of Bobby Labonte (18) and Tony Stewart (20). Running first and third when the 12th caution appeared, Stewart pitted for tires along with second-place Hamilton, but Labonte elected to stay on the track and took the lead for good.

(Left) Celebrating in victory lane are (from left) team owner Joe Gibbs, crew chief Jimmy Makar, Miss Winston Cielo Garcia and Bobby Labonte. Labonte's 19th career win was his first on a short track.

Virginia 500 final race results

Fin. Pos.	Start Pos.	Car No.	Driver	Team
1	15	18	Bobby Labonte	Interstate Batteries Pontiac
2	26	17	Matt Kenseth	DeWalt Power Tools Ford
3	8	20	Tony Stewart	Home Depot Pontiac
4	31	88	Dale Jarrett	UPS Ford
5	3	8	Dale Earnhardt Jr.	Budweiser Chevrolet
6	4	5	Terry Labonte	Kellogg's Chevrolet
7	13	28	Ricky Rudd	Havoline Ford
8	17	6	Mark Martin	Pfizer/Viagra Ford
9	23	99	Jeff Burton	CITGO SUPERGARD Ford
10	20	97	Kurt Busch	Sharpie/Rubbermaid Ford
11	19	19	Jeremy Mayfield	Dodge Dealers/UAW Dodge
12	29	40	Sterling Marlin	Coors Light Dodge
13	33	15	Michael Waltrip	NAPA Chevrolet
14	36	22	Ward Burton	Caterpillar Dodge
15	22	23	Hut Stricklin	Hills Bros Coffee Dodge
16	5	2	Rusty Wallace	Miller Lite Ford
17	25	77	Dave Blaney	Jasper Engines Ford
18	16	14	Stacy Compton	Conseco Pontiac
19	39	10	Johnny Benson	Valvoline Pontiac
20	27	45	Kyle Petty	Sprint Dodge
21	9	41	Jimmy Spencer	Target Dodge
22	38	30	Jeff Green	America Online Chevrolet
23	1	24	Jeff Gordon	DuPont Chevrolet
24	32	1	Steve Park	Pennzoil Chevrolet
25	12	4	Mike Skinner	Kodak Film Chevrolet
26	30	11	Brett Bodine	Hooters Ford
27	2	55	Bobby Hamilton	Schneider Electric Chevrolet
28	37	21	Elliott Sadler	Motorcraft Ford
29	35	02	Hermie Sadler	Virginia Lottery Chevrolet
30	18	32	Ricky Craven	Tide Ford
31	6	9	Bill Elliott	Dodge Dealers/UAW Dodge
32	7	29	Kenny Wallace	GM Goodwrench Service Chevrolet
33	28	44	Buckshot Jones	Georgia Pacific Dodge
34	11	31	Robby Gordon	Cingular Wireless Chevrolet
35	14	48	Jimmie Johnson	Lowe's Chevrolet
36	40	36	Ken Schrader	M&M's Pontiac
37	42	90	Rick Mast	Duke's Mayonnaise/Sauer's Ford
38	34	7	Casey Atwood	Sirius Satellite Radio Dodge
39	24	25	Jerry Nadeau	UAW-Delphi Chevrolet
40	41	26	Frank Kimmel	Advance Auto Parts Ford
41	10	12	Ryan Newman	ALLTEL Ford
42	21	43	John Andretti	Cheerios Dodge
43	43	71	Andy Hillenburg	Warranty Gold Chevrolet

Aaron's 499

The tightly-packed field rounds the fourth turn at mammoth Talladega Superspeedway led by the DEI duo of Michael Waltrip in his NAPA Chevrolet and Dale Earnhardt Jr. in the Budweiser Monte Carlo.

PEPSI
HILLS BROS
CAT
TARGET

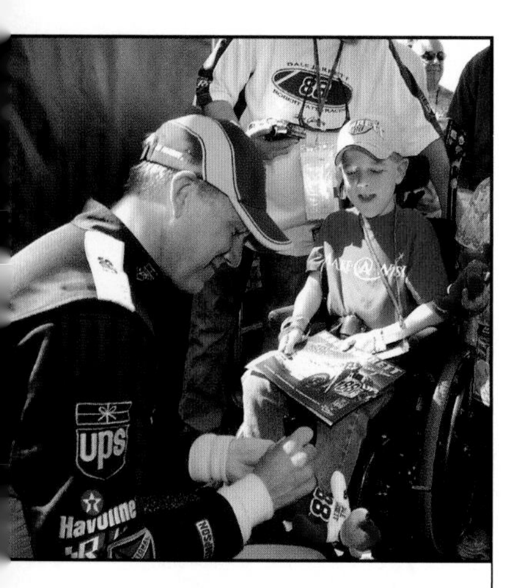

(Above) Dale Jarrett, his spirits bolstered by his first top-five finish of the season last week at Martinsville, gladly signs autographs for the Talladega fans. Another strong showing netted the UPS driver a sixth place and a jump of eight positions in the standings over the past two events.

(Right) Michael Waltrip and Dale Earnhardt Jr. scoot through the tri-oval with nearly the entire field rumbling behind, all within a second or two of the leaders. Little E put on quite a show in this one, leading the race on 10 different occasions for a total of 133 laps – more than 350 of the 500-mile distance.

(Below Right) Kevin Harvick ponders his GM Goodwrench Chevrolet along with team member Mike Moore in the Talladega garage. Harvick was in need of a good run after sitting out the weekend at Martinsville, but luck was not on his side as Harvick was caught in the backstretch melee on lap 164.

There's always a challenge built into the NASCAR Winston Cup Series schedule. For example, it may be a road-course race scheduled right after an event on an "intermediate" track or a 500-mile run on a superspeedway following 500 grueling laps on a short track. Throughout the season, teams are tested in a variety of ways, and it is this crucible that forges the true championship contenders.

OK, it may be an overused cliché, but it is what separates the men from the boys.

Team chemistry, preparation and planning, having the right cars prepared at the right time, scheduling test sessions, building the ideal engine for the right moment of competition – all are part of what determines who is left standing when the time comes to make the final run toward the brass ring.

In this case, the fastest superspeedway on the circuit followed the slowest short track on the schedule, and drivers had little time to mentally transition from the cut-and-thrust of the Virginia 500 at Martinsville, Va., to the Aaron's 499 at Talladega, Ala.

After being "parked" at Martinsville, Kevin Harvick was back behind the wheel of the No. 29 GM Goodwrench Chevrolet at Talladega. The lost points from the event dropped him from 22nd to 29th in the standings, and he was well aware he needed to put together a season full of solid finishes from here on out if he wanted to climb back into any form of contention for the championship.

Bobby Labonte's Martinsville victory vaulted him from 17th to 12th in the point standings, but it was the combination of Matt Kenseth's Rock of Gibraltar runner-up finish and Sterling Marlin's 12th-place showing that made things interesting at the top of the point ladder. Kenseth's rush had closed the gap between himself and Marlin to a mere 27 points, and the DeWalt Tools driver was beginning to make people believe that he was a bona fide championship contender. Mark Martin's eighth place moved him from fifth to third in the standings, while Rusty Wallace maintained fourth place. Tony Stewart's fighting third place at Martinsville moved him from eighth to fifth in

Martinsville to move up two spots to a tie with Ricky Rudd for ninth in the point standings.

While the youth brigade (Kenseth, Johnson, Busch, Ryan Newman) had been the toast of the media over the past several races, veteran Ricky Rudd was quietly putting together a three-race string of top-seven finishes that made the Havoline Ford driver smile as he made his way to the Robert Yates Racing hauler at Talladega. If he could continue those finishes, Rudd believed he would contend for the championship he had sought throughout his career.

the standings, while Kurt Busch moved up one notch to sixth place.

Jimmie Johnson lost a lot of ground with his 35th-place finish; he fell from third in the standings to seventh, while Jeff Gordon also dropped a couple of spots to eighth. Dale Earnhardt Jr., chomping at the bit like a stallion in rut to get to the next restrictor-plate race, used his fifth at

In another portion of the garage area, Steve Grissom was sliding into the Petty Enterprises Georgia Pacific-sponsored Intrepid. Petty had released Buckshot Jones after crashing out of the Martinsville event, and Grissom now had the opportunity to show he should be back in a NASCAR Winston Cup Series ride.

Jimmie Johnson toured the 2.66-mile track at

(Left) Mark Martin considers the nuances of his Ford with help from team engineer Bob Osborne (left) and crew chief Ben Leslie between practice sessions. A third at Texas and an eighth at Martinsville had pushed Martin into the top 10 in points, but Talladega was not as kind to him.

(Below) A four-wide Ford quartet with Hut Stricklin (23), Mark Martin (6), Kurt Busch (97) and Geoffrey Bodine (09) tackles the 33-degree Talladega high banks. On the whole, the group did well; Busch took third place in the race, with Stricklin and Bodine just missing the top 10. Martin, on the other hand, was caught up in the multi-car wreck, his first DNF of the year.

"ANGEL" RESCUES ROUSH

Following the end of qualifying for the Aaron's 499 NASCAR Winston Cup Series event, team owner Jack Roush and a group of friends began celebrating Jack's 60th birthday by taking to the skies in a variety of aircraft. A veteran pilot, Roush was piloting an unfamiliar twin-engined Air Cam – a lightweight aircraft designed for aerial photography – when the plane hit a partially-obscured power line, flipped and crashed upside down into a lake in a subdivision near Troy, Ala.

Luckily for Roush, a "guardian angel" was close by at the time. Larry Hicks, a state conservation officer and retired U.S. Marine, saw the accident from his home on the lake. Hicks told his wife to call 911 and immediately ran to his boat, paddled it the 30 yards to the crash site and began diving in the eight feet of water to try to rescue Roush.

On his third dive he found Roush jammed into the front of the plane. Hicks unhooked the safety harness and pulled Roush, who was not breathing, to the surface. Surrounded by floating – and potentially explosive – aviation fuel, Hicks began CPR. On the fifth breath, Roush began responding and Hicks then was assisted by rescue workers, who transported the severely battered racer to the hospital. He had head injuries, a compound fracture of the left leg and fractured ribs. Stabilized at Troy Regional Medical Center, Roush was then airlifted to the University of Alabama-Birmingham Medical Center, where he underwent surgery and began what could only be called a miraculous recovery.

"It's simply a wonderful feeling to save another human being, especially an individual who touches so many people," said Hicks, who was overcoming a life-threatening bout with cancer. "Now, if I were to get cancer back and pass away tomorrow, my whole life has been blessed by this event."

Terry Labonte (5) and outside pole-winner Robby Gordon (31) form a double-file draft leading Jeff Gordon (24), Dale Earnhardt Jr. (8), Rusty Wallace (2) and Jerry Nadeau (25), leaving Kurt Busch (97) looking for help on the high side. Gordon pulled off his second top five of the year and moved up one spot in the standings to seventh.

186.532 mph in his Lowe's Chevrolet to win the pole, and Robby Gordon put his Cingular Chevrolet on the outside of the front row. Michael Waltrip and "Little E" made it a Dale Earnhardt Inc. second row, with Ward Burton and Stacy Compton grabbing the third-row starting positions from Johnny Benson and Ryan Newman. Steve Park and Jeff Gordon completed the top 10, edging Terry Labonte and Kyle Petty for the fifth-row starting slots.

Kenseth headed the list of drivers needing provisionals to make the race. He was joined by Bill Elliott, Rudd, Elliott Sadler, Dale Jarrett, Mike Skinner and Bobby Hamilton. Shawna Robinson, Rick Mast, Dick Trickle (in a Ray Evernham-prepared Dodge) and Bobby Gerhart all failed to make the 43-car field.

The NASCAR Winston Cup Series garage area, at first stunned by the news of Jack Roush's airplane accident and then heartened by the news of his progress (see inset story) turned to "business as usual" for the Aaron's 499.

And it turned out it was the "usual business" for the DEI efforts of Little E and Michael Waltrip during the running of the 500-mile event on the mammoth Talladega Superspeedway. With wins in two of the last three restrictor-plate races, Earnhardt Jr. was thoroughly enjoying his jaunts to Talladega. With Waltrip – an accomplished restrictor-plate racer as teammate – Earnhardt knew if he could stay in the hunt throughout the afternoon, the Budweiser Chevrolet would have a chance to visit victory lane for the third time in the last four "plate" races.

That's the way it turned out at the end, with Little E at the point and Waltrip second when the race was red-flagged with just a handful of laps left. Waltrip felt he had a chance to win, but when drafting help didn't materialize in the closing laps, Waltrip was left to protect Little E's rear bumper as the duo rolled to a DEI one-two finish.

Throughout the contest, drivers had white-knuckled their way around the track, lap after lap, hoping the "Big One" would not occur as they drafted inches apart. But on lap 164 it

Johnny Benson's Valvoline Pontiac goes up in flames after the battery caught fire while the car was on the track under caution. Benson, who had just pitted for tires following the lap-164 incident, was assisted by members of several teams on pit road and was later treated and released from the infield care center.

happened, triggered when Mike Wallace nudged Tony Stewart against the outside wall. When the backstretch smoke had wafted into the pristine Alabama air, a total of 24 cars had been involved in the accident, ending victory hopes for many.

The mess was cleared away and the green flag waved again on lap 176, but when Sterling Marlin's Coors Light Dodge stalled in the third turn on lap 181, the final caution waved. On lap 183, the red flag was displayed, stopping the event until the track could be cleared and leaving Michael Waltrip to ponder if he had enough in his NAPA Chevrolet to beat his teammate. When the green flew again, Jimmie Johnson, Jeff Burton and Geoff Bodine were behind Waltrip for the short sprint. None could help him enough to pass Little E in the closing laps.

Kurt Busch fought his way to third place ahead of Jeff Gordon and Marlin. Dale Jarrett claimed sixth ahead of Johnson, with Rusty Wallace charging to eighth place. Jeff Burton and Kyle Petty rounded out the top 10.

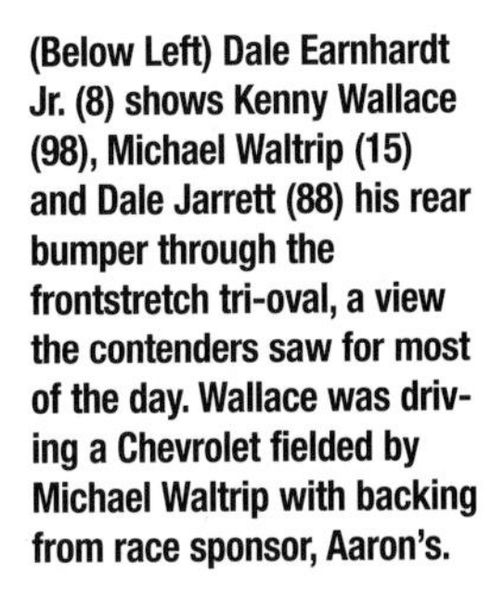

(Below Left) Dale Earnhardt Jr. (8) shows Kenny Wallace (98), Michael Waltrip (15) and Dale Jarrett (88) his rear bumper through the frontstretch tri-oval, a view the contenders saw for most of the day. Wallace was driving a Chevrolet fielded by Michael Waltrip with backing from race sponsor, Aaron's.

(Below) Little E pumps his fist in victory as the celebration begins. The win, the sixth of his career, was the first for the Bud driver since his triumph at Talladega in October 2001.

Aaron's 499 final race results

Fin. Pos.	Start Pos.	Car No.	Driver	Team
1	4	8	Dale Earnhardt Jr.	Budweiser Chevrolet
2	3	15	Michael Waltrip	NAPA Chevrolet
3	20	97	Kurt Busch	Rubbermaid Ford
4	10	24	Jeff Gordon	DuPont Chevrolet
5	33	40	Sterling Marlin	Coors Light Dodge
6	41	88	Dale Jarrett	UPS Ford
7	1	48	Jimmie Johnson	Lowe's Chevrolet
8	13	2	Rusty Wallace	Miller Lite Ford
9	25	99	Jeff Burton	CITGO SUPERGARD Ford
10	12	45	Kyle Petty	Sprint Dodge
11	22	23	Hut Stricklin	Hills Bros Coffee Dodge
12	23	09	Geoffrey Bodine	Miccosukee Indian Resort Ford
13	24	11	Brett Bodine	Hooters/Wells Fargo Financial Ford
14	38	28	Ricky Rudd	Havoline Ford
15	5	22	Ward Burton	Caterpillar Dodge
16	30	30	Jeff Green	America Online Chevrolet
17	32	41	Jimmy Spencer	Target Dodge
18	35	32	Ricky Craven	Tide Ford
19	39	9	Bill Elliott	Dodge Dealers/UAW Dodge
20	11	5	Terry Labonte	Kellogg's Chevrolet
21	27	98	Kenny Wallace	Aaron's Chevrolet
22	43	55	Bobby Hamilton	Schneider Electric Chevrolet
23	42	4	Mike Skinner	Kodak Chevrolet
24	36	36	Ken Schrader	M&M's Pontiac
25	34	44	Steve Grissom	Georgia Pacific Dodge
26	16	7	Casey Atwood	Sirius Satellite Radio Dodge
27	6	14	Stacy Compton	Conseco Pontiac
28	14	29	Kevin Harvick	GM Goodwrench Service Chevrolet
29	26	20	Tony Stewart	Home Depot Pontiac
30	37	17	Matt Kenseth	DeWalt Power Tools Ford
31	21	77	Dave Blaney	Jasper Engines & Transmissions Ford
32	15	25	Jerry Nadeau	UAW-Delphi Chevrolet
33	2	31	Robby Gordon	Cingular Wireless Chevrolet
34	9	1	Steve Park	Pennzoil Chevrolet
35	29	26	Frank Kimmel	Advance Auto Parts Ford
36	31	19	Jeremy Mayfield	Dodge Dealers/UAW Dodge
37	19	6	Mark Martin	Pfizer/Viagra Ford
38	28	43	John Andretti	Cheerios Dodge
39	7	10	Johnny Benson	Valvoline Pontiac
40	40	21	Elliott Sadler	Motorcraft Ford
41	17	18	Bobby Labonte	Interstate Batteries Pontiac
42	18	33	Mike Wallace	Preen Chevrolet
43	8	12	Ryan Newman	ALLTEL Ford

NAPA Auto Parts 500

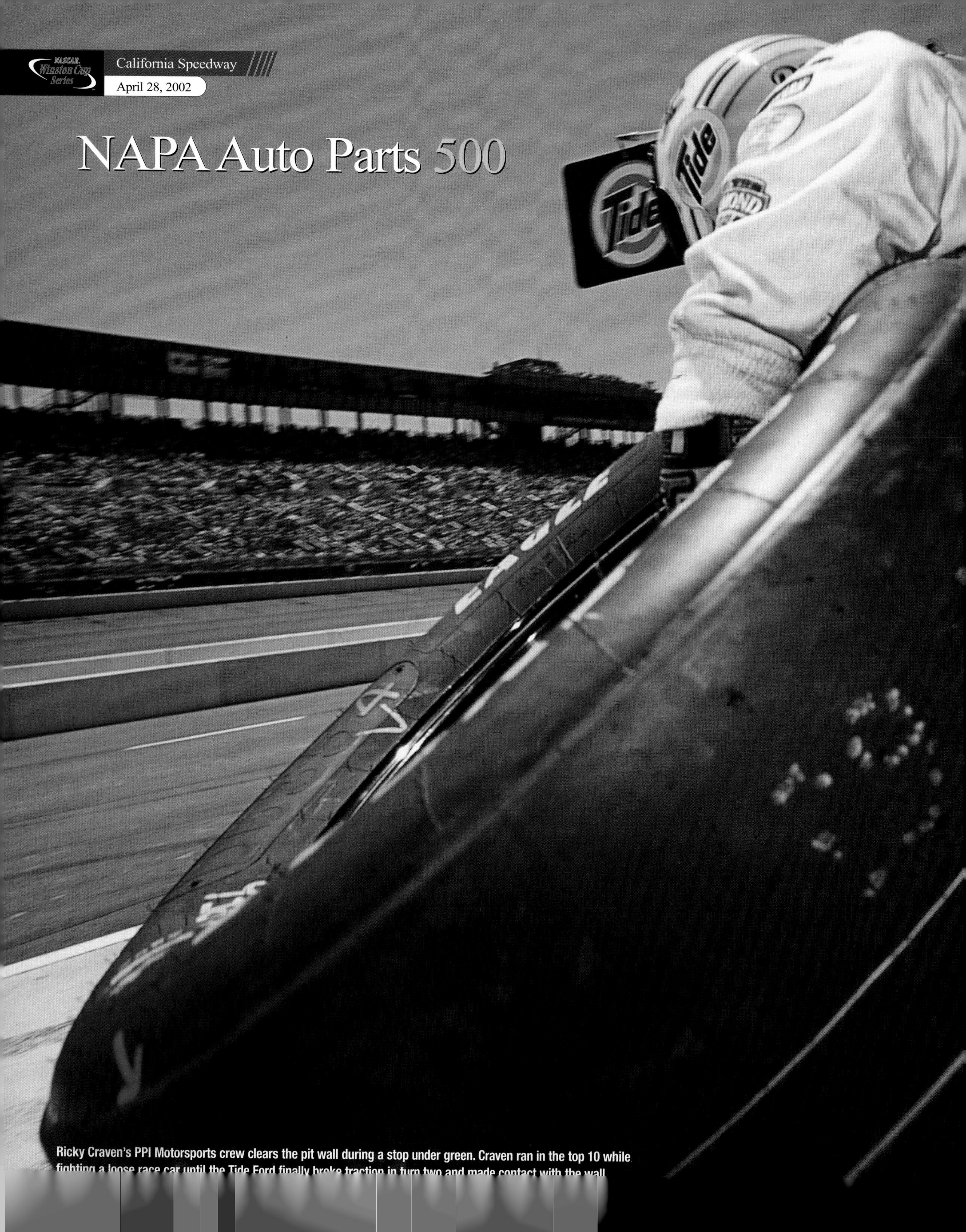

Ricky Craven's PPI Motorsports crew clears the pit wall during a stop under green. Craven ran in the top 10 while fighting a loose race car until the Tide Ford finally broke traction in turn two and made contact with the wall.

32
Tide

The "Big One" in the final portion of the Aaron's 499 at Talladega Superspeedway had scrambled the point standings – but instead of an expected battle for the top spot in the points at California in the NAPA Auto Parts 500, Sterling Marlin had not simply held onto the point lead, he had expanded it.

Marlin's drive to fifth place in his silver No. 40 Coors Light Dodge at Talladega, coupled with Matt Kenseth's 30th-place finish, cost the DeWalt Tools driver more than 70 points, although Kenseth managed to hold onto second place in the standings. Rusty Wallace moved to third, while Mark Martin, who had held third place heading into Talladega, plummeted to ninth in the standings after his 37th-place finish.

Tony Stewart also took a point hit after being involved in the multi-car accident, falling from fifth to eighth in the standings after his 29th-place finish. On the other hand, Kurt Busch used his third-place Talladega finish to move from sixth to fourth in the point standings, and Dale Earnhardt Jr.'s victory vaulted him from a ninth-place tie to fifth in the points, just 14 behind Busch. Jimmie Johnson continued his torrid rookie pace, moving up a spot to sixth in the standings after his seventh-place Talladega effort, while Ricky Rudd dropped from a ninth-place tie to 10th, ahead of Jeff Burton and Bill Elliott.

With Jack Roush firmly on the road to recovery following his aviation mishap in Alabama and with Talladega behind them, the teams arrived at the two-mile California Speedway ready to contest the NAPA Auto Parts 500. Since the opening of the track five years ago, the jewel of a facility has become one of the favorite stops on the tour. Impeccably maintained, it is one of the finest facilities on the schedule.

(Above) Jimmie Johnson collects his first NASCAR Winston Cup Series trophy, which came in his 13th career start and in his native state of California. Johnson, who led on four different occasions throughout the race, took the lead for good after a call for fuel only by crew chief Chad Knaus during the final caution.

(Right) Jimmy Spencer, one of those who pitted on the first caution at lap 20, heads back into action after service from his Target crew.

(Far Right) Sterling Marlin splits the difference between John Andretti (43) and Jerry Nadeau (25) in his Coors Dodge, this week painted in the gold of Coors Original. Marlin continued his season of consistency at California by posting his eighth top-10 finish.

Few were surprised to find Penske Racing South driver Ryan Newman securely on the pole at the conclusion of Bud Pole qualifying. With one of the fastest Fords on the circuit, and although classified as a Raybestos NASCAR Rookie of the Year contender, the eye-opening performances Newman posted in a few races last year had not abated in 2002. His pole lap was 187.432 mph – merely a new track record.

(Left) Joe Nemechek (26), Jimmy Spencer (41) and Jeremy Mayfield (19) spread out three wide on California's frontstretch with Dale Earnhardt Jr. (8) and Matt Kenseth (17) looking for an opening from behind. Nemechek was behind the wheel of the Haas Carter Motorsports Ford after missing the previous three events.

Kurt Busch continued on a roll in the Roush Racing/Rubbermaid Ford, claiming the outside front row and certainly giving his car owner reason to smile during his recovery period. Dale Jarrett posted the third-fastest lap, and the former champion hoped to get his United Parcel Service Ford untracked on the two-mile oval. After finishing sixth at Talladega, Jarrett hoped his team finally had some momentum.

Jimmie Johnson arrived in his native California in sixth place in the standings and immediately claimed the outside of the second row during qualifying. Jerry Nadeau and Michael Waltrip made up the third row for the start of the race, ahead of Elliott Sadler and Tony Stewart. Dale Earnhardt Jr. and Rusty Wallace completed the top 10 ahead of Johnny Benson and Casey Atwood.

Ricky Rudd led the list of those forced to use provisionals to make the field, joined by Jeff Burton, Bill Elliott, Robby Gordon and Steve Grissom, in his second outing in the Petty Enterprises/Georgia Pacific Dodge. Rick Mast and Shawna Robinson completed the provisional list, leaving Brendan Gaughan, Chad Little and Hermie Sadler on the sidelines for the race.

In the track's inaugural race in 1997, native son Jeff Gordon rocketed to victory, giving the California media members plenty to hang their headlines on for Monday's papers. How fitting then, that Jimmie Johnson, in his first NASCAR Winston Cup Series outing on the two-mile oval, should also find a way to the winner's circle – and in a car partially owned by Gordon. It was a perfect way to end the Southern California weekend.

And it came when crew chief Chad Knaus made the right call at a critical moment in the event, putting Johnson in position to score the first NASCAR Winston Cup Series victory of his brief career and give long-suffering Lowe's Home Improvement stores their first victory as a team sponsor after years of trying.

The final caution of the race, setting the stage for Knaus' late-race decision, came on lap 230 after Little E and Kevin Harvick tangled. Earnhardt took a hard lick when he hit the outside wall but was all right after groggily shaking his head to clear the cobwebs and collecting the breath that had been knocked from him.

Kurt Busch was the race leader at the time, trailed by Johnson and Rudd. The leaders headed for pit road and Johnson was the first of the group to exit after Knaus called for fuel only. All of the others who pitted took at least two tires, and when Johnson lined up for the restart, the only driver in front of him was Bill Elliott, who had eschewed a trip to pit road.

Johnson wasted no time in grabbing the lead. He moved past Elliott on the backstretch when the green flag flew and then had to fight off challenges from both Busch and Rudd in the closing laps to claim the flagman's checkered banner. The

Kurt Busch (97), Jimmie Johnson (48) and Michael Waltrip (15), who qualified second, fourth and sixth, respectively, vie for position in early race action. Busch led six times for 101 laps to take the five-point, lap-leader bonus and finally took second place behind Johnson. Waltrip came home in 10th place for car and event sponsor NAPA.

Elated Lowe's team members give an assist to Jimmie Johnson on the way to victory lane after Johnson, while celebrating his initial victory with burnouts, broke the motor in his Chevrolet.

battle between Busch and Rudd for second place was decided when Busch passed Rudd for the final time on lap 248, while Johnson eased to a six car-length victory.

The 21-year-old Californian had been a threat to win several times earlier in the season, but had saved the best for his native state. As he cut doughnuts and did the now seemingly obligatory burnout to celebrate the victory, one could almost hear the strains of California Dreamin' wafting through the air.

Bill Elliott claimed fourth place behind Rudd, while Mark Martin made it two Jack Roush-owned cars in the top five. Jarrett was sixth with another strong performance, and point-leader Sterling Marlin clawed his way to seventh in a gold Coors Original paint scheme. Rusty Wallace was eighth ahead of Dave Blaney, while Michael Waltrip brought his NAPA Chevrolet home 10th in his sponsor's event.

NAPA Auto Parts 500 final race results

Fin. Pos.	Start Pos.	Car No.	Driver	Team
1	4	48	Jimmie Johnson	Lowe's Chevrolet
2	2	97	Kurt Busch	Sharpie/Rubbermaid Ford
3	37	28	Ricky Rudd	Havoline Ford
4	39	9	Bill Elliott	Dodge Dealers/UAW Dodge
5	26	6	Mark Martin	Pfizer/Viagra Ford
6	3	88	Dale Jarrett	UPS Ford
7	25	40	Sterling Marlin	Coors Light Dodge
8	10	2	Rusty Wallace	Miller Lite Ford
9	32	77	Dave Blaney	Jasper Engines Ford
10	6	15	Michael Waltrip	NAPA Chevrolet
11	16	30	Jeff Green	America Online Chevrolet
12	40	31	Robby Gordon	Cingular Wireless Chevrolet
13	29	16	Greg Biffle	jr.com/Volvo Trucks Ford
14	1	12	Ryan Newman	ALLTEL Ford
15	11	10	Johnny Benson	Valvoline Pontiac
16	17	24	Jeff Gordon	DuPont Chevrolet
17	19	45	Kyle Petty	Sprint Dodge
18	27	22	Ward Burton	Caterpillar Dodge
19	38	99	Jeff Burton	CITGO SUPERGARD Ford
20	20	17	Matt Kenseth	DeWalt Power Tools Ford
21	34	5	Terry Labonte	Kellogg's Chevrolet
22	18	1	Steve Park	Pennzoil Chevrolet
23	36	11	Brett Bodine	Hooters Ford
24	24	43	John Andretti	Cheerios Dodge
25	13	26	Joe Nemechek	Checker/Shuck's/Kragen Auto Parts Ford
26	5	25	Jerry Nadeau	UAW-Delphi Chevrolet
27	22	41	Jimmy Spencer	Target Dodge
28	12	7	Casey Atwood	Sirius Satellite Radio Dodge
29	8	20	Tony Stewart	Home Depot Pontiac
30	30	55	Bobby Hamilton	Schneider Electric Chevrolet
31	33	4	Mike Skinner	Kodak Film Chevrolet
32	42	90	Rick Mast	Duke's Mayonnaise/Sauer's Ford
33	41	44	Steve Grissom	Georgia Pacific Dodge
34	28	18	Bobby Labonte	Interstate Batteries Pontiac
35	21	29	Kevin Harvick	GM Goodwrench Service Chevrolet
36	9	8	Dale Earnhardt Jr.	Budweiser Chevrolet
37	15	32	Ricky Craven	Tide Ford
38	14	19	Jeremy Mayfield	Dodge Dealers/UAW Dodge
39	7	21	Elliott Sadler	Motorcraft Ford
40	31	23	Hut Stricklin	Hills Bros Coffee Dodge
41	35	14	Stacy Compton	Conseco Pontiac
42	43	49	Shawna Robinson	BAM Racing Dodge
43	23	36	Ken Schrader	M&M's Pontiac

Pontiac Excitement 400

Tony Stewart (20) and Jimmie Johnson (48) chase Jeff Gordon (24) on the inside, with Mark Martin (6) and Jeff Green (30) holding the upper groove on Richmond's smooth, three-quarter-mile speedway.

VIAGRA
(sildenafil citrate) tablet
6
VIAGRA
(sildenafil citrate) tablets
6
VIAGRA
Pfizer
Ford
AMERICA ONLINE
HOME DEP
48
LOWE'S
LOWE'S
48
LOWE'S
Visit Lowesracing.com

Ricky Rudd (28) takes the field under green for a restart on lap 164, leading (in order) Ward Burton, Jimmy Spencer, Jeff Green and Jeff Burton, with Matt Kenseth (17) leading the lap-down cars of Frank Kimmel (26) and Michael Waltrip (15) on the inside. Ward Burton, who set a new track record of 127.389 mph in qualifying, led 125 of the first 150 laps before transmission problems ended his challenge.

For the past several events, reporters had plenty of stories to develop and offer up to a hungry public. Among them were: Initial NASCAR Winston Cup Series career victories for Kurt Busch and now Jimmie Johnson; the surge to the front of Matt Kenseth; Sterling Marlin's dogged persistence in holding onto his lead in the points, and the aircraft accident that nearly claimed Jack Roush. All had garnered their share of headlines.

Now, with more than two-thirds of the season still to be completed, "silly season" had reared its head.

As teams arrived in the "Capital of the Confederacy" to compete in the Pontiac Excitement 400, Virginian Elliott Sadler's request for a release from his contract with Wood Brothers Racing went through the NASCAR Winston Cup Series garage like a cannon shot.

The Woods, of Stuart, Va., were not pleased with Sadler's request, to say the least. Eddie Wood told media members he expected that the 22-year-old from Emporia would continue to drive the Motorcraft Ford for the remainder of the season.

What Sadler had in mind – or why he asked to be let out of his contract – was yet unclear. Still there was plenty of fuel for the rumor mill, which also included Hendrick Motorsports, Robert Yates Racing and Dale Earnhardt, Inc., to name just a few.

It had become increasingly clear that the atmosphere wasn't one of total amity at DEI, where Michael Waltrip and Steve Park appeared on tenterhooks. Waltrip had run well in restrictor-plate races, but his NAPA-sponsored team had not exhibited any consistency. Park, in the six races since his return to the wheel at Darlington, S.C., had not yet rounded into the form he displayed before an accident in a NASCAR Busch Series race last September put him on the sidelines. Could Sadler be a possible replacement for one of them?

Or was Sadler headed for Robert Yates Racing, where he would replace Ricky Rudd? Rudd had already stated he would not sign another long-

term contract at this stage of his career and would prefer to ink year-to-year agreements if he decided to continue racing. Or, Rudd, 45, noted, he just might call it a career after 25 years behind the wheel.

In another scenario, Sadler could ease over to Hendrick Motorsports and slip into the window of the No. 25 car. Things already seemed tense with that team and crew chief Tony Furr had already left. Was Jerry Nadeau next? And if so, could Sadler fit into that program?

No one would clarify anything – and few would deny silly-season musings. It was an interesting way to start the Richmond weekend.

After the dramas of Talladega and California, teams appeared ready to contest the last of three short-track races on the first half of the schedule. Sterling Marlin had turned in another championship-winning performance at California, working his way to a solid seventh place, and when he arrived at Richmond he found a different car parked next to his in the garage area. Kurt Busch, on the strength of his recent performances, had moved into second place in the standings, but Marlin's margin had increased to 143 points over his closest challenger.

Matt Kenseth was now third in points, while Rusty Wallace was fourth, just two points ahead

(Left) The UPS Ford sits behind the wall for repairs after Dale Jarrett got loose near the exit to turn four and was hit hard by Bobby Labonte. Jarrett eventually returned to the race, but lost nearly 100 laps and ended a string of three straight top-six finishes.

(Below) The Home Depot crew wraps up work on Tony Stewart's Pontiac as Jimmy Spencer and Jimmie Johnson blast away from their pits. With 14 cautions for 103 laps, teams had lots of opportunity to adjust – and repair – their cars, which played well into Stewart's hands.

(Right) Mark Martin's Viagra Ford ignites some fuel upon entering the corner on Saturday night. Martin drove a smart race to fourth place, which moved him from sixth to fourth in the point standings.

(Below) Jimmy Spencer (41) and Jeff Burton (99) engage in some side-by-side racing through the corners. Spencer led 59 laps in the second half of the race and looked like a strong contender for the win until a tangle with Jimmie Johnson dropped him from the point to a 10th-place run. Burton narrowly avoided serious problems and took third in the race to nail down his first top five of the season.

of California winner Jimmie Johnson. Mark Martin had moved from ninth back to sixth, making it three Jack Roush-owned cars in the top six in the standings. Jeff Gordon remained seventh in the points, while Ricky Rudd's third place at California moved him from 10th to eighth on the point table. Dale Earnhardt Jr. slalomed from fifth place to ninth after his 36th-place finish at California, and although beaten and bruised from his hard lick with the California concrete, said he was ready to race at Richmond. Tony Stewart, Bill Elliott, Jeff Burton and Dale Jarrett, now 13th in points, were all waging their weekly war for 10th place.

Virginian Ward Burton gave his home-state fans plenty to anticipate when he put the Caterpillar Dodge on the inside of the front row at the conclusion of Bud Pole qualifying, and Little E showed he was ready to race by grabbing the outside of the front row. Pre-event favorite Tony Stewart plunked the Home Depot Pontiac on the inside of the second row, beating Jeff Gordon for the spot, while Park responded to his situation by qualifying fifth fastest. Kyle Petty surprised the garage area by putting the Sprint Dodge on the outside of the third row ahead of Matt Kenseth and Bobby Labonte, while Rusty Wallace and Ricky Craven beat Ryan Newman and Ricky Rudd for the fifth row.

Using provisionals to make the field were Kurt Busch, Bill Elliott, Dale Jarrett, Jimmy Spencer, John Andretti, Frank Kimmel (in Travis Carter's No. 26) and Randy Renfrow. Only Kevin Grubb failed to make the field.

The Pontiac Excitement 400 took two days to complete after being stopped via a red flag for rain on lap 68 at 9:40 p.m. Saturday evening. Teams scrambled for places to sleep and when the green flag flew the following afternoon, Dale Jarrett held the lead over Michael Waltrip, Bobby Hamilton, Rusty Wallace and David Green.

Back in the pack, working his way through traffic after being forced to start at the rear after an engine change, was Stewart. Not known as the most patient driver in the field, Stewart took a page from teammate Bobby Labonte's book and eased his way through traffic. As contenders wrecked and spun and as leaders found a way to lose the race, Stewart eased and picked his way toward the front.

The orange Pontiac finally surfaced at the point with just 28 laps to go when Stewart fought his way past Ryan Newman, and once in the

(Left) In the late stages of the race, Tony Stewart (20) stalks Ryan Newman, his final victim of the day. Stewart qualified third for the race but was forced to start at the rear of the field after an engine change. Once under green, the Home Depot driver, with two wins and five top 10s in his six previous starts at Richmond, patiently went from worst to first to capture his second win of the season.

(Below Left) Media members gather around the colorful Stewart before the Richmond event.

lead, Stewart motored away to a 1.48-second margin over runner-up Newman. The victory was his second of the season and was a fitting reward for the patience he had displayed throughout the marathon event. It was also testimony to his crew and crew chief Greg Zipadelli, who made subtle change after subtle change during pit stops to tune the chassis to the track.

Jeff Burton fought to third place ahead of Mark Martin and Jeremy Mayfield, while Matt Kenseth took sixth place. Jeff Gordon was seventh ahead of Steve Grissom, Ricky Craven and Jimmy Spencer.

Pontiac Excitement 400 final race results

Fin. Pos.	Start Pos.	Car No.	Driver	Team
1	3	20	Tony Stewart	Home Depot Pontiac
2	11	12	Ryan Newman	ALLTEL Ford
3	23	99	Jeff Burton	CITGO Ford
4	18	6	Mark Martin	Pfizer/Viagra Ford
5	17	19	Jeremy Mayfield	Dodge Dealers/UAW Dodge
6	7	17	Matt Kenseth	DeWalt Power Tools Ford
7	4	24	Jeff Gordon	DuPont Chevrolet
8	20	44	Steve Grissom	Georgia Pacific Dodge
9	10	32	Ricky Craven	Tide Ford
10	40	41	Jimmy Spencer	Target Dodge
11	35	40	Sterling Marlin	Coors Light Dodge
12	16	10	Joe Nemechek	Valvoline/Maxlife Pontiac
13	14	30	Jeff Green	America Online Chevrolet
14	38	9	Bill Elliott	Dodge Dealers/UAW Dodge
15	22	36	Ken Schrader	M&M's Pontiac
16	32	23	Hut Stricklin	Hills Bros Coffee Dodge
17	36	55	Bobby Hamilton	Schneider Electric Chevrolet
18	30	02	Hermie Sadler	Virginia Lottery Chevrolet
19	33	11	Brett Bodine	Hooters Restaurants Ford
20	41	43	John Andretti	Cheerios Dodge
21	21	21	Elliott Sadler	Motorcraft Ford
22	29	7	Casey Atwood	Sirius Satellite Radio Dodge
23	6	45	Kyle Petty	Sprint Dodge
24	27	15	Michael Waltrip	NAPA Chevrolet
25	9	2	Rusty Wallace	Miller Lite Ford
26	31	14	Stacy Compton	Conseco Pontiac
27	37	97	Kurt Busch	Rubbermaid Ford
28	19	4	Mike Skinner	Kodak Chevrolet
29	28	77	Dave Blaney	Jasper Engines & Transmissions Ford
30	1	22	Ward Burton	Caterpillar Dodge
31	26	48	Jimmie Johnson	Lowe's Chevrolet
32	8	18	Bobby Labonte	Interstate Batteries Pontiac
33	15	5	Terry Labonte	Kellogg's Chevrolet
34	5	1	Steve Park	Pennzoil Chevrolet
35	24	90	Rick Mast	Duke's Mayonnaise/Sauer's Ford
36	2	8	Dale Earnhardt Jr.	Budweiser Chevrolet
37	34	31	Robby Gordon	Cingular Wireless/Spiderman Chevrolet
38	39	88	Dale Jarrett	UPS Ford
39	12	28	Ricky Rudd	Havoline Ford
40	25	29	Kevin Harvick	GM Goodwrench Service Chevrolet
41	13	25	Jerry Nadeau	UAW-Delphi Chevrolet
42	42	26	Frank Kimmel	Pork The Other White Meat Ford
43	43	59	Randy Renfrow	Price Motorsports Dodge

The Winston

Ryan Newman (12) makes a hole up the middle between Tony Stewart (20) and Joe Nemechek (25) as he charges toward the front in The Winston. Newman made the all-star field by virtue of his win in the 16-lap No Bull Sprint.

(Right) Jeremy Mayfield (19) and Ryan Newman (12) bring the field around for the only restart in Winston Open. Mayfield clearly had the car to beat and proved it by taking the win in convincing fashion.

(Below Right) Jeremy Mayfield shows off his trophy with Miss Winston Cielo Garcia following his flag-to-flag victory in the Winston Open. Mayfield looked like a contender in the main event as well, driving from 26th to fourth in the first segment, but his luck ran out when he was collected in an accident before the second segment was completed.

(Below) Ryan Newman takes a quick breather after sprinting to the win in the final qualifying event to become the last driver entered in the 18th running of The Winston.

By the time teams assembled at Lowe's Motor Speedway in Concord, N.C., for the annual running of The Winston, the NASCAR Winston Cup Series' all-star event, ripples of change had begun to become evident in the garage area.

Jerry Nadeau had been released from the No. 25 Hendrick Motorsports/UAW-Delphi Chevrolet and then immediately found another ride for the weekend's events. Crew Chief Tony Furr had left the No. 25 team just a couple of weeks earlier, and two days after the Pontiac Excitement 400 in Richmond, Va., Nadeau found himself with an out-of-date contract and no ride.

At the same time, Johnny Benson had suffered a broken rib in an accident during the NASCAR Busch Series event at Richmond and was unable to compete in the NASCAR Winston Cup Series event. Joe Nemechek filled in for Benson at Richmond and when Nadeau became available for The Winston weekend, he was quickly hired to drive the No. 10 Valvoline Pontiac normally chauffeured by Benson.

Nemechek also found work. He was named as the driver for the Chevrolet vacated by Nadeau, with Ken Howes working as the interim crew chief for that effort. Nemechek was quite naturally happy to get a shot with one of Hendrick's powerhouse teams and called it a "golden opportunity" at this point in his career. He had started the season with high hopes in Travis Carter's Kmart-sponsored "26," but when funding disappeared (Kmart filed federal bankruptcy papers and ended its racing spon-

sorships), he found himself on the outside looking in. Nemechek was expected to drive the car for the remainder of this season.

Since the first running of The Winston in 1985, it had been a showcase event for drivers and teams with rich rewards for the winner. While points are not awarded, the "fans' race" has, through the years, developed a tradition of providing plenty of close action for competitors and plenty of fireworks for the thousands of spectators who circle the date on their calendars a year in advance.

The Winston has always had a different format than a "normal" NASCAR Winston Cup Series race, and that format has been changed and tweaked on nearly an annual basis as the event's organizers try to make an already fun-filled evening at LMS even more of a show for fans.

This year was no different. A total of 25 drivers and car owners were qualified for the race, with the winners of the Winston Open and the No Bull Sprint "consolation" races each earning a berth in the 90-lap running of The Winston. Drivers who had not already made the show would have two chances to get into The Winston.

And the 90-lap event itself underwent a tweak or two this year. The purse was boosted, with the

(Left) Matt Kenseth is happy to know that he will get the jump on the competition in The Winston by starting on the pole for the lucrative race. The DeWalt Tools team – the reigning pit crew champions – beat everyone on pit road with a 13.23-second four-tire stop, helping Kenseth to the fastest three-lap average.

(Below) Michael Waltrip, the 1996 The Winston champion, clicked off the second-fastest time in qualifying to place the NAPA Chevrolet on the front row next to Kenseth.

(Below) Bobby Hamilton's battered Square D Chevrolet grinds to a stop after a hard hit during the race's first segment. Also involved in the incident were Rusty Wallace, Dale Jarrett and Sterling Marlin, all of whom were finished for the night.

(Bottom) Jimmie Johnson (48) and Bill Elliott (9) lead the field toward a restart during the second segment of the race. Johnson drove from 17th to first in the first segment, and then led wire to wire in the second. But when the field of 10 was inverted for the start of the final 20-lap sprint, Johnson only had time to fight back to fifth before the checkers flew.

winner's share a whopping $750,000. That in itself would help the fireworks! All 27 cars would start the first 40-lap segment, and only the top 20 finishers would advance to the second segment of the race. That 30-lap segment would then reward only the first 10 finishers, turning the 20-lap, all green-flag shootout into a battle among the best – and perhaps hungriest – 10 drivers of the evening.

The elimination aspect of the second segment of the race meant that if drivers wanted a chance to win the event – and cash the huge check – they would have to flat-out sprint that second segment and hope they were not collected in someone else's mistake.

Qualifying for The Winston was also unique. Drivers started with a four-tire pit stop and then completed three laps at speed on the track. The fastest elapsed time earned the team the pole for the start of the race and a $50,000 bonus.

Michael Waltrip's NAPA Chevrolet was fast on the track, but Matt Kenseth's crew was a second faster on pit road, sending the DeWalt Tools driver to the top of the scoring pylon.

Jeremy Mayfield won the pole for the Winston Open and then went wire to wire to record his first victory of any type in Ray Evernham's Dodge. Ryan Newman used his last possible chance to enter The Winston by rolling to victory in the No Bull Sprint.

Those wins put Mayfield and Newman in the final starting slots for The Winston, and at the end of the first 40-lap segment – won by Jimmie Johnson – Newman had barely made it to the next part of the race. He was 20th – the final driver to move from the first segment to the second. During the second segment of the race, however, Newman found the right rhythm. He passed Jeff Gordon, Ricky Rudd, Terry and Bobby Labonte and eventually worked his way to finish seventh, while Johnson won again.

Others, like three-time event winner Jeff Gordon, would watch the final segment from the sidelines, not able to make it into the final 10. While Gordon was in the pits during a caution period, a rubber windshield-cleaning blade got loose from its long handle and fell off. Gordon left the pits with the offending piece on the ground in the pit box, a violation of the rules. He was sent to the rear of the field and ended up 11th in segment No. 2.

Sterling Marlin, Dale Jarrett, Rusty Wallace and Bobby Hamilton had already gone to the garage area after an accident ended their evening in the first segment. Mark Martin, Jeff Burton, Michael Waltrip, Joe Nemechek and Mayfield, along with Elliott Sadler, were victims of the second segment.

That left Johnson, Dale Earnhardt Jr., Bill Elliott, Ricky Craven, Kenseth, Kurt Busch, Kevin Harvick, Robby Gordon and Tony Stewart ready to do battle with Newman for the winner's share of the glory.

Fans voted to invert the entire field for the start of the final 20 laps, and Newman found himself starting fourth, and he wasted no time in getting his ALLTEL Ford to the front. Newman rocketed past Harvick and Robby Gordon and then wrestled the lead from Stewart. Newman flew away from the field, building a three-second lead that evaporated when Kurt Busch and Robby Gordon got together on the backstretch, bringing out a yellow flag. Little E was the only driver who could challenge Newman when the flags went green for the final time, but the

(Above) Rookie Ryan Newman enjoys the biggest win of his young NASCAR Winston Cup Series career, worth more than $794,000! Newman became the second rookie to capture the all-star crown, matching Dale Earnhardt Jr., who won it as a rookie in 2000.

(Left) Ryan Newman uses the low groove on LMS' fourth turn to slip past Tony Stewart on his way to the big win. By virtue of the inverted field, Stewart started the final sprint in the first position and led the first three laps before Newman worked past to lead the final 17 circuits.

Budweiser Chevrolet driver couldn't find what he needed to win a second straight all-star race.

Newman won by more than a car-length, with Little E second and Kenseth third. Busch was fourth ahead of Jimmie Johnson and Stewart, while Robby Gordon, Harvick and Craven finished ahead of Elliott.

Newman's winnings were nearly $800,000 – nearly as much as he had won in the first 11 point races of the season, combined.

The Winston final race results

Segment 1 (40 laps)

Fin. Pos.	Start Pos.	Driver
1	17	Jimmie Johnson
2	4	Jeff Burton
3	18	Bill Elliott
4	26	Jeremy Mayfield
5	5	Mark Martin
6	9	Ricky Craven
7	7	Jeff Gordon
8	11	Kurt Busch
9	8	Ricky Rudd
10	24	Dale Earnhardt Jr.
11	16	Robby Gordon
12	1	Matt Kenseth
13	3	Kevin Harvick
14	2	Michael Waltrip
15	6	Elliott Sadler
16	10	Terry Labonte
17	23	Tony Stewart
18	12	Joe Nemechek
19	13	Bobby Labonte
20	27	Ryan Newman
21	25	Ward Burton
22	22	Steve Park
23	19	Mike Wallace
24	14	Sterling Marlin
25	20	Bobby Hamilton
26	15	Dale Jarrett
27	21	Rusty Wallace

Segment 2 (30 laps)

Fin. Pos.	Start Pos.	Driver
1	1	Jimmie Johnson
2	10	Dale Earnhardt Jr.
3	3	Bill Elliott
4	6	Ricky Craven
5	12	Matt Kenseth
6	8	Kurt Busch
7	20	Ryan Newman
8	13	Kevin Harvick
9	11	Robby Gordon
10	17	Tony Stewart
11	7	Jeff Gordon
12	14	Michael Waltrip
13	9	Ricky Rudd
14	18	Joe Nemechek
15	16	Terry Labonte
16	19	Bobby Labonte
17	4	Jeremy Mayfield
18	5	Mark Martin
19	15	Elliott Sadler
20	2	Jeff Burton

Segment 3 (20 laps)

Fin. Pos.	Start Pos.	Car No.	Driver	Team
1	4	12	Ryan Newman	ALLTEL Ford
2	9	8	Dale Earnhardt Jr.	Budweiser Chevrolet
3	6	17	Matt Kenseth	DeWalt Tools Ford
4	5	97	Kurt Busch	Rubbermaid Ford
5	10	48	Jimmie Johnson	Lowe's Chevrolet
6	1	20	Tony Stewart	Home Depot Pontiac
7	2	31	Robby Gordon	Cingular Wireless Chevrolet
8	3	29	Kevin Harvick	GM Goodwrench Chevrolet
9	7	32	Ricky Craven	Tide Ford
10	8	9	Bill Elliott	Dodge Dealers/UAW Dodge

Coca-Cola Racing Family 600

Dale Jarrett attacks the fourth turn in his UPS Ford as the longest race of the year gets underway at Lowe's Motor Speedway.

(Above) Mark Martin emerges from his car with a huge grin and a lot of relief, having finally put an end to his winless streak of 73 races dating back to the spring of 2000.

(Right) Ricky Rudd (28) brings the field to the green flag ahead of Jimmie Johnson and Matt Kenseth for a restart on lap 136 after the fifth of nine cautions in the race. Jeff Burton (99) leads the lap-down cars after an unscheduled pit stop due to a vibration in his car.

It's one thing to nudge a driver and send him into a spin, bringing out a caution when the leader is running away from the field in an event like The Winston. It's quite another to admit to the activity when the television cameras are rolling during post-event interviews.

Roush Racing driver Kurt Busch learned the cost of talking about putting the chrome horn to Robby Gordon during the final segment of The Winston. NASCAR officials promptly created a vacant space in Busch's wallet to the tune of $10,000 in the days following The Winston.

While Ryan Newman was still trying to absorb the enormity of his accomplishment of capturing The Winston, it was time to return to the everyday battle of trying to win the NASCAR Winston Cup Series championship. The "fans' race" was history, Busch accepted his role as a chastised youngster, and the teams prepared for the Coca-Cola Racing Family 600.

Jeff Gordon, after not making the final segment of The Winston and being forced to watch from the sidelines, figured there was no better place to end the longest winless streak of his career. Lowe's Motor Speedway had been good to him so many times in the past, and Gordon hoped he could put an end to the streak of 19 races without a win he was carrying from track to track, much like the doomed Jacob Marley lugging his chains into Eb Scrooge's London flat on Christmas eve.

If Gordon was haunted by not winning since Sept. 30 at Kansas, he could empathize with Mark Martin, who had gone since April of 2000 without driving into a NASCAR Winston Cup Series victory lane. Martin's winless string was now at 73 events, and Jack Roush's Viagra Ford driver hoped the cards would finally turn for him at the end of the longest race of the season.

Martin had another reason to hope for victory. The Coca-Cola Racing Family 600 was also a No Bull 5 event, and if he could find a way to win, he would cash Winston's huge $1 million bonus check – and at the same time make a fan a millionaire, as well. The other drivers eligible for Winston's No Bull 5 bonus at Lowe's Motor Speedway were Newman, Jeremy Mayfield, Sterling Marlin and Tony Stewart.

The event also marked Ricky Rudd's 656th consecutive start in a NASCAR Winston Cup Series race, breaking the mark set by Terry Labonte. Rudd remembered when he drove a family-entered and prepared Ford in his early NASCAR Winston Cup Series outings in the mid-1970s. The sport – and Rudd's career – had certainly come a long way from those initial forays.

Marlin maintained the point lead he had held throughout most of the first third of the season, and as a result of the Richmond race, Kenseth moved back into second place in the standings. The DeWalt Tools Ford driver trailed Marlin by 132 points, while Kurt Busch held third place, 59 points behind his Jack Roush teammate.

Martin had moved to fourth in the standings, just two points behind Busch, and with Jeff Burton ensconced in ninth place in the standings, the four Roush drivers all occupied places within the top 10.

Rusty Wallace, slightly hobbled by three cracked toes as a result of hitting the wall in The Winston, was fifth in the standings, just 10 points behind Martin, while Gordon was solidly in sixth place, just 13 points behind Wallace.

Jimmie Johnson, who had nearly won The Winston, was seventh in the standings, seven points behind Gordon and 28 points ahead of Richmond winner Stewart. Rudd held 10th place, 13 points behind Jeff Burton and 31 points ahead of Bill Elliott.

Johnson left no doubt he was ready to rumble once again at Lowe's when he put his Monte Carlo on the pole during the Bud Pole qualifying session while setting a new track record at a blistering 186.464 miles per hour. He beat Elliott Sadler for the inside of the front row, while Ricky Craven and Ryan Newman were forced to settle for the second-row starting positions. Bill Elliott cranked up his Dodge and notched the fifth-fastest lap, just edging Dale Earnhardt Jr., while Jerry Nadeau made himself at home in the injured Johnny Benson's Valvoline Pontiac and grabbed the inside of the fourth row. Jeff Burton

(Above) Michael Waltrip (15) and Jeff Gordon (24) duel through the turns in a battle of Chevrolets. Neither driver led the race, but both scored top-10 finishes with Gordon fifth and Waltrip eighth in the final running order.

(Top Left) Jeremy Mayfield takes a lick on the fourth-turn wall and punctures the water barrier designed to dull the impact. Mayfield, who had to start at the rear of the field following an engine change, finished his frustrating weekend in the garage after this incident on lap 257.

(Bottom Left) Sterling Marlin (40) uses the outside line to sneak up on Rusty Wallace (2) and Terry Labonte (5), already going at it side by side through the turn. The trio finished the race together, with Wallace edging Marlin for 10th place and Labonte in 12th.

Mark Martin streaks through the first turn under the bright lights at LMS. Martin picked up a total of 24 positions over the course of the night and, on the strength of an outstanding 14-second pit stop by his crew, took the lead with 40 laps remaining and held on for the win.

was eighth with Ken Schrader and Tony Stewart beating Michael Waltrip and Robby Gordon for the final top-10 starting positions.

Robby Gordon knew no matter where he qualified, he would end up starting the Coca-Cola Racing Family 600 from the back of the pack. He was scheduled for "double duty" by running the Indianapolis 500 earlier in the day and then heading back to Charlotte to compete in the 600 that evening.

Ward Burton, Dale Jarrett, Jeff Green, Steve Grissom, Brett Bodine, Hermie Sadler and Ron Hornaday (in the BAM Racing Dodge usually driven by Shawna Robinson) used provisionals to make the field. Chad Little, Carl Long, Derrike Cope and Randy Renfrow were left to watch from the sidelines.

After finishing eighth at Indy, Robby Gordon arrived on the infield grass via helicopter in time to sprint to his Cingular Chevrolet, buckle in and flick the ignition switch to start the 600. And as the late afternoon turned into twilight - and then into evening – Jimmie Johnson merely picked up where he had left off the previous weekend, threatening to turn the 600 into a personal benefit. He led six different times for 263 laps as he tried to turn the event into a yawner – but in the end it was a pair of his own rookie mistakes that cost him his second career victory and opened the door for the veteran Martin.

Johnson, in the No. 48 Lowe's Chevrolet, was leading the event with 40 laps remaining when he made contact with Hut Stricklin's Hills Bros Dodge. He had been following Stricklin for more than a dozen laps and finally got too impatient.

When Stricklin spun, the leaders headed for pit road and Johnson agonizingly slid out of the front of his pit box, forcing his crew to push him backwards before they could get to work. By the time service was completed, Johnson found himself mired in the middle of the pack.

Martin's crew turned him back out after one of the Viagra team's best pit stops of the race. He had the lead, clean air, four sticker Goodyears and a Ford capable of fronting the field. When the green flag flew, he headed off into the bright lights.

Kenseth closed on his Roush teammate, getting all the way to Martin's rear bumper more than once. But he simply could not find a way to make the winning move as "aero push" reared its ugly head. During the final laps, Martin rocketed his way through lapped traffic with abandon, and Kenseth could do nothing other than settle for second place, about five car-lengths behind.

Martin heads for the finish line and the checkered flag with a half-second margin over second-place Matt Kenseth. The win, the 33rd of Martin's career, also bumped him into third in the standings and established him as a serious championship contender.

Martin's joyful doughnuts through the infield grass underscored his delight at finally winning, not to mention claiming the first Winston No Bull 5 $1 million bonus of his career. He was delighted to have also made Janet Hogan of Sterling, Va., an instant Winston millionaire, as well. Hogan was the fan paired with him as a result of Winston's fan sweepstakes held in conjunction with each Winston No Bull 5 race.

Craven finished ahead of Rudd, who celebrated his record-breaking start with fourth place. Jeff Gordon was fifth, beating Tony Stewart in a torrid battle for the position, and Jimmie Johnson fought his way back to seventh. Michael Waltrip was eighth, Bill Elliott ninth and Rusty Wallace 10th.

Coca-Cola Racing Family 600 final race results

Fin. Pos.	Start Pos.	Car No.	Driver	Team
1	25	6	Mark Martin	Pfizer/Viagra Ford
2	21	17	Matt Kenseth	DeWalt Power Tools Ford
3	3	32	Ricky Craven	Tide Ford
4	19	28	Ricky Rudd	Havoline Ford
5	16	24	Jeff Gordon	DuPont Chevrolet
6	10	20	Tony Stewart	The Home Depot Pontiac
7	1	48	Jimmie Johnson	Lowe's Chevrolet
8	11	15	Michael Waltrip	NAPA Chevrolet
9	5	9	Bill Elliott	Dodge Dealers/UAW Dodge
10	31	2	Rusty Wallace	Miller Lite Ford
11	35	40	Sterling Marlin	Coors Light Dodge
12	34	5	Terry Labonte	Cheez-It/Kellogg's Chevrolet
13	32	45	Kyle Petty	Sprint Dodge
14	23	18	Bobby Labonte	Interstate Batteries Pontiac
15	28	43	John Andretti	Cheerios/Star Wars Dodge
16	12	31	Robby Gordon	Cingular Wireless Chevrolet
17	17	7	Casey Atwood	Sirius Satellite Radio Dodge
18	9	36	Ken Schrader	Pedigree/M&Ms Pontiac
19	38	88	Dale Jarrett	UPS Ford
20	39	30	Jeff Green	America Online/Scooby Doo Chevrolet
21	14	77	Dave Blaney	Jasper Engines & Transmissions Ford
22	36	23	Hut Stricklin	Hills Bros. Coffee Dodge
23	29	55	Bobby Hamilton	Schneider Electric/Square D Chevrolet
24	13	4	Mike Skinner	Kodak Chevrolet
25	30	41	Jimmy Spencer	Target Dodge
26	33	26	Frank Kimmel	Pork the Other White Meat Ford
27	41	11	Brett Bodine	Hooters Restaurants Ford
28	7	10	Jerry Nadeau	Eagle One/Valvoline Pontiac
29	42	90	Hermie Sadler	Duke's Mayonnaise/Sauer's Ford
30	18	25	Joe Nemechek	UAW-Delphi Chevrolet
31	24	97	Kurt Busch	Rubbermaid Ford
32	40	44	Steve Grissom	Georgia Pacific/Brawny Dodge
33	2	21	Elliott Sadler	Motorcraft/U.S. Air Force Ford
34	26	29	Kevin Harvick	GM Goodwrench Service Chevrolet
35	6	8	Dale Earnhardt Jr.	Budweiser Chevrolet
36	43	49	Ron Hornaday	BAM Racing Dodge
37	15	14	Stacy Compton	Conseco Pontiac
38	20	1	Steve Park	Pennzoil Chevrolet
39	27	19	Jeremy Mayfield	Dodge Dealers/UAW Dodge
40	8	99	Jeff Burton	CITGO SUPERGARD Ford
41	4	12	Ryan Newman	ALLTEL Ford
42	37	22	Ward Burton	Caterpillar Dodge
43	22	38	Kevin Lepage	GEICO Direct Ford

MBNA Platinum 400

Jimmie Johnson's Lowe's Chevrolet flies past the grandstands at Dover Downs International Speedway on its way to victory lane for the second time in the 2002 NASCAR Winston Cup Series season.

LOWE'S
1-800-MARROW-2
QUAKER STATE
GMAC
EDS
HAAS
Econo Lodge
TOP CHOICE
LUMBER PRODUCTS
American Tradition
One Coat Paints

Jimmie Johnson leads (in order) Jeff Gordon, Ricky Rudd, Sterling Marlin, Dale Earnhardt Jr. and Dale Jarrett under the green flag for a restart on lap 221 following the fourth of seven cautions in the event. Jerry Nadeau, who qualified third while subbing for Johnny Benson in the Valvoline Pontiac, leads the inside line under the flagstand.

With his 73-race winless streak finally broken, Mark Martin was all smiles as he arrived in Delaware's capital city for the MBNA Platinum 400. Not only had he proven the circuit's "over-40" bunch weren't sleeping in the sun on the front porch, but he had also served notice that there was plenty of bite remaining in the veterans.

Rusty Wallace, Dale Jarrett, Ricky Rudd, Bill Elliott and Terry Labonte, among others in what some considered the "old dog" category, took heart with Martin's performance at Lowe's Motor Speedway. Would one of them be the next to teach the young whippersnappers in the NASCAR Winston Cup Series garage not to discount the talent of veteran drivers?

In the days between the Coca-Cola Racing Family 600 and the opening of practice for the MBNA Platinum 400, Elliott Sadler and the Wood Brothers had come to an agreement to cancel the three remaining years on Sadler's contract and make the Emporia, Va., driver a free agent. Many assumed Sadler was headed for the Texaco Havoline Ford presently driven by Rudd, but car owner Robert Yates said that the car and the ride were Rudd's, particularly if Ricky decided to extend his contract with Yates for the 2003 season. Rudd said he would make that decision by July 15 – also the deadline for Michael Waltrip and Steve Park at Dale Earnhardt, Inc. Both Waltrip and Park knew they were on tenterhooks, and Waltrip had begun to run better than in the early stages of the season. His eighth-place finish at LMS in the NAPA Chevrolet moved him to 14th in the point standings.

Whatever questions there were about Dale

Bobby Labonte (18) tries to get position on Dale Earnhardt Jr. (8) entering the first turn, with Terry Labonte (5) and Tony Stewart (20) coming from behind.

Jarrett moving from the UPS Ford to another team were quickly squelched by both Jarrett and car owner Yates. Jarrett said he had no intention of leaving the UPS team, and in fact, extensions were being worked on that would keep driver, team and sponsor together through 2006. No word, though, on how long the "Big Brown Truck" TV ad campaign would continue.

While Mark Martin's No. 6 Roush Racing team was anteing up the $50,000 fine imposed for Martin's Viagra Ford being one-eighth of an inch too low during the post-race inspection following his Winston No Bull 5 victory the previous week, all Roush teams welcomed car owner Jack Roush back to the garage area at Dover. It was Roush's first appearance at a track following his airplane accident during the Talladega weekend. True to form, Roush had flown himself to Dover and planned to fly himself back to his home following the MBNA Platinum 400.

Junie Donlavey, a NASCAR Winston Cup Series team owner since 1950, found himself searching for sponsorship for his No. 90 Ford after being notified that C.F. Sauer expected to cease backing his team following the upcoming Pocono, Pa., race. While Donlavey was on the sponsor hunt, Travis Carter rolled out his Discover Card Ford for Todd Bodine. The Dover race marked the first of a six-event sponsorship program for Discover, and Carter hoped strong performances might encourage Discover to continue its program.

Martin was not the only driver on a roll at the "Monster Mile." Matt Kenseth's fighting second place in the 600 continued to fuel the confidant fires within the DeWalt Tools team, and Matt gave his teammates yet another boost by claiming the Bud Pole during qualifying. Bill Elliott gave the "Dodge Boys" plenty to cheer about by claiming the outside front row, while Jerry Nadeau, released from the No. 25 Hendrick Motorsports team and filling in behind the wheel of the Valvoline Pontiac for the wounded Johnny Benson, qualified third.

Waltrip continued to try to save his job by putting the NAPA Chevrolet on the outside of the second row ahead of Kurt Busch and Ricky

(Above) The UPS team springs into action as Dale Jarrett brings his Ford to a stop under caution. With the help of great pit work, Jarrett was able to pick up a net gain of 26 positions over the 400 laps and post his second top-five finish of the season.

(Right) Bill Elliott's bright red Dodge worked well on the Dover concrete all weekend. Elliott captured the outside pole in qualifying and was an early leader in the race. As the laps wound down, he put on a stirring charge to catch Jimmy Johnson but ran out of laps.

Craven. Rudd and Sadler made up the fourth row, while Jeff Gordon and Jimmie Johnson beat Kyle Petty and Robby Gordon for the final top-10 starting positions.

Terry Labonte, Ryan Newman, Dave Blaney, Hut Stricklin, Steve Grissom, John Andretti and Todd Bodine used provisionals to make the field, leaving Derrike Cope, Hermie Sadler and Randy Renfrow on the sidelines for the event.

During the first quarter of the MBNA Platinum 400, it appeared Martin was headed for his second straight victory. He led handily, but then found his hopes for victory dashed when he was involved in the aftermath of a collision between Ryan Newman and Steve Park on lap 125. Martin continued, but finished 41st.

Jimmy Johnson, Jarrett and Rudd then established themselves as contenders for victory, as did Elliott in his red Dodge. Johnson finally took the lead from Rudd on lap 363 of the 400-lap event, and then saw his chances for a second career NASCAR Winston Cup Series win cemented when the caution flag flew for the final time on lap 373.

Ken Schrader's Pontiac dumped oil on the track when the rear end failed between the first and second turns, and crew chiefs had to decide whether to pit for tires and fuel for the final 25 laps or hope what they had would do the trick.

Johnson's crew chief, Chad Knaus, made the decision to gamble, leaving the rookie driver on the track with his Lowe's Chevrolet, while many of the other drivers on the lead lap headed for pit road. With 18 cars on the lead lap, "sticker" tires could play a big part in posting a strong finishing position during those final laps, but Johnson was

(Far Left) Jimmie Johnson's Chevrolet took the lead for the first time on lap 125. From there, Johnson led four times for 188 of the remaining 275 laps, including stints of 73, 75 and 38 laps, on his way to the win.

(Left) Jimmie Johnson signals his second win in 16 career NASCAR Winston Cup Series starts from Dover's victory lane. As in his initial victory at California, a gutsy call by crew chief Chad Knaus to forego new tires in favor of track position late in the race was a critical element in the win.

told to remain on the track. Knaus believed track position and clean air would be more beneficial in the short sprint to the checkered flag.

It turned out that he was right – but it's a good thing there were not one or two more laps remaining at the end. Johnson handled the crowd, moving to his second career victory during his first season, but Elliott thrilled the mass of spectators with a brilliant charge that netted a fighting second place. Rudd, running second and ready to challenge Johnson, was forced to pit road with a loose rear tire, opening the door for Elliott's spectacular charge. At the checkered flag, the Redhead's Intrepid lost by a half-second. Elliott felt that if the race had gone a lap or two longer, he would have been able to pass Johnson.

Jeff Burton battled to third place ahead of Ryan Newman and Jarrett, with Jeff Gordon, Ricky Craven and Robby Gordon all having their private battle for sixth place. Bobby Hamilton and Sadler completed the top-10 finishers.

MBNA Platinum 400 final race results

Fin. Pos.	Start Pos.	Car No.	Driver	Team
1	10	48	Jimmie Johnson	Lowe's Chevrolet
2	2	9	Bill Elliott	Dodge Dealers/UAW Dodge
3	33	99	Jeff Burton	CITGO Ford
4	38	12	Ryan Newman	ALLTEL Ford
5	31	88	Dale Jarrett	UPS Ford
6	9	24	Jeff Gordon	DuPont Chevrolet
7	6	32	Ricky Craven	Tide Ford
8	12	31	Robby Gordon	Cingular Wireless Chevrolet
9	19	55	Bobby Hamilton	Schneider Electric Chevrolet
10	8	21	Elliott Sadler	Motorcraft Ford
11	25	20	Tony Stewart	Home Depot Pontiac
12	5	97	Kurt Busch	Sharpie/Rubbermaid Ford
13	27	40	Sterling Marlin	Coors Light Dodge
14	23	7	Casey Atwood	Sirius Satellite Radio Dodge
15	37	5	Terry Labonte	Kellogg's Chevrolet
16	16	18	Bobby Labonte	Interstate Batteries Pontiac
17	21	2	Rusty Wallace	Miller Lite Ford
18	43	26	Todd Bodine	Discover Card Ford
19	7	28	Ricky Rudd	Havoline Ford
20	11	45	Kyle Petty	Sprint Dodge
21	4	15	Michael Waltrip	NAPA Chevrolet
22	20	4	Mike Skinner	Kodak Chevrolet
23	18	41	Jimmy Spencer	Target Dodge
24	32	14	Stacy Compton	Conseco Pontiac
25	41	44	Steve Grissom	Georgia Pacific Dodge
26	40	23	Hut Stricklin	Hills Bros Coffee Dodge
27	3	10	Jerry Nadeau	Valvoline Pontiac
28	34	29	Kevin Harvick	GM Goodwrench Service Chevrolet
29	39	77	Dave Blaney	Jasper Engines Ford
30	30	8	Dale Earnhardt Jr.	Budweiser Chevrolet
31	17	73	Tony Raines	BACE Motorsports Chevrolet
32	42	43	John Andretti	Cheerios Dodge
33	36	74	Chad Little	Staff America Chevrolet
34	26	11	Brett Bodine	Hooters Ford
35	24	19	Jeremy Mayfield	Dodge Dealers/UAW Dodge
36	15	36	Ken Schrader	M&M's Pontiac
37	14	22	Ward Burton	Caterpillar Dodge
38	35	30	Jeff Green	America Online Chevrolet
39	22	1	Steve Park	Pennzoil Chevrolet
40	1	17	Matt Kenseth	DeWalt Power Tools Ford
41	13	6	Mark Martin	Pfizer/Viagra Ford
42	29	71	Dick Trickle	Continental Fire & Safety Chevrolet
43	28	25	Joe Nemechek	UAW-Delphi Chevrolet

Pocono 500

Dale Earnhardt Jr. prepares to climb aboard his Budweiser Monte Carlo during practice at Pocono. The day before the Pocono 500, Earnhardt told members of the press he was close to signing a contract that would keep him with DEI for an extended period, perhaps the remainder of his career.

(Right) Jeff Green (30) and Mark Martin (6) go at it on Pocono's sweeping third turn in front of a tightly bunched, side-by-side pack of cars.

(Above) Dale Jarrett signals victory from Pocono's winner's circle after snatching a win in the final laps and ending a winless string of 31 races dating back to July 2001 at New Hampshire. Jarrett had to be feeling his team was turning things around with five top-six finishes in their last seven starts.

(Right) Steve Park hugs the inside with Ken Schrader and Sterling Marlin applying heavy pressure from behind. Speculation had been swirling through the Pocono garage regarding Park's future with DEI, and the Pennzoil driver was looking for a solid showing on the track.

Jeff Gordon's protégé, Jimmie Johnson, may have been the giddiest person in the garage area after the running of the MBNA Platinum 400 at Dover International Speedway. After all, he was the driver standing in victory lane spraying the champagne and collecting the hardware.

If Johnson, a Raybestos Rookie of the Year contender, was the happiest, then perhaps the most frustrated was Ricky Rudd. For the second straight week, the driver of Robert Yates' No. 28 Havoline Ford had seen his chances for victory disappear in the late going. The aura of disappointment surrounding the Havoline team was palpable. Rudd had been in the hunt – but in the end, another driver had stolen his thunder.

Johnson's second victory of his "debutante" season moved him from fifth place into the runner-up spot in the NASCAR Winston Cup Series point standings as teams assembled at Pennsylvania's Pocono Raceway for the first of two tests on the unique 2.5-mile triangular superspeedway. Although Johnson now occupied second place in the points, Sterling Marlin's 13th place at Dover kept him handily in the lead. Marlin's consistent finishes provided him with a 136-point bulge over Johnson, while Jeff Gordon continued to gather his forces and inch upward in the standings.

Although Gordon was working a 21-race winless streak, it was clear the storm was gathering around the No. 24 team. Some racing insiders were betting it would not be long before the DuPont Chevrolet was back in the winner's circle.

Matt Kenseth dropped from second to fourth place in the standings after his 40th-place finish at Dover, while Rusty Wallace held fifth place. Mark Martin plummeted from third place to sixth after finishing 41st at Dover, while Tony Stewart maintained his seventh place in the standings. Kurt Busch remained in eighth place, while Bill

Elliott and Rudd exchanged places, with Elliott moving to ninth after his stirring second-place run at Dover. Jeff Burton, Ricky Craven, Dale Jarrett, Dale Earnhardt Jr. and Ryan Newman occupied the 11th through 15th positions in the championship points after the first 13 races of the season.

In the week between the Dover and Pocono races, two teams had shuffled crew members in hopes of becoming more competitive. At Petty Enterprises, Brandon Thomas, formerly of Joe Gibbs Racing, was named crew chief for John Andretti's No. 43 Cheerios Dodge, and Greg Steadman, formerly crew chief of the "43," was named head wrench for Steve Grissom and the Georgia Pacific No. 44. Bryant Frazier, who had been crew chief for the "44," was reassigned as the car chief for the team.

Richard Childress went one step further. He exchanged the entire crews of the Nos. 29 and 31 cars, with Kevin Hamlin and his band of merry men now assigned to the Cingular Chevrolet and driver Robby Gordon. The Gil Martin-led gang switched to the GM Goodwrench effort and driver Kevin Harvick. Only time would tell if any

(Left) Tony Stewart challenges Mark Martin (6) for position on Pocono's long front straight. Martin just edged Stewart in qualifying to start sixth, and then drove his Viagra Ford to a strong second-place finish to jump from sixth to fourth in the points. Stewart notched a top 10 in the race with a seventh place and moved up a spot in the standings to sixth.

(Below) The DuPont crew sends driver Jeff Gordon on his way after a stop during the first caution of the race. Gordon was leading when the yellow flew, but lost track position when several cars already in the pits moved to the front for the restart. Gordon was able to climb back to fifth and continue his strong performances of late.

(Above) Ricky Rudd (28) hunts down Jeff Burton (99), the leader on the final restart with less than 25 laps to go in the race. Rudd, fourth on the restart, already had passed Stewart and Marlin and took the point from Burton at the entrance to turn one, seemingly on his way to the victory.

(Below) The Fords of Robert Yates Racing teammates Dale Jarrett (88) and Ricky Rudd (28) were both formidable at Pocono. Rudd, the defending race champion, led 60 of the final 80 laps, but Jarrett had luck on his side and led the final six laps to snatch the win.

of the changes would have the desired effect.

Rain and seeping water forced teams to start the Pocono 500 by points, which put Sterling Marlin and Jimmie Johnson on the front row for the 200-lapper at Drs. Rose and Joe Mattioli's scenic facility. Set in the Pocono Mountains and occupying land that was once a spinach farm, Pocono offers a challenge to drivers unlike any other track on the circuit. All three corners have different degrees of banking, and the three straightaways are of varying lengths. The chassis setup for Pocono is a huge compromise, and with the water problems, drivers and crew chiefs were forced to build-in the opportunity for considerable change within their race-day chassis setups. The winner might be determined by which crew chief and driver had decided on the best "combination" Saturday afternoon and Sunday morning.

Rudd's frustration level deepened at the end of "happy hour" when an oil leak forced an engine change. That meant the Virginian would have to give up his 10th-place starting position and go to the back of the field for the start of the Pocono 500.

The veteran didn't let anxiety affect his skill as a racer. In fact, he used it to bolster his charge to the front and by the midpoint of the race, Rudd was in his accustomed challenging position in the lead pack of cars. He moved under teammate Dale Jarrett to take the lead on lap 121, and then reeled off the laps, headed toward what appeared to be his first victory of the season.

The final caution flag appeared at the starter's stand on lap 169 when debris was spotted in the third turn. The lead-lap cars headed for pit road for the final time, and when they lined up behind the pace car to take the green flag on lap 173, Jeff Burton was the leader. Behind him were Marlin, Stewart, Rudd, Rusty Wallace, Michael Waltrip, Jarrett, Martin, Dave Blaney and Johnson.

Rudd wasted no time. He bolted under Marlin for second place and within three laps erased Burton's lead and rocketed past the CITGO Ford to take the lead. Elliott lost the engine in his Intrepid and headed for pit road, and Jarrett used the Robert Yates power under the hood of his UPS Ford to move to second place, more than 1.2 seconds behind teammate Rudd.

With 10 laps to go and with Jarrett closing, Rudd had the first inkling that all was not right with his Havoline Ford. With five laps to go, Jarrett made his move, and Ricky had no defense. The brown-white-and-yellow UPS Taurus fought to the point, and Rudd realized he had a slowly deflating rear tire. Jarrett forged ahead, while Rudd tried to nurse the tire to the best finish he could get in the final five laps.

It almost worked, but on the next-to-last lap, the tire let go and Rudd whacked the outside of the first-turn wall when the tire came off the wheel. Jarrett was home free after a stirring drive, and Rudd was once again left with the frustration of what might have been.

The victory was the first for Jarrett in 30 races and came just one race after he finished in the top five for just the second time in the season. It marked his 29th career NASCAR Winston Cup Series victory and made him the 10th different winner in the first 14 races of the season.

Martin fought to second place – his fourth top-five finish in the last five races – with Jimmie Johnson and Sterling Marlin finishing third and fourth. Jeff Gordon overcame pit problems to finish fifth ahead of Jeff Burton and Stewart, while Michael Waltrip was eighth. Rusty Wallace and Dave Blaney completed the top 10, while Rudd was forced to accept 17th place in the final rundown.

A satisfied Dale Jarrett holds his first trophy of the 2002 season, his third at Pocono and the 29th of his NASCAR Winston Cup Series career. Jarrett had climbed from 24th to 12th in the standings over the last seven races and felt his UPS team was ready to break into the top 10 and stake their claim as challengers for the rest of the season.

Pocono 500 final race results

Fin. Pos.	Start Pos.	Car No.	Driver	Team
1	13	88	Dale Jarrett	UPS Ford
2	6	6	Mark Martin	Pfizer/Viagra Ford
3	2	48	Jimmie Johnson	Lowe's Chevrolet
4	1	40	Sterling Marlin	Coors Light Dodge
5	3	24	Jeff Gordon	DuPont Chevrolet
6	11	99	Jeff Burton	CITGO Ford
7	7	20	Tony Stewart	Home Depot Pontiac
8	17	15	Michael Waltrip	NAPA Chevrolet
9	5	2	Rusty Wallace	Miller Lite Ford
10	21	77	Dave Blaney	Jasper Engines Ford
11	37	7	Casey Atwood	Sirius Satellite Radio Dodge
12	14	8	Dale Earnhardt Jr.	Budweiser Chevrolet
13	20	45	Kyle Petty	Sprint Dodge
14	12	32	Ricky Craven	Tide Ford
15	25	21	Elliott Sadler	Motorcraft Ford
16	38	36	Ken Schrader	M&M's Pontiac
17	10	28	Ricky Rudd	Havoline Ford
18	39	26	Todd Bodine	Discover Card Ford
19	28	31	Robby Gordon	Cingular Wireless Chevrolet
20	27	10	Johnny Benson	Valvoline Pontiac
21	18	41	Jimmy Spencer	Target Dodge
22	31	23	Hut Stricklin	Hills Bros Coffee Dodge
23	32	1	Steve Park	Pennzoil Chevrolet
24	36	11	Brett Bodine	Hooters Ford
25	19	18	Bobby Labonte	Interstate Batteries Pontiac
26	34	44	Steve Grissom	Georgia Pacific Dodge
27	26	55	Bobby Hamilton	Schneider Electric Chevrolet
28	40	14	Stacy Compton	Conseco Pontiac
29	41	90	Hermie Sadler	Duke's Mayonnaise/Sauer's Ford
30	9	9	Bill Elliott	Dodge Dealers/UAW Dodge
31	35	43	John Andretti	Cheerios Dodge
32	15	12	Ryan Newman	ALLTEL Ford
33	22	22	Ward Burton	Caterpillar Dodge
34	23	30	Jeff Green	America Online Chevrolet
35	4	17	Matt Kenseth	DeWalt Power Tools Ford
36	24	19	Jeremy Mayfield	Dodge Dealers/UAW Dodge
37	29	4	Mike Skinner	Kodak Chevrolet
38	16	5	Terry Labonte	Kellogg's Chevrolet
39	30	29	Kevin Harvick	GM Goodwrench Service Chevrolet
40	8	97	Kurt Busch	Sharpie/Rubbermaid Ford
41	33	25	Joe Nemechek	UAW-Delphi Chevrolet
42	42	85	Carl Long	Mansion Mtspts/Juvenile Diabetes Dodge
43	43	46	Frank Kimmel	Advance Auto Parts Ford

Sirius Satellite Radio 400

The grandstands are packed at beautiful Michigan International Speedway for the running of the Sirius Satellite Radio 400.

SIRIUS
Satellite Radio
400

(Right) Jeremy Mayfield waits for new tires form his crew on pit road. Struggling to get the team out of a recent slump, Mayfield felt his luck might turn at Michigan, but a couple of unscheduled pit stops under green due to tire problems dropped him several laps off the pace.

performances, earning the outside of the front row and beating teammate Dale Earnhardt Jr. for the second-fastest lap. Bill Elliott, at the track where he dominated not that long ago, slapped his Dodge on the outside of the second row, while Ward Burton and Ryan Newman claimed the third-row starting positions. Elliott Sadler and Ricky Craven posted the seventh- and eighth-fastest laps ahead of Mark Martin and Tony Stewart.

Morgan Shepherd withdrew his car from competition, leaving just 43 cars in the garage area. Starting in the final seven positions were Sterling Marlin, Terry Labonte, Casey Atwood, Steve

On the final restart with just three laps to go, Matt Kenseth (17) gets the jump on (in order) Jimmie Johnson, Ryan Newman, Ricky Rudd, Kurt Busch and Bill Elliott. While Kenseth pulled away, Dale Jarrett set sail from ninth place in his UPS Ford and charged past all but the DeWalt driver, who took the win.

Grissom, Jason Small, Derrike Cope and Gary Bradberry, in Junie Donlavey's Ford.

With Todd Bodine making the decision to remain in Kentucky for the rain-delayed NASCAR Busch Series race (which he won), older brother Geoffrey Bodine slid into Todd's seat in the Discover Card Ford for the Sirius Satellite Radio 400. With no practice, Geoffrey turned in a credible job in the substitute's role, earning a 19th-place finish on the two-mile Michigan oval.

Throughout its history, Michigan, with its wide straights and expansive turns, has been the site of some of the most exciting races of the season. At times, the battle for the lead has resembled a restaging of the Oklahoma Land Rush, and this year's edition of the Sirius Satellite Radio 400 was no different.

Ten different drivers led the race at one time or another, but Jarrett and Kenseth established themselves early as the fastest of the fast. Jimmie Johnson continued his torrid run, and Kurt Busch and Ryan Newman also showed flashes of strength at the front.

The stage seemed set when the third caution flag flew on lap 139, affording teams the chance to set up for the run to the checkers. The only problem was the timing of the caution. No team could make it to the end on fuel, necessitating green-flag stops in the closing laps to determine the winner.

With just over 15 laps to go, Jimmie Johnson turned over the point when he headed for pit road as the leaders began making their stops under green. Three laps later, Kenseth gave up the lead and stopped for just four seconds to get the needed fuel to finish. He was back in the lead on lap 192 when Dave Blaney made his last stop, and the DeWalt Tools Ford appeared headed for its third win of the season.

Then Elliott Sadler spun in the second turn on lap 196, and NASCAR officials displayed the red flag so fans could have a chance to see a race for the finish rather than watching the field circle behind the pace car for the remaining few laps.

After a seven-minute cleanup, the event was ready for a three-lap shootout, and on the restart, Kenseth tried his best to bolt from the field. Behind him, Jarrett was carving through the cars after stopping for new tires, with Michael Waltrip right behind. In one lap, Jarrett and Waltrip cracked the top five, and with one lap remaining, Jarrett rocketed past Ryan Newman to move into second place.

That, however, was as far as he could get in the remaining time. Kenseth was just too far ahead with only two miles to go, and Kenseth held off the challenge and moved to his fourth career victory, his third of the season.

Jarrett was forced to settle for second, while Newman held off Waltrip for third place. Jeff Gordon fought back from a lap behind to claim fifth place ahead of a now-healthy Johnny Benson and Rusty Wallace. Ricky Rudd was eighth after not stopping for tires, while Mark Martin took ninth and Kurt Busch finished 10th.

(Left) The DeWalt Tools team, led by crew chief Robbie Reiser, cheers its third victory of the season while TV crews catch the pit road celebration. Kenseth's was one of three Jack Roush-owned teams to finish in the top 10, joined by those of Mark Martin and Kurt Busch.

(Below) In the winner's circle, driver Matt Kenseth shows off this latest mantelpiece. Not only had he become the only three-time winner so far this season, but he also just jumped from seventh to fifth in the points.

Sirius Satellite Radio 400 final race results

Fin. Pos.	Start Pos.	Car No.	Driver	Team
1	20	17	Matt Kenseth	DeWalt Power Tools Ford
2	1	88	Dale Jarrett	UPS Ford
3	6	12	Ryan Newman	ALLTEL Ford
4	2	15	Michael Waltrip	NAPA Chevrolet
5	24	24	Jeff Gordon	DuPont Chevrolet
6	30	10	Johnny Benson	Valvoline Pontiac
7	25	2	Rusty Wallace	Miller Lite Ford
8	26	28	Ricky Rudd	Havoline Ford
9	9	6	Mark Martin	Pfizer/Viagra Ford
10	12	97	Kurt Busch	Sharpie/Rubbermaid Ford
11	4	9	Bill Elliott	Dodge Dealers/UAW Dodge
12	27	45	Kyle Petty	Sprint Dodge
13	23	77	Dave Blaney	Jasper Engines Ford
14	14	48	Jimmie Johnson	Lowe's Chevrolet
15	8	32	Ricky Craven	Tide Ford
16	10	20	Tony Stewart	Home Depot Pontiac
17	22	23	Hut Stricklin	Hills Brothers Coffee Dodge
18	34	30	Jeff Green	America Online Chevrolet
19	17	26	Geoffrey Bodine	Discover Card Ford
20	32	99	Jeff Burton	CITGO Ford
21	37	40	Sterling Marlin	Coors Light Dodge
22	3	8	Dale Earnhardt Jr.	Budweiser Chevrolet
23	11	43	John Andretti	Cheerios Dodge
24	18	18	Bobby Labonte	Interstate Batteries Pontiac
25	36	36	Ken Schrader	M&M's Pontiac
26	7	21	Elliott Sadler	Motorcraft Ford
27	19	29	Kevin Harvick	GM Goodwrench Service Chevrolet
28	13	41	Jimmy Spencer	Target Dodge
29	29	25	Joe Nemechek	UAW-Delphi Chevrolet
30	15	4	Mike Skinner	Kodak Chevrolet
31	38	5	Terry Labonte	Kellogg's Chevrolet
32	16	1	Steve Park	Pennzoil Chevrolet
33	35	31	Robby Gordon	Cingular Wireless Chevrolet
34	21	11	Brett Bodine	Hooters Ford
35	33	14	Stacy Compton	Conseco Pontiac
36	31	19	Jeremy Mayfield	Dodge Dealers/UAW Dodge
37	28	55	Bobby Hamilton	Schneider Electric Chevrolet
38	42	37	Derrike Cope	WNR/Alabama Ford
39	39	7	Casey Atwood	Sirius Satellite Radio Dodge
40	40	44	Steve Grissom	Georgia Pacific Dodge
41	41	59	Jason Small	Key West Aloe Dodge
42	5	22	Ward Burton	Caterpillar Dodge
43	43	90	Gary Bradberry	Duke's Mayonnaise/Sauer's Ford

Dodge/Save Mart 350

Dale Earnhardt Jr. backs the Budweiser Chevrolet into the fence that lines the road course at Infineon Raceway. Little E was able to right his Monte Carlo without need for a caution, but lost a lap as a result of the mishap.

Remington
ARMS
weiser
EAGLE
The Outlaw
Snap-on
8

(Right) Much of the work done by Speedway Motorsports at newly named Infineon Raceway over the years had been to increase sight lines for fans, making it somewhat unique among road courses. Here, Ken Schrader (36) paces a single-file pack of cars up the hill and through the second corner on the 11-turn circuit.

(Right Below) Tony Stewart (20), defending race champion and pole winner of this year's event, leads second-fastest qualifier Kurt Busch through the esses. Both Stewart and Busch led laps in the middle portions of the event, and both came away with top-five results.

Since the second race of the season, Sterling Marlin had been ensconced in the catbird's seat atop the NASCAR Winston Cup Series point standings. He had driven his Coors Dodge to a pair of victories, and then put together solid finishes week after week while watching his fellow competitors battle to try to reach the top rung of the ladder.

With 10 winners in 15 races, Marlin's smile was a self-satisfied one, knowing that behind him, no driver had really stepped out of the pack and established himself as a true contender for the championship.

Yet Marlin also knew the vagaries of NASCAR Winston Cup Series racing. A seasoned veteran, Marlin knew that in a single race, his point lead could be erased and that a dogfight for the championship could easily ensue during the upcoming second half of the season. His lead was 110 points – a nice number, to be sure – but a number that certainly was not erasable. With 140 points available between first and last in a given weekend, Sterling knew full well the quest for his first NASCAR Winston Cup Series championship was a long way from being over.

Since the first time NASCAR Winston Cup Series teams visited Sears Point Raceway in 1989, the venue has established itself as one of the most unique on the circuit. The beauty of the Sonoma and Napa Valleys, the opportunity to spend time in spectacular San Francisco and Marin County, the charm of cable car rides, visits to Fisherman's Wharf and the fine restaurants overlooking the harbors are all part of a trip to Sears Point.

So is re-learning the course every year. The road-racing course has changed almost annually since Ricky Rudd won the first race in 1989, and this year was no different. Speedway Motorsports Inc. continues to pour money into the facility and has found ways to work with the environmentalists who have been involved with all of the course developments.

This year, the track went through extensive changes, and when drivers arrived they found many of their former braking and shifting landmarks gone. The two-mile track, always a problem for drivers who were used to turning left, was another challenge to overcome.

Road-racing specialists Ron Fellows and Boris Said were on hand in one-off appearances, with Fellows driving Joe Nemechek's NEMCO Chevrolet and Said in a second Jasper Motorsports Ford. And Jerry Nadeau took over the Petty Enterprises Georgia Pacific entry normally driven by Steve Grissom. Some have forgotten that Nadeau's background includes several years of

Remington
ARMS
weiser
EAGLE
8
The
OUTLAW
Snap-on

(Right) Much of the work done by Speedway Motorsports at newly named Infineon Raceway over the years had been to increase sight lines for fans, making it somewhat unique among road courses. Here, Ken Schrader (36) paces a single-file pack of cars up the hill and through the second corner on the 11-turn circuit.

(Right Below) Tony Stewart (20), defending race champion and pole winner of this year's event, leads second-fastest qualifier Kurt Busch through the esses. Both Stewart and Busch led laps in the middle portions of the event, and both came away with top-five results.

Since the second race of the season, Sterling Marlin had been ensconced in the catbird's seat atop the NASCAR Winston Cup Series point standings. He had driven his Coors Dodge to a pair of victories, and then put together solid finishes week after week while watching his fellow competitors battle to try to reach the top rung of the ladder.

With 10 winners in 15 races, Marlin's smile was a self-satisfied one, knowing that behind him, no driver had really stepped out of the pack and established himself as a true contender for the championship.

Yet Marlin also knew the vagaries of NASCAR Winston Cup Series racing. A seasoned veteran, Marlin knew that in a single race, his point lead could be erased and that a dogfight for the championship could easily ensue during the upcoming second half of the season. His lead was 110 points – a nice number, to be sure – but a number that certainly was not erasable. With 140 points available between first and last in a given weekend, Sterling knew full well the quest for his first NASCAR Winston Cup Series championship was a long way from being over.

Since the first time NASCAR Winston Cup Series teams visited Sears Point Raceway in 1989, the venue has established itself as one of the most unique on the circuit. The beauty of the Sonoma and Napa Valleys, the opportunity to spend time in spectacular San Francisco and Marin County, the charm of cable car rides, visits to Fisherman's Wharf and the fine restaurants overlooking the harbors are all part of a trip to Sears Point.

So is re-learning the course every year. The road-racing course has changed almost annually since Ricky Rudd won the first race in 1989, and this year was no different. Speedway Motorsports Inc. continues to pour money into the facility and has found ways to work with the environmentalists who have been involved with all of the course developments.

This year, the track went through extensive changes, and when drivers arrived they found many of their former braking and shifting landmarks gone. The two-mile track, always a problem for drivers who were used to turning left, was another challenge to overcome.

Road-racing specialists Ron Fellows and Boris Said were on hand in one-off appearances, with Fellows driving Joe Nemechek's NEMCO Chevrolet and Said in a second Jasper Motorsports Ford. And Jerry Nadeau took over the Petty Enterprises Georgia Pacific entry normally driven by Steve Grissom. Some have forgotten that Nadeau's background includes several years of heavy-duty road racing, but Kyle Petty hadn't. The moment Jerry was released from Hendrick Motorsports earlier this year, Kyle made the decision he wanted Nadeau for Sears Point.

Others had also forgotten that Rudd and Terry Labonte have been among the most successful road racing drivers in NASCAR's history. Both would gently jog the faded memories of many before the weekend was complete.

Tony Stewart, who won last year's Sears Point event, claimed the Bud Pole for this year's edition, scoring his first pole of the year and putting the Home Depot Pontiac into the Bud Shootout next February. Stewart needed everything he could squeeze from the orange-and-white Tin Indian to keep Kurt Busch's Ford at bay. Jeff Burton and local favorite Jeff Gordon made up the second row ahead of Bill Elliott and Matt Kenseth, while Rudd and Rusty Wallace grabbed the fourth-row spots. Robby Gordon, who nearly won last year's race until a contretemps with now teammate Kevin Harvick ended his chances, was ninth fastest. Said was the best of the road-racing interlopers, grabbing the 10th-fastest lap and keeping Ward Burton from the position.

Three NASCAR Winston West Series competitors – Jim Inglebright, Austin Cameron and Brandon Ash – tried to make the field, with Inglebright and Cameron succeeding. That meant that Stacy Compton, in A.J. Foyt's Conseco Pontiac, failed to make the grid. Using provisionals for the field were Dale Jarrett, Ricky Craven, Terry Labonte, Elliott Sadler, Hut Stricklin, Steve Park and Casey Atwood.

Those who had been at the track Friday and Saturday were in for a surprise when they arrived Sunday morning. Overnight, speedway president Steve Page and his tireless workers had transformed the track from the familiar red-and-white colors to the blue and white of Infineon, a semi-

(Left) Dave Blaney pilots the Jasper Engines Ford ahead of Jimmy Spencer's Target Dodge. Despite front-end damage to his Taurus, Blaney maintained position on the lead lap, while Spencer was one of several cars that suffered broken rear-end gears.

(Below) Jeff Gordon (24) gets a nudge from Jeff Burton's CITGO Ford with the entire pack charging uphill toward the second turn. Gordon, an accomplished road racer with three wins and six top fives in his nine career starts at Sonoma, charged to the point on the second lap and led the next 31 circuits until the rear end broke in his Monte Carlo.

(Above Right) Dale Earnhardt Jr. takes an off-road excursion in his Budweiser Chevrolet while the field weaves through the esses. Earnhardt recovered and continued without the need for a full-course caution.

(Right Below) The powerful Ford of Kurt Busch pulls the right-front wheel off the pavement as the young Roush driver stays ahead of Bill Elliott and Bobby Labonte. Busch showed great skill on the road course, leading twice including one stretch of 28 laps, before taking fourth place at the finish.

conductor manufacturing company. Infineon had bought the track-naming rights in a multi-year deal, and the new track sponsor's presence was everywhere.

And the surprises for spectators continued all the way through the afternoon.

For many drivers – including Rudd – the strategy for the road course was to run the car as easily as possible, stay in touch with the early "rabbit" leaders and try to be positioned in the lead group to make a charge in the closing laps. For others, the strategy was to run at the front and let those behind take their chances trying to play catch-up.

Local favorite Jeff Gordon, who had moved into a tie with Jimmie Johnson for second in the point standings after Michigan, watched as Sterling Marlin headed his Coors Dodge onto pit road after just 13 laps. Marlin had run over some rocks tossed on the course by Jeff Green's Chevrolet and had knocked the water pump belt off the engine. The engine fried, Marlin saw his 44-race streak of running at the finish come to an end. Gordon, anticipating the chance to catch Marlin in the point battle, then made his own trip to pit road on lap 33 with a broken ring gear.

After the third caution of the race, Bill Elliott found himself at the point, leading Nadeau, Jeff Green, Terry Labonte and Jeremy Mayfield. On lap 88, however, Elliott headed through the dirt while battling Nadeau for the lead, and Jerry emerged at the point in the blue-and-white Georgia Pacific Dodge. Terry Labonte fought his way through to second on lap 93, but was more than 4.3 seconds behind as the race began winding toward its conclusion.

Rudd, cagily measuring the race, made his move toward the front. He battled past Labonte into second place with 10 laps to go, but by then, Nadeau was long gone. More than six seconds separated the two, and Rudd knew the best he could do was finish second. Nadeau, one of the longest shots in the field, appeared ready to write a storybook finish at the newly named Infineon Raceway.

Oops.

Just three laps from the end of the event, Nadeau pulled to the asphalted infield area of the final turn. Like several others (including Gordon), Jerry had broken the ring gear and had no power to the rear wheels. Frustrated with seeing his victory snatched away, Jerry could only look out the side window of his car and watch Rudd flash past.

After a month of frustration, Rudd motored to victory, the 23rd of his long NASCAR Winston Cup Series career. Stewart finished more than two seconds behind Rudd, and Terry Labonte posted the first top-five finish in 47 races for the Kellogg's team by claiming third. Kurt Busch was a solid fourth ahead of Jeff Green and Elliott Sadler, while Mark Martin, Bill Elliott, Ryan Newman and John Andretti filled out the final top-10 positions.

At the end of the day, the race belonged to Havoline Ford driver Ricky Rudd, who posted his fourth road-course win, the 23rd of his career and the first in a season that had seen its share of bad racing luck. This time, lady luck smiled on Rudd when he assumed the point for the first time with three laps remaining after Jerry Nadeau stripped a rear-end gear.

Dodge/Save Mart 350 final race results

Fin. Pos.	Start Pos.	Car No.	Driver	Team
1	7	28	Ricky Rudd	Havoline Ford
2	1	20	Tony Stewart	Home Depot Pontiac
3	39	5	Terry Labonte	Kellogg's Chevrolet
4	2	97	Kurt Busch	Sharpie/Rubbermaid Ford
5	33	30	Jeff Green	America Online Chevrolet
6	40	21	Elliott Sadler	Motorcraft Ford
7	12	6	Mark Martin	Pfizer/Viagra Ford
8	5	9	Bill Elliott	Dodge Dealers/UAW Dodge
9	17	12	Ryan Newman	ALLTEL Ford
10	13	43	John Andretti	Cheerios Dodge
11	9	31	Robby Gordon	Cingular Wireless Chevrolet
12	16	4	Mike Skinner	Kodak Chevrolet
13	14	18	Bobby Labonte	Interstate Batteries Pontiac
14	24	29	Kevin Harvick	GM Goodwrench Chevrolet
15	37	88	Dale Jarrett	UPS Ford
16	30	10	Johnny Benson	Valvoline Pontiac
17	27	45	Kyle Petty	Sprint Dodge
18	28	25	Joe Nemechek	UAW-Delphi Chevrolet
19	38	32	Ricky Craven	Tide Ford
20	21	77	Dave Blaney	Jasper Engines Ford
21	43	7	Casey Atwood	Sirius Satellite Radio Dodge
22	20	15	Michael Waltrip	NAPA Chevrolet
23	42	1	Steve Park	Pennzoil Chevrolet
24	25	11	Brett Bodine	Hooters Ford
25	19	87	Ron Fellows	Cellular One Chevrolet
26	29	26	Todd Bodine	Discover Card Ford
27	8	2	Rusty Wallace	Miller Lite Ford
28	26	19	Jeremy Mayfield	Dodge Dealers/UAW Dodge
29	3	99	Jeff Burton	CITGO Ford
30	23	8	Dale Earnhardt Jr.	Budweiser Chevrolet
31	31	55	Bobby Hamilton	Schneider Electric Chevrolet
32	34	0	Jim Inglebright	Jelly Belly Chevrolet
33	41	23	Hut Stricklin	Hills Bros Coffee Dodge
34	22	44	Jerry Nadeau	Georgia Pacific/Brawny Dodge
35	15	48	Jimmie Johnson	Lowe's Chevrolet
36	35	41	Jimmy Spencer	Target Dodge
37	4	24	Jeff Gordon	DuPont Chevrolet
38	18	36	Ken Schrader	M&M's Pontiac
39	6	17	Matt Kenseth	DeWalt/AT&T Broadband Ford
40	11	22	Ward Burton	Caterpillar Dodge
41	10	67	Boris Said	Jasper Engines Ford
42	32	62	Austin Cameron	NAPA Hand Tools Chevrolet
43	36	40	Sterling Marlin	Coors Light Dodge

Pepsi 400

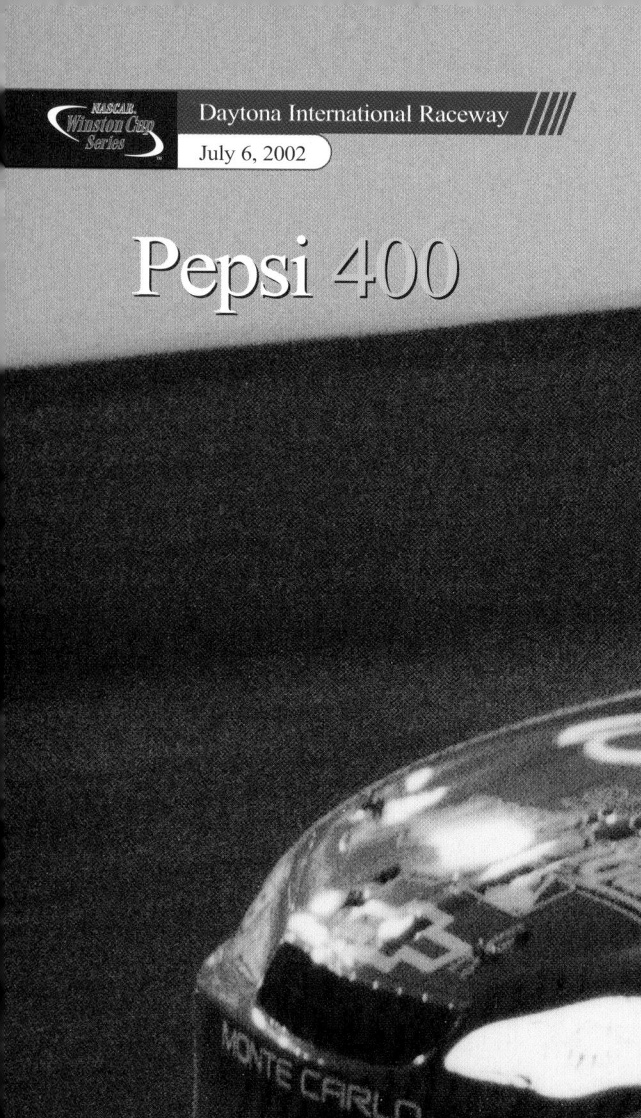

Bud
MONTE CARLO
GOODYEAR
MOOG
True Value
GOODYEAR
INFOGRAMES
MOOG
76
CLEVITE
Edelbrock
WIX
COMP

Now in their second full season as restrictor-plate tag-team titleholders, "Little E" Earnhardt and "Big Mikey" Waltrip body-slammed all comers, this time under the bright lights at Daytona International Speedway in the Independence Day classic, the Pepsi 400.

(Above) Michael Waltrip and wife "Buffy" smile for the cameras during victory lane celebrations at Daytona. The win was the second of Michael's career, both at Daytona, and his sixth top-10 finish in the last nine events.

(Above Right) Jeff Burton (left) and Rusty Wallace ease the pre-race tension with a couple of laughs. Burton had the only Ford that managed to lead the race - 23 laps during the first third of the event - but Jeff later got together with Dale Jarrett which triggered the biggest accident of the evening on lap 137.

(Right) Richard Childress Racing teammates Robby Gordon (31) and Kevin Harvick (29) slip between Ricky Rudd (28) and Dale Earnhardt Jr. while coming through the tri-oval. Harvick captured the Bud Pole for the event, his first of the season, and led the first 13 laps, while Gordon started fourth in his Cingular Monte Carlo.

If anything had become "perfectly clear" after the Sonoma, Calif., experience, it was that the NASCAR Winston Cup Series championship was there for the taking.

Series point-leader Sterling Marlin finished dead last in the field after a broken power steering belt ended the Coors Light Dodge's day early.

It was a golden opportunity for someone to unseat Marlin from the top of the point ladder, and although Jimmie Johnson and Jeff Gordon stumbled in their quest to seize the moment, veteran Mark Martin made the most of Marlin's problems. Martin's seventh place boosted him into second place in the battle for the championship, and for the first time all season, Mark could actually catch a whiff of Marlin's exhaust pipes. The Viagra Ford driver was now just 62 points behind the Tennessean, and Mark knew he had a real fighting chance to make a run at the title that has eluded him throughout his storied NASCAR Winston Cup Series career.

For all intents and purposes there were seven drivers in contention for the championship as the season prepared to start the grueling marathon run toward the title. Beginning with the Pepsi 400, teams would fight and claw their way through 20 consecutive events.

Gordon and Johnson, who had entered the West Coast race tied for second place, now occupied third and fourth, with Gordon just 20 points behind Martin and a mere four markers ahead of Johnson. Tony Stewart, after his fighting second at Sonoma, was in a virtual dead heat for fourth place, just two points behind Johnson. Rusty Wallace remained sixth in the standings despite his 27th-place finish in California, now 56 points behind Stewart, while Ricky Rudd's victory moved him from eighth place to seventh, only four points behind the Miller Lite driver. Matt Kenseth fell to eighth place and was suddenly well within reach of Kurt Busch, only 17 points behind his Roush Racing teammate. Bill Elliott's eighth place kept him 10th in the standings, 31 points behind Busch.

The season's schedule had juxtaposed the 2.5-mile Daytona International Speedway right on top of the winding Sonoma road course, and drivers and teams had to make the adjustment from the brown-green California wine country to the

steamy beachside superspeedway. Two drivers who couldn't wait to get to The Beach were Dale Earnhardt Jr. and Michael Waltrip. Their Chevrolets have been the class of the field at restrictor-plate tracks, and the generally accepted question was not ***if*** a Dale Earnhardt Inc. car would win the Pepsi 400, but rather, ***which*** DEI car would win.

Just a few short months ago, Michael Waltrip had been on the ropes with the team, struggling to find the key to consistent finishes with his NAPA Chevrolet. Many speculated that Michael would not return to the team next season, and then Waltrip and crew chief Slugger Labbe began pulling the magic rabbits out of their hats. Week after week, Michael qualified better, raced better and finished better. His gritty performances were rewarded when NAPA re-upped its sponsorship and Michael was retained to continue to drive the car.

Now, teams were at Daytona, and if it came down to a battle between Little E and Mikey, many expected Waltrip would not dally in a bid for victory. As it turned out, Michael didn't have to make the bid. Instead, he fought off the challenge of Little E.

(Above) Elliott Sadler (21), Mike Skinner (4) and Kyle Petty (45) make it three abreast along the frontstretch. Sadler's Ford was damaged when he got together with Tony Stewart on lap 2, but the Wood Brothers team was able to patch it sufficiently enough to keep their driver on the lead lap where he gutted out a 12th-place finish.

(Left) A puff of tire smoke blows from between the cars of Geoffrey Bodine (09) and Ryan Newman as they rub fenders near the wall, while Todd Bodine (26), Ward Burton (22) and Elliott Sadler (21) look for a little extra room on the inside.

(Right) Rusty Wallace's Miller Lite Ford was truly a hot rod at Daytona. After taking a provisional start in 37th position, Wallace worked his way through 35 spots and picked up a Daytona career-high second place at the end of the night, jumping from sixth to fourth in the point standings.

(Below) Brett Bodine (11) tucks in behind Sterling Marlin's Dodge as the two draft past Mike Wallace (33), driving a Chevrolet for team owner Andy Petree. Marlin gained a handful of points on his closest competitors in the standings with a strong, third-place run.

The two drivers locked up together as they have time and again at restrictor-plate tracks over the past couple of years, and this time Michael and Dale both had time to think about what they needed to do.

But we're getting ahead of ourselves.

Kevin Harvick, headed for a contract extension with Richard Childress Racing, claimed the Pepsi 400 Bud Pole, beating a surprising Geoffrey Bodine for the inside of the front row. The Gordons – Jeff and Robby – made up the second row ahead of Dale Jarrett and Johnny Benson. Michael qualified seventh with DEI teammate Steve Park on his right, and Little E slotted perfectly into ninth place, right behind Waltrip, by chance, for the start of the Pepsi 400. Casey Atwood was the fastest Dodge qualifier, taking the outside of the fifth row, while provisionals were used by Rusty Wallace, Matt Kenseth, Ryan Newman, Jeff Green, Daytona 500-winner Ward Burton, Jeremy Mayfield and Joe Nemechek. Steve Grissom failed to make the field in the Georgia Pacific Dodge, as did Ed Berrier in Junie Donlavey's Ford.

Part of racing at Daytona is trying to get to the front of the pack, where clean air and track position play themselves out lap after lap, making it even more difficult for those behind to pass. And part of getting to that clean air at the front is fighting your way through the massed traffic brought about by the restrictor plates – and not being caught in TBO (The Big One) that seems to happen when bunched cars and fiercely competitive drivers battle for inches.

TBO happened on lap 136 of the 160-lap event when Dale Jarrett and Jeff Burton touched as Burton tried to pass Jarrett, while Dale tried to

protect his turf. Within split seconds, 14 cars were involved, and those at the front breathed a sigh of relief. Those at the front were Michael and Little E, who had worked their way to the point and, as a duo, led from lap 61 until the end of the race.

Waiting for the accident to be cleared, Michael pondered his fate. Did he try to win the race, or let his teammate win? Little E was in the same predicament. His guys worked hard all week to prepare the Budweiser Chevrolet and they expected their driver to give them his very best on the track. His very best meant trying to win the race. Dale thought about it, talked with crew chief Tony Eury about it, and in the end, forsook a certain second place to make a bid for victory.

It might not have been the best thing to do for DEI – after all, a one-two finish is something to take home and boast about quietly. But to take a sure second place and not try for the win is something Dale Junior had learned long ago that real drivers don't do. And make no mistake; Dale Junior is a real driver.

So when push came to shove with just six laps left after the final yellow flag for debris, Dale Jr. made his run at Michael. It wasn't enough, and as he tried Michael's outside with just three laps remaining, it opened the door for Rusty Wallace, Sterling Marlin, Jimmy Spencer and Mark Martin. Little E could manage just sixth place as the yellow flew to bring the battle to a close when Ryan Newman cut a tire and collected Jeff Green and Dave Blaney.

Michael had ridden to his second career victory and became the 12th different winner of the first half of the season. He was the seventh straight different driver to win as the series readied for the stretch run, and Dale Junior could only whack the steering wheel in frustration.

Michael had won – and Dale Jr. had tossed aside a sure second place for his team. But he had tried. And he knew inside that if he hadn't made that decision it would have stayed with him for a long time. After all, Earnhardts are real racers. And they always try to win. Particularly at Daytona.

Brothers Michael and Darrell Waltrip share the joy of victory in Daytona's winner's circle. Darrell, winner of the 1989 Daytona 500, moved to the broadcast booth for FOX television, where they completed their portion of the 2002 broadcast schedule at the Pepsi 400.

Pepsi 400 final race results

Fin. Pos.	Start Pos.	Car No.	Driver	Team
1	7	15	Michael Waltrip	NAPA Chevrolet
2	37	2	Rusty Wallace	Miller Lite/Harley Davidson Ford
3	20	40	Sterling Marlin	Coors Light Dodge
4	25	41	Jimmy Spencer	Target Dodge
5	18	6	Mark Martin	Pfizer/Viagra Ford
6	9	8	Dale Earnhardt Jr.	Budweiser Chevrolet
7	24	26	Todd Bodine	Discover Card Ford
8	16	48	Jimmie Johnson	Lowe's Chevrolet
9	41	22	Ward Burton	Caterpillar Dodge
10	2	09	Geoffrey Bodine	Miccosukee Resort Ford
11	1	29	Kevin Harvick	GM Goodwrench Service Chevrolet
12	31	21	Elliott Sadler	Motorcraft Ford
13	42	19	Jeremy Mayfield	Dodge Dealers/UAW Dodge
14	36	5	Terry Labonte	Kellogg's Chevrolet
15	12	28	Ricky Rudd	Havoline Ford
16	11	55	Bobby Hamilton	Schneider Electric Chevrolet
17	14	9	Bill Elliott	Dodge Dealers/UAW Dodge
18	33	14	Stacy Compton	Conseco Pontiac
19	22	45	Kyle Petty	Sprint/Men in Black II Dodge
20	10	7	Casey Atwood	Sirius Satellite Radio Dodge
21	40	30	Jeff Green	America Online Chevrolet
22	3	24	Jeff Gordon	DuPont/Pepsi Chevrolet
23	26	32	Ricky Craven	Tide Ford
24	32	43	John Andretti	Honey Nut Cheerios Dodge
25	19	36	Ken Schrader	M&M's Pontiac
26	34	23	Hut Stricklin	Hills Bros Coffee Dodge
27	39	12	Ryan Newman	ALLTEL Ford
28	30	77	Dave Blaney	Jasper Engines & Transmissions Ford
29	4	31	Robby Gordon	Cingular Wireless Chevrolet
30	38	17	Matt Kenseth	DeWalt/AT&T Broadband Ford
31	28	97	Kurt Busch	Rubbermaid Ford
32	21	18	Bobby Labonte	Interstate Batteries Pontiac
33	35	99	Jeff Burton	CITGO Ford
34	8	1	Steve Park	Pennzoil Chevrolet
35	5	88	Dale Jarrett	UPS Ford
36	43	25	Joe Nemechek	UAW-Delphi Chevrolet
37	23	4	Mike Skinner	Kodak Chevrolet
38	17	11	Brett Bodine	Hooters Restaurants Ford
39	29	20	Tony Stewart	Home Depot Pontiac
40	27	49	Shawna Robinson	dakotaimaging/Life 02 Dodge
41	13	33	Mike Wallace	1-800-CALLATT Chevrolet
42	15	98	Kenny Wallace	Stacker2 Chevrolet
43	6	10	Johnny Benson	Valvoline Pontiac

(Above) Roush Racing and Kurt Busch's Sharpie Ford team had a very busy weekend. After Busch turned the second-fastest lap in qualifying, he blew two motors in practice, forcing him to the rear of the field with engine No. 3 for the race. But Busch paid them back with an impressive run to sixth place.

(Right) Jerry Nadeau (left) gets his buddy, Ricky Craven, laughing as they prepare to go racing at Chicagoland. Nadeau was on hand to drive a Chevrolet fielded by Michael Waltrip.

Michael Waltrip's Pepsi 400 victory was greeted with delight at NAPA's Atlanta headquarters – and at the "Garage Mahal" outside of Kannapolis. It couldn't have come at a better time because on July 9, Dale Earnhardt Inc. officials announced that NAPA – and Michael – would be around for two more years.

High fives greeted the entire NAPA team when they arrived at Chicagoland Speedway for the second running of the Tropicana 400, and Michael's news wasn't the only story occupying reporters. Discover Card, after a six-race "trial balloon" with

Travis Carter and Todd Bodine, stepped up to the plate with full sponsorship for the remainder of the season.

Carter's share of the good tidings brought him full circle. He had opened the season with a pair of teams carrying Kmart sponsorship, and when the retail giant went kerflop, Travis was left with nothing. He scratched and clawed and now had put together the deal to keep one of his teams intact for the remainder of the season. One step at a time.

Ward Burton had made the decision to remain at Bill Davis Racing and Caterpillar had renewed its yellow-and-black sponsorship of the Dodges driven by the Virginian. He had been the object of several other offers, but chose to stay with Davis and the Dodge camp. Richard Childress and Kevin Harvick were on the verge of extending their relationship, while Ricky Rudd still had not made a decision regarding what he would do at the end of the season. Several enticing offers were on the table and Rudd hoped to have an answer in the immediate future.

On the other side of the fence, Bobby Hamilton told reporters he would be leaving Andy Petree's team at the end of the season and

there was considerable speculation he would return to Petty Enterprises to drive the Georgia Pacific Dodge. Sprint had announced it would withdraw from primary sponsorship of Kyle Petty's Dodge, with the company feeling the heat of the slumping telecom economy.

One of the biggest stories to emerge was the confirmed rumor that Joe Gibbs Racing would switch from Pontiacs to Chevrolets, and that the team would not wait until the 2003 season to do it. After doing the development work on the new Pontiac for next year, Gibbs' decision to switch to the Bowtie Brigade raised many eyebrows of those speculating about the competitiveness of the new Poncho.

Sterling Marlin's third place at Daytona enabled him to pad his series point lead slightly over Mark Martin, who finished fifth at The Beach. Jimmy Johnson's eighth place moved him from fourth to third in the point standings, while Rusty Wallace's fighting second place at Daytona vaulted him from sixth in the standings to fourth, where he trailed Johnson by 30 points. Jeff Gordon, after a 22nd-place finish at Daytona, plummeted from third

(Left) Jeremy Mayfield looks for a little room on the inside of Ryan Newman, who captured his second pole of the season with a lap in excess of 183 miles per hour. Newman was the man to beat in the race, leading 87 laps and clearly in control until a tire went flat with 27 laps remaining. Still, he stayed on the lead lap and managed to climb back to fifth place at the end.

(Below) Robby Gordon's crew provides fresh rubber under green for their Cingular Wireless Chevrolet. Gordon took a late-race gamble for track position with older tires and matched his best finish of the season with an eighth place.

(Top Right) Jimmie Johnson smacks the wall during the weekend's first practice session and was forced to go to his backup car for the remainder of the weekend. Determined not to let a little adversity spoil his championship bid, Johnson went out on Sunday and picked up 33 positions to finish a very respectable fourth.

(Middle Right) Although Jeff Gordon did not lead the race, he stayed among the top 10 all day and then stayed out on the final caution, opting for track position over fresh tires. The move paid off with a runner-up finish and moved him up yet another slot to fourth in the points.

(Bottom Right) Fans were treated to a perfect day in Joliet, Ill., for the second NASCAR Winston Cup Series visit to beautiful Chicagoland Speedway.

place to fifth, while Ricky Rudd eased up one notch on the ladder to sixth.

Few were really paying much attention to the Redhead. Yet Bill Elliott was quietly putting together a string of top-10 finishes and had eased his way up to ninth in the standings. He was a long way from the front, but Bill was gradually re-establishing the missing "Awesome" part of his nickname, and one wondered just how soon Elliott would put together the race that would see him back at the front of the field.

Jerry Nadeau, who had nearly won the Sears Point event in the Petty Enterprises Georgia Pacific Dodge, found himself with a four-event substitute role for Johnny Benson, but the package didn't begin at Chicagoland. Nadeau, for the

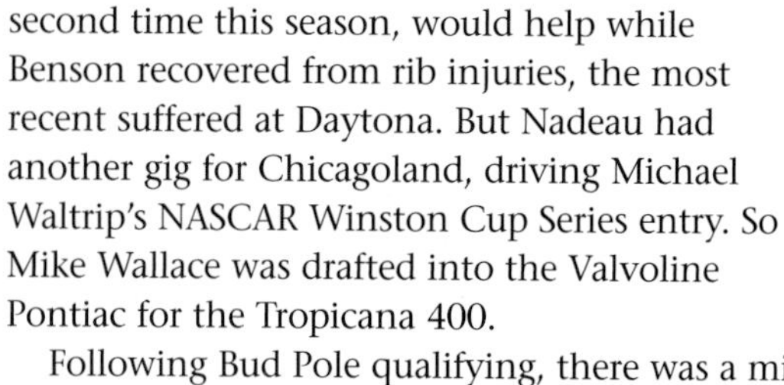

second time this season, would help while Benson recovered from rib injuries, the most recent suffered at Daytona. But Nadeau had another gig for Chicagoland, driving Michael Waltrip's NASCAR Winston Cup Series entry. So Mike Wallace was drafted into the Valvoline Pontiac for the Tropicana 400.

Following Bud Pole qualifying, there was a mix of new and veteran faces in the first two rows for the start of the 267-lap event on the 1.5-mile track. Ryan Newman claimed his third career pole and his second of the season, while Kurt Busch grabbed the outside of the front row. Bill Elliott and Sterling Marlin led the Dodge Boys with their second-row starting slots ahead of Michael Waltrip and Tony Stewart. Dave Blaney gave his Jasper Motorsports Ford a good ride to the seventh-fastest spot, and Rusty Wallace lined up alongside in eighth. Dale Earnhardt Jr. made it a pair of DEI Chevrolets in the top 10 by grabbing the ninth position, and Joe Nemechek became the fastest Hendrick Motorsports entry with his 10th-fastest lap.

Surprisingly, Jimmie Johnson was forced to use a provisional to make the field, as did Ricky Rudd, Jimmy Spencer, Bobby Hamilton, Casey Atwood, Steve Grissom and Stacy Compton. Those failing to make the field included Ron Hornaday, Kirk Shelmerdine, Tony Raines in a BACE Motorsports entry and Scott Wimmer, trying to put a third Bill Davis Dodge into the field.

A wild and wooly Tropicana 400 greeted fans and Ryan Newman continued his impressive performance by leading twice for 87 laps, but a flat tire ended his chances for victory. Dale Earnhardt Jr. led four times for 81 laps, but a decision to take four tires on his final pit stop slapped him back in mid-pack and all he could manage was a 10th at the end.

Clean air was the ticket to victory lane, and when the final caution flew with just over 25 laps remaining in the race, Harvick and crew chief Gil Martin gambled that track position was more important than new tires. Harvick was at the point when the green flag flew for the final time and once he headed the field, it was a matter of waiting to see if he would make a mistake or not. Jeff Gordon also gambled on track position, as did Robby Gordon, and it paid off.

No one had an answer for Harvick, who didn't set a wheel wrong in the remaining laps. His margin of victory over Jeff Gordon was more than eight-tenths of a second, while Tony Stewart rode a charging Home Depot Pontiac to third place. Jimmie Johnson finished fourth ahead of Newman, while Kurt Busch was sixth. Bill Elliott flogged his Intrepid to seventh place while Robby Gordon faded slightly to eighth place, yielding positions to those on new tires in the final sprint to the checkered flag. Mark Martin and Little E completed the top 10.

(Left) Kevin Harvick and company didn't wait to arrive in victory lane before the celebration began. Instead, they started the party on the frontstretch grass when Harvick climbed atop his Monte Carlo and saluted the cheering crowd.

(Below) An elated Richard Childress escorts his driver to the formal celebration with Kevin's wife, DeLana, alongside. With one top five, two top 10s and a one-race suspension in the first 17 events of the year, the victory was welcome relief, although Childress maintained he never gave up on his sophomore driver.

Tropicana 400 final race results

Fin. Pos.	Start Pos.	Car No.	Driver	Team
1	32	29	Kevin Harvick	GM Goodwrench Service Chevrolet
2	15	24	Jeff Gordon	DuPont Chevrolet
3	6	20	Tony Stewart	Home Depot Pontiac
4	37	48	Jimmie Johnson	Lowe's Chevrolet
5	1	12	Ryan Newman	ALLTEL/Mobil 1 Ford
6	2	97	Kurt Busch	Rubbermaid Ford
7	3	9	Bill Elliott	Dodge Dealers/UAW/Muppet Show Dodge
8	21	31	Robby Gordon	Cingular Wireless Chevrolet
9	13	6	Mark Martin	Pfizer/Viagra Ford
10	9	8	Dale Earnhardt Jr.	Budweiser Chevrolet
11	11	88	Dale Jarrett	UPS/Muppet Show Ford
12	33	30	Jeff Green	America Online Chevrolet
13	24	5	Terry Labonte	Kellogg's/got milk? Chevrolet
14	16	17	Matt Kenseth	DeWalt Power Tools Ford
15	40	55	Bobby Hamilton	Square D/Inside Traxx Chevrolet
16	4	40	Sterling Marlin	Coors Light Dodge
17	7	77	Dave Blaney	Jasper Engines & Transmissions Ford
18	12	18	Bobby Labonte	Interstate Batteries/Muppet Show Pontiac
19	38	28	Ricky Rudd	Havoline/Muppet Show Ford
20	25	32	Ricky Craven	Tide Ford
21	19	21	Elliott Sadler	Motorcraft Ford
22	30	43	John Andretti	Cheerios Dodge
23	17	4	Mike Skinner	Kodak Chevrolet
24	35	45	Kyle Petty	Sprint Dodge
25	8	2	Rusty Wallace	Miller Lite Ford
26	14	26	Todd Bodine	Discover Card Ford
27	22	1	Steve Park	Pennzoil Chevrolet
28	41	7	Casey Atwood	Sirius Satellite Radio/Muppet Show Dodge
29	28	98	Kenny Wallace	Stacker2 Chevrolet
30	23	11	Brett Bodine	Hooters Restaurants Ford
31	42	44	Steve Grissom	Georgia Pacific/Brawny Dodge
32	39	41	Jimmy Spencer	Target Dodge
33	10	25	Joe Nemechek	UAW-Delphi Chevrolet
34	20	19	Jeremy Mayfield	Dodge Dealers/UAW/Muppet Show Dodge
35	43	14	Stacy Compton	Conseco Pontiac
36	29	23	Hut Stricklin	Hills Bros Coffee Dodge
37	34	00	Jerry Nadeau	Aaron's Sales & Lease Chevrolet
38	36	10	Mike Wallace	Valvoline/Pitbull Pontiac
39	18	99	Jeff Burton	CITGO Ford
40	27	36	Ken Schrader	M&M's Pontiac
41	31	22	Ward Burton	Caterpillar Dodge
42	5	15	Michael Waltrip	NAPA Chevrolet
43	26	57	Stuart Kirby	CLR Ford

NASCAR Winston Cup Series
New Hampshire International Speedway
July 21, 2002
New England 300
MOOG
CLEVITE

Ward Burton salutes the crowd from his Caterpillar Dodge after outsmarting the competition and out-driving the track to take the win at New Hampshire.

(Below) Bill Elliott (9) and Mike Skinner (4) bring the field of 43 under the green flag to begin 300 laps on the 1.058-mile New Hampshire oval. Elliott pulled into a tie with Jimmie Johnson for the season-long Bud Pole Award by capturing his third pole of the season with a lap at 131.468 miles per hour (right). Unfortunately for Elliott, a carburetor problem 40 laps into the event forced him to pit road, where he lost 13 laps waiting for repairs.

When Sterling Marlin slid to a mid-race, green-flag stop outside his pit box at Chicagoland Speedway, the ensuing penalty cost him a lap and sent him to a 16th-place finish in the Tropicana 400. Marlin's mistake cost him a lap, but not the point lead. Sterling remained on the top rung of the point ladder where he has viewed the chase behind him since the second race of the season.

While Marlin was finishing 16th, Mark Martin, Jimmie Johnson, Jeff Gordon and Tony Stewart all seized the opportunity to cut into the Coors Light driver's lead, and when the points were totaled at the conclusion of the Chicagoland event, Martin had closed to 49 points behind Marlin.

Johnson was now just 40 points behind Martin, and Jeff Gordon's second place in the Tropicana 400 moved him from fifth to fourth place in the standings, where he trailed Johnson by just six points. Tony Stewart's third place moved him to fifth in the standings, up two positions, while Rusty Wallace fell from fourth to sixth after his 25th-place finish. Ricky Rudd slumped to seventh in the points, down one slot, while Bill Elliott continued his climb, moving to eighth place after finishing seventh at Chicago.

Kurt Busch moved to ninth place while Roush Racing teammate Matt Kenseth fell from eighth to 10th.

Kevin Harvick's successful defense as the event champion at Chicago made him the 13th different driver to win in the first 19 races of the season and he became the eighth straight different driver to win an event on the tour. Despite his victory, however, Harvick was still mired in the bottom 20 of the point standings, where he stood 27th. His total was not helped by the fact that he had been parked at Martinsville by NASCAR officials and had gained no points.

Crews go head to head on pit road during pit stops en masse under caution. Although the race was just 300 laps, crews had plenty of work as 14 caution flags flew during the day.

Drivers weren't sure what to expect when they arrived at New Hampshire International Speedway for the New England 300. Bob Bahre and his energetic group of workers had ground down and replaced asphalt in the third and fourth turns, in hopes of eliminating complaints about the surface in those areas from the last race held there. When the wear and tear of 43 heavy and powerful NASCAR Winston Cup Series cars was finished at the end of the weekend, Bahre would have to go back to the drawing board.

Bill Elliott climbed into a tie with Jimmie Johnson at the top of the Bud Pole standings following qualifying at New Hampshire when he notched his third pole position of the season. His red Dodge Intrepid was clocked at more than 131.4 miles per hour during his pole-winning lap. Mike Skinner turned in a strong performance behind the wheel of the Kodak Chevrolet to grab the outside of the front row.

(Right) Ward Burton directs his Caterpillar Dodge into the turn ahead of Matt Kenseth (17) and Dale Earnhardt Jr. While Kenseth and Earnhardt fought for the lead, Burton picked his way through the field after starting 31st, driving with care on the slick asphalt and using pit strategy to gain valuable track position.

(Below) Kenseth's DeWalt crew slaps a new set of tires on the specially painted Ford, trying desperately to save positions after a flat tire forced him to pit just two laps from the finish. Kenseth led six times for 77 laps to take the lap-leader bonus and was in position to pick up his fourth win of the season, but dropped to a very disappointing 33rd-place finish after the tire went down.

Rusty Wallace and Bobby Labonte made up the second row, while Dave Blaney had another superb qualifying session in the Jasper Motorsports Ford to grab the inside of the third row with Matt Kenseth on his right. Ryan Newman and Ricky Rudd occupied the fourth row, while Ricky Craven and Bobby Hamilton completed the top 10. With only 43 cars in the garage area, no driver or team was sent home. Provisionals were used by Kyle Petty, Elliott Sadler, Hut Stricklin, Stacy Compton, Geoffrey Bodine (helping out with Travis Carter's Discover Card Ford), Kirk Shelmerdine and Morgan Shepherd, both in Fords fielded by their own teams.

When the green flag fell on the New England 300, the drama began. Dave Blaney's third-turn spin brought out the first yellow flag on the third lap, and Jimmy Spencer spun on the backstretch to make the caution wave for the second time on lap 20. It was only the beginning. With the new asphalt surface feeling like ice to the drivers, Elliott Sadler spun off the fourth turn and then Casey Atwood lost control of his Sirius Dodge and collected John Andretti. Kyle Petty hit the fourth-turn wall and Mike Skinner did the same right behind him.

Then it was Tony Stewart's turn followed by Steve Park in the Pennzoil Chevrolet. Jeff Gordon somehow saved his DuPont Chevrolet when it appeared he would join the wall-banging brigade. Drivers were white-knuckling their way through the turns, trying to race as hard as possible yet tippy-toe at the same time. It was a situation where you simply couldn't have it both ways.

Michael Waltrip spun in the fourth turn and then Atwood spun and hit the wall between the first and second turn. By that point, Dale Jarrett had worked his way to the front with Elliott Sadler, Ward Burton, Matt Kenseth, Jeff Green and Rusty Wallace behind him.

Kenseth, determined to snake his way through the field in victorious style, moved past Sadler into second place on lap 282 and then, two laps later, rocketed past Jarrett to take the point. Ward Burton followed the DeWalt Ford as Kenseth made his move, and the Virginian moved to second place.

Just two laps after Kenseth took the lead, Dale Earnhardt Jr. collided with Todd Bodine, with Junior spinning down the backstretch after the second-turn accident, which also found Marlin, Rudd and Hut Stricklin involved, bringing out the final caution of the race on lap 286.

Kenseth held the point on the restart, and just three laps after the green flag flew, Kenseth felt something wrong with his tires. He knew one of them was going flat and was forced to ease off the throttle with just 10 laps to go. There was nothing wrong with Ward Burton's Caterpillar Dodge, however, and Ward tuned the black-and-yellow Intrepid into the low groove and into the lead in the second turn on lap 291. Kenseth went as long as he could on the tire, but finally limped to pit road two laps from the end of the race.

Jeff Green worked his way past Jarrett to claim second place while the UPS Ford driver held on to finish third. A post-race inspection showed his car one-eighth of an inch too low, and it cost Jarrett 25 championship points.

Rusty Wallace fought to fourth place ahead of Penske teammate Ryan Newman. Todd Bodine turned in a sparkling performance to grab sixth ahead of Robby Gordon, Kurt Busch, Kevin Harvick and Elliott Sadler.

Ward Burton gives a happy thumbs-up while son Jeb hangs on to Dad's newest trophy, his second of the year and the fifth of his career. The win was welcome relief for Burton and the entire Bill Davis-owned team after a frustrating string of races since their victory in the season-opening Daytona 500.

New England 300 final race results

Fin. Pos.	Start Pos.	Car No.	Driver	Team
1	31	22	Ward Burton	Caterpillar Dodge
2	30	30	Jeff Green	America Online Chevrolet
3	33	88	Dale Jarrett	UPS Ford
4	3	2	Rusty Wallace	Miller Lite Ford
5	7	12	Ryan Newman	ALLTEL Ford
6	32	26	Todd Bodine	Discover Card Ford
7	26	31	Robby Gordon	Cingular Wireless Chevrolet
8	23	97	Kurt Busch	Rubbermaid Ford
9	24	29	Kevin Harvick	GM Goodwrench Service Chevrolet
10	38	21	Elliott Sadler	Motorcraft Ford
11	34	41	Jimmy Spencer	Target Dodge
12	21	99	Jeff Burton	CITGO SUPERGARD Ford
13	4	18	Bobby Labonte	Interstate Batteries Pontiac
14	18	40	Sterling Marlin	Coors Light Dodge
15	13	48	Jimmie Johnson	Lowe's Chevrolet
16	17	6	Mark Martin	Pfizer/Viagra Ford
17	8	28	Ricky Rudd	Havoline Ford
18	15	10	Jerry Nadeau	Valvoline Pontiac
19	14	19	Jeremy Mayfield	Dodge Dealers/UAW Dodge
20	16	15	Michael Waltrip	NAPA Chevrolet
21	9	32	Ricky Craven	Tide Ford
22	19	5	Terry Labonte	Kellogg's Chevrolet
23	28	8	Dale Earnhardt Jr.	Budweiser Chevrolet
24	20	36	Ken Schrader	M&Ms Pontiac
25	27	43	John Andretti	Cheerios/Betty Crocker Dodge
26	10	55	Bobby Hamilton	Schneider Electric/Square D Chevrolet
27	36	11	Brett Bodine	Hooters Restaurants Ford
28	25	44	Steve Grissom	Georgia Pacific/Brawny Dodge
29	11	24	Jeff Gordon	DuPont Chevrolet
30	40	14	Stacy Compton	Conseco Pontiac
31	39	23	Hut Stricklin	Hills Bros Coffee Dodge
32	22	1	Steve Park	Pennzoil Chevrolet
33	6	17	Matt Kenseth	DeWalt Power Tools Ford
34	1	9	Bill Elliott	Dodge Dealers/UAW Dodge
35	5	77	Dave Blaney	Jasper Engines & Transmissions Ford
36	35	7	Casey Atwood	Sirius Satellite Radio Dodge
37	37	45	Kyle Petty	Sprint Dodge
38	2	4	Mike Skinner	Kodak Chevrolet
39	12	20	Tony Stewart	The Home Depot Pontiac
40	43	89	Morgan Shepherd	Redline Oil/Berlin City Ford
41	29	25	Joe Nemechek	UAW-Delphi Chevrolet
42	42	27	Kirk Shelmerdine	Naturally Fresh Foods Ford
43	41	66	Geoffrey Bodine	Discover Card Ford

Rolling through the inspection sticks after the New Hampshire event and finding the UPS Ford Taurus was one-eighth of an inch too low led NASCAR officials to dock the team 25 championship points, and Jarrett was emphatic the white-brown-and-yellow-clad team would not have that occur again.

Jarrett, fighting an uphill battle toward contention for the NASCAR Winston Cup Series championship, felt the sting of the lost points when the driver standings were posted after the New Hampshire race. Instead of being ninth in the standings after his well-judged, third-place run, he was listed as 11th, seven points behind Bill Elliott and nine points behind Matt Kenseth.

Sterling Marlin managed to maintain the point lead despite a less than spectacular finish at New Hampshire as teams arrived at Pocono Raceway for the second go-round of the season. Marlin finished 14th at New Hampshire but his closest challengers, Mark Martin and Jimmie Johnson, had finishes similar to that posted by the Coors Light Dodge. Martin was 16th and now trailed Sterling by 55 points, while Johnson finished 15th and found himself 37 points behind Martin. Rusty Wallace's fourth place boosted him from sixth to fourth in the standings, while Jeff Gordon fell to fifth and Ricky Rudd moved up to sixth. Tony Stewart's disastrous 39th-place finish dropped him to seventh in the point standings, while steady Kurt Busch remained eighth.

(Above Right) Ricky Rudd gladly signs autographs for his fans at Pocono Raceway. Rudd, after three straight finishes of 15th or worse, was ready to get back to his winning ways at the track he dominated in June 2001.

(Middle Right) Dale Jarrett manages a smile as he helps bring his UPS Ford to the line. Not happy after his Taurus failed post-race inspection the week before at New Hampshire, Jarrett was pleased to be at Pocono where he had posted 12 top-five finishes in his last 14 appearances, including three wins, one of which was earlier this season.

As teams rolled into the old spinach farm in the lovely Pocono Mountains, Johnny Benson readied to return to the Valvoline Pontiac after recovering from broken ribs for the second time this season. That freed up Jerry Nadeau, who moved over to the Georgia Pacific-sponsored

(Below Right) With puddles of standing water still visible around the track during a rainy, Pennsylvania weekend, competitors roll through the Adam Petty Garage on their way to the track during a much needed practice session.

Dodge fielded by Petty Enterprises, and Nadeau was elated to find he would be in the blue-and-white Intrepid for the remainder of the season.

Mike Wallace was slotted into A.J. Foyt's Conseco Pontiac for the 500-mile Pocono event, with regular driver Stacey Compton relieved of his driving duties for the team. From Compton's standpoint, it was a bizarre situation. On July 18, Foyt sent a certified letter to Compton telling him he was released from the team. Compton received it July 22, the day after the New Hampshire event. Compton had actually driven the car at New Hampshire without knowing he had been fired!

For the second straight week, Bill Elliott slapped his red Dodge Intrepid on the pole with a

(Far Left) Two-time Pocono winner Jeremy Mayfield was encouraged after turning the fourth-fastest lap in qualifying, nearly matching his teammate Bill Elliott, who grabbed the Pocono pole. With just two finishes in the top 10 so far this season, a strong run would go far in boosting his team, but an accident spoiled his bid.

(Above Left) The Budweiser Chevrolet of Dale Earnhardt Jr. and the Coors Light Dodge of point-leader Sterling Marlin bring the beer to the starting grid. Marlin, struggling of late with two top 10s in his last nine events, felt ready to notch his third win of the season – and he nearly did.

(Below Left) Although Mark Martin has yet to win at Pocono, his record boasts top-10 finishes in 13 of his last 14 starts. That string was broken this time with a 13th place, but it was still good enough to keep him second in points for the fifth straight week.

(Bottom) Kurt Busch (97) is chased by (in order) Jimmy Spencer, Jerry Nadeau and Kevin Harvick through the third-turn sweeper. Busch, in his fourth career start at Pocono, put on a strong charge late in the race, passing all challengers except Elliott to take second place and move from eighth to fifth in the point standings.

(Below) Ryan Newman (12) hugs the inside in front of Dave Blaney and Bill Elliott. In only his second Pocono appearance, Newman looked like an old pro, qualifying eighth and driving to his third straight fifth-place finish in an impressive performance at the tricky superspeedway.

(Bottom) Ricky Rudd (28) gets pressure from behind in the person of Joe Nemechek (25) with Dale Jarrett (88) in tow. Rudd, the outside pole winner, led the first nine laps of the race and then settled in for a top-10 run.

"show-me-what-you-got" lap at more than 170.5 miles per hour. The Pennsylvania 500 pole boosted him into the lead for the yearlong Bud Pole Award bonus with four, breaking him out of a tie with Jimmie Johnson for the most poles in the first 20 races of the season.

Ricky Rudd, still trying to make his decision regarding next year, grabbed the outside pole with his Havoline Ford, while Michael Waltrip and Jeremy Mayfield took positions in the second row after their qualifying runs. John Andretti gave the Cheerios folks something to cheer about with his fifth-place starting position, and Benson marked his return to the wheel by taking the outside of the third row. Jimmie Johnson and Ryan Newman were side by side in the fourth row, while Rusty Wallace and Tony Stewart beat Dale Earnhardt Jr. and Nadeau for the final top-10 qualifying positions.

Provisionals for the Pennsylvania 500 went to Bobby Labonte, Kyle Petty, Mike Skinner, Brett Bodine, Derrike Cope, Kirk Shelmerdine and Morgan Shepherd. That left Carl Long as the only driver not to make the Pocono field.

Most of the huge throng of fans mobbing the unique 2.5-mile triangular superspeedway wondered if they were going to see the full 500-mile running of the race when a first-lap accident between teammates Dale Earnhardt Jr. and Steve Park brought a red-flag delay. Park was pushed into the inside guardrail and when he hit it, the Pennzoil Chevrolet was launched into the air and flipped before coming down on its roof. Little E was unable to get untangled from the sliding Park and the force of the accident damaged the guardrail to such an extent that it took more than an hour to repair.

Only 17 more laps were in the books when rain swept over the area, delaying the race for more than two hours before the track was raceable again. It was clear to all that when the race started again, it would be difficult to get the entire distance in the books given the remaining daylight.

As the racing resumed, Sterling Marlin appeared determined to get to the checkered flag – whenever it came – first. The Coors Light Dodge driver dominated the running of the Pennsylvania 500 and led 106 laps. Right behind him, doing his best job of playing possum, was Bill Elliott, who proved his pole-winning qualifying lap was not a fluke. Bill was dialed in and simply rolled around the track a la David Pearson in his heyday behind the controls of the Wood Brothers Purolator Mercury. Waiting and using his experience to put himself in the position to win, Elliott finally made his move with just 19 laps left in the shortened 175-lap event.

It wasn't a timid move either. When Elliott went, the red

(Left) Bill Elliott (9) closes in on race-leader Sterling Marlin (40) with about 25 laps remaining in the rain-shortened event. Elliott had settled in among the leaders and watched as Marlin set the pace for most of the day. He then let the reigns out on his red Dodge and moved the point with 19 laps to go in the race.

Dodge swept to the high side of the track in the scary first turn, and Bill made it stick. He drove past Marlin and Sterling had no answer. Once in the clean air at the front of the field, Elliott steadily increased his lead, and when he flashed across the finish line for his first victory of the season, he was more than 1.7 seconds ahead. Elliott's 42nd career NASCAR Winston Cup Series victory gave Dodge back-to-back wins and put a Dodge in victory lane at Pocono for the first time since Richard Petty won the 1976 running of the Purolator 500.

Kurt Busch also worked his way past Marlin and was a distant second at the end of the event, while Marlin took third ahead of Dale Jarrett.

(Below) Coming to Pocono, Bill Elliott's Dodge had qualified in the top 10 in seven of the last eight events, but the final results had been inconsistent with a single top five during that span. This week, it all came together with a win from the pole, the first victory of the season for Elliott and Evernham Motorsports.

Ryan Newman was fifth with a strong showing, and Chicagoland-winner Kevin Harvick fought his way from the 29th starting position to finish sixth. Tony Stewart was seventh ahead of Matt Kenseth, Terry Labonte and Ricky Rudd.

Pennsylvania 500 final race results

Fin. Pos.	Start Pos.	Car No.	Driver	Team
1	1	9	Bill Elliott	Dodge Dealers/UAW Dodge
2	23	97	Kurt Busch	Rubbermaid Ford
3	13	40	Sterling Marlin	Coors Light Dodge
4	15	88	Dale Jarrett	UPS Ford
5	8	12	Ryan Newman	ALLTEL Ford
6	29	29	Kevin Harvick	GM Goodwrench Service Chevrolet
7	10	20	Tony Stewart	The Home Depot Pontiac
8	22	17	Matt Kenseth	DeWalt Power Tools Ford
9	30	5	Terry Labonte	Kellogg's Chevrolet
10	2	28	Ricky Rudd	Havoline Ford
11	37	18	Bobby Labonte	Interstate Batteries Pontiac
12	28	24	Jeff Gordon	DuPont Chevrolet
13	17	6	Mark Martin	Pfizer/Viagra Ford
14	34	22	Ward Burton	Caterpillar Dodge
15	7	48	Jimmie Johnson	Lowe's Chevrolet
16	33	99	Jeff Burton	CITGO SUPERGARD Ford
17	16	32	Ricky Craven	Tide Ford
18	3	15	Michael Waltrip	NAPA Chevrolet
19	18	55	Bobby Hamilton	Schneider Electric/Square D Chevrolet
20	25	36	Ken Schrader	M&M's Pontiac
21	32	21	Elliott Sadler	Motorcraft/U.S. Air Force Ford
22	21	77	Dave Blaney	Jasper Engines & Transmissions Ford
23	5	43	John Andretti	Cheerios/Betty Crocker Dodge
24	20	25	Joe Nemechek	UAW-Delphi Chevrolet
25	27	31	Robby Gordon	Cingular Wireless Chevrolet
26	26	30	Jeff Green	America Online Chevrolet
27	38	45	Kyle Petty	Sprint Dodge
28	19	7	Casey Atwood	Sirius Satellite Radio Dodge
29	39	4	Mike Skinner	Kodak Chevrolet
30	6	10	Johnny Benson	Eagle One/Valvoline Pontiac
31	31	23	Hut Stricklin	Hills Bros Coffee Dodge
32	35	41	Jimmy Spencer	Target Dodge
33	40	11	Brett Bodine	Hooters Restaurants Ford
34	24	26	Geoffrey Bodine	Discover Card Ford
35	41	37	Derrike Cope	MNR/Poison Ford
36	12	44	Jerry Nadeau	Georgia Pacific/Brawny Dodge
37	11	8	Dale Earnhardt Jr.	Budweiser Chevrolet
38	4	19	Jeremy Mayfield	Dodge Dealers/UAW Dodge
39	36	14	Mike Wallace	Conseco Pontiac
40	9	2	Rusty Wallace	Miller Lite Ford
41	42	27	Kirk Shelmerdine	Naturally Fresh Foods Ford
42	43	89	Morgan Shepherd	LifeXProgram.com/Berlin City Ford
43	14	1	Steve Park	Pennzoil Chevrolet

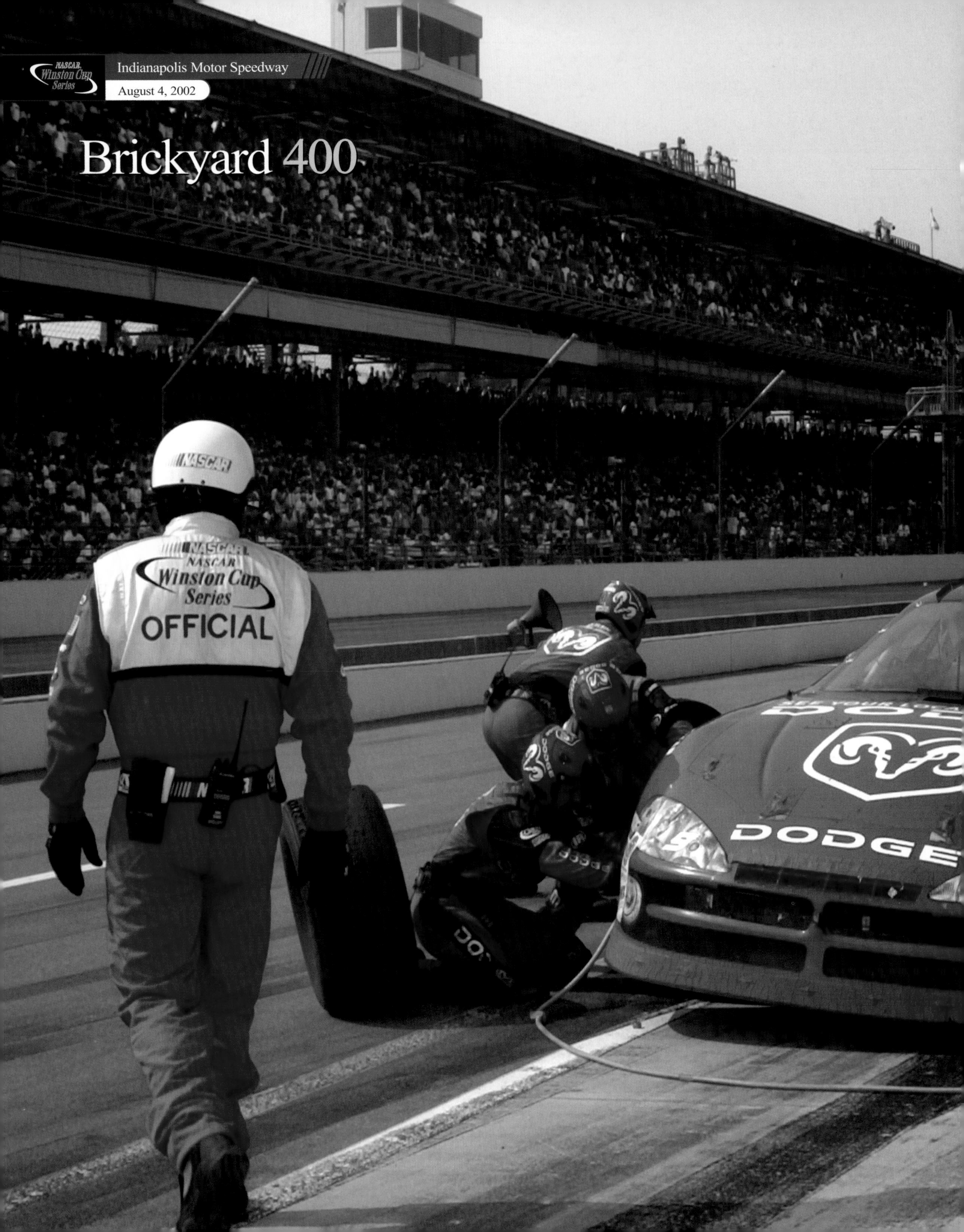
NASCAR Winston Cup Series
Indianapolis Motor Speedway
August 4, 2002
Brickyard 400
NASCAR
NASCAR
NASCAR
Winston Cup
Series
OFFICIAL
DODGE

Bill Elliott's crew works another fine stop for new tires and fuel during the ninth running of the Brickyard 400. They did a superb job on pit road, turning the Dodge out of the pits with sub-15-second stops to keep their driver in contention for a win in one of the biggest events of the year.

(Above) Bill Elliott salutes the fans during his post-race parade laps. His second straight win, the 43rd of his career, served notice to all that the 1988 NASCAR Winston Cup Series champion was back in winning form.

(Right) The DEI team for driver Steve Park pushes their Pennzoil Chevrolet toward the track on race day. Park, who had been struggling since his return to the wheel in the fifth race of the season, put on a solid performance at Indianapolis with a sixth-place qualifying run and a seventh-place finish, his first top 10 of the season.

(Below Right) The covered frontstretch grandstand that reaches all the way to the entrance of the first turn provides relief for fans from the hot August sun. Estimated crowds of close to 400,000 annually attend the summer classic at the storied superspeedway.

Many veteran garage watchers had seen the Red Storm gathering for several weeks as Bill Elliott and Ray Evernham put the building blocks in place. Elliott's Pocono victory surprised some, but others had predicted the Redhead would be in victory lane soon. And they were delighted it happened at Pocono.

Elliott was overjoyed with his win on the triangular superspeedway for several reasons. First, it showed he had not lost any of the "fire in the belly" needed to emerge victorious in the highly competitive world of NASCAR Winston Cup Series racing. Second, and perhaps more important to Bill at this stage of his career, was the importance of winning for his crew. Elliott has been through it all – from the highs of the late 1980s when he proved over and over he was the best fighter pilot in the field of aces – to the lows of the 1990s when he went to battle as a car owner and driver. He will be the first to tell you the only things he has ever wanted to do through his illustrious career are to work on cars and drive them.

And when he went to the fledgling Ray Evernham Dodge team, some felt Ray was just using Elliott in the twilight of his career to help get the team off on a solid foundation. In truth, Evernham saw that Bill could be "Awesome Bill" again. Perhaps not every week, but with the problems of putting together a new team and bringing Dodge back to the sport, not every week would be a good one, Evernham believed. And the weeks prior to Pocono saw the red-clad team learning how to challenge for victory, and then understanding what it took to go out and claim that win.

The confidence from the Pocono win was evident from the very first moment Elliott and the Evernham Dodge team arrived at Indianapolis for the Brickyard 400, one of the most important races on the NASCAR Winston Cup Series schedule. Elliott and the team had spent two days testing at the 2.5-mile oval, and Bill admitted the crew flogged him during those two days, running as many laps as humanly possible. But when the group returned for the real thing, Elliott also knew they were ready.

Bill was near the top of the charts during every practice session, and when Bud Pole qualifying was complete, Elliott had posted the second-fastest lap to claim the outside of the front row. He couldn't beat Tony Stewart's lap that saw the Home Depot Pontiac driver thrill his Indiana fans, but Elliott's smile was much broader than usual when he was asked about his chances during the race.

Dale Earnhardt Jr. and Robby Gordon grabbed the second-row starting positions ahead of Ryan Newman and Steve Park, while Kevin Harvick and NASCAR Winston Cup Series point-leader Sterling Marlin lined up in the fourth row following qualifying. Mark Martin and Joe Nemechek completed the top 10 qualifiers.

The Brickyard event traditionally draws one of the largest

entries of the year, and this season was no exception. A total of 50 cars took timed laps and Jimmie Johnson, Kurt Busch, Elliott Sadler, Bobby Labonte, Hut Stricklin, Brett Bodine and Mike Wallace, driving A.J. Foyt's Conseco Pontiac, all were forced to use provisionals to make the field.

Ron Hornaday, driving the BAM Racing Dodge instead of Shawna Robinson, was unable to qualify fast enough to make the field, and Derrike Cope suffered the same fate with his own Ford.

Scott Wimmer, in a third Bill Davis Racing Dodge, didn't make the field, nor did Tony Raines in a BACE Motorsports Chevrolet. Also unable to qualify fast enough to make the race were Jim Sauter, Stuart Kirby and P.J. Jones in a second Foyt entry.

Many of the eyes in the enormous throng were on Kevin Harvick as the Brickyard 400 field rolled under the green flag. With three straight top-10 finishes, including the Chicagoland victory, Harvick was suddenly back in the element that made him a crowd favorite last year. He also rolled to the International Race of Champions title the previous day at The Brickyard in just his first year of competition in the series, and many hoped he would be able to make it a sweep of the weekend's events.

It wasn't to be.

Instead, the momentum built by the Red Storm simply overpowered the field on the brutally hot afternoon. Elliott and Stewart waged a furious battle throughout the race, with the red Dodge and the orange-black-and-white Pontiac clearly the class of the field. There were other challengers, of course, but Elliott and Stewart cagily tested each other, knowing that if everything went right, the battle might very well be between them in the closing laps of the race.

Time after time, Elliott's red-clad crew did their job on pit road. Four times they turned Bill back out of the pits in 14.5 seconds or less. And on the track, Elliott did his work as well, running at the point or in the lead pack throughout the afternoon.

(Far Left) Jeff Gordon chases the side-by-side duo of Robby Gordon (left) and Kevin Harvick, with Dale Jarrett, Ryan Newman and Sterling Marlin following as the cars head toward the backstretch. IMS' "soft wall" can be seen here in the exit of the second turn.

(Left) Bill Elliott (9) brings the tightly bunched field down the frontstretch in front of (in order) Robby Gordon, Mark Martin, Ryan Newman, Kevin Harvick, Ward Burton, Steve Park and Matt Kenseth, with Jeff Gordon's DuPont Chevrolet leading a second pack of cars.

(Right) At lap 138, Rusty Wallace has his Miller Lite Ford out front with Tony Stewart in second and Bill Elliott closing from third. It took Elliott only another 11 laps to dispose of Stewart's Pontiac the Wallace's Ford before moving into the lead for the last time in the race.

(Below) Robby Gordon looks inside of Bill Elliott's Dodge, but to no avail, as Elliott clearly had the strongest mount, leading five times for 93 of the race's 160 laps. Gordon, who qualified in fourth, capitalized on his experience at IMS and turned in an eighth-place run, his third top 10 in the last four races.

The seventh caution of the afternoon came when Sadler cut a right-front tire on his Motorcraft Ford, and with just over 30 laps to go, teams headed for pit road making decisions on whether to take two tires or four. Two might help with track position and four would certainly help with grip. Elliott took four tires and fuel in 14.3 seconds while Mark Martin and Dale Jarrett took just two tires. Jarrett left with the fuel catch can dangling from the left rear of his UPS Taurus, and although he shook the offending can off, he was ordered to pit road for a stop-and-go penalty. During that stop, his crew changed the other two tires to give him four fresh Goodyear Eagles, but he was mired back in the field.

Martin headed the field for the restart followed by Stewart, Rusty Wallace and Kevin Harvick. Elliott was fifth, and as far as the Redhead was concerned, it was time to let the dogs off the porch.

Wallace flashed past Martin to take the point, and Rusty hoped it was finally his turn to win at Indy after finishing second twice before. While Wallace was moving to the front, Elliott dove past Harvick and set sail after Stewart. He got the Pontiac driver two laps later and then set off after Wallace. Rusty looked in the mirror and groaned. Elliott was coming hard.

Elliott stalked Wallace for nearly 10 laps and finally decided to make his move on the backstretch with just 11 laps to go. Wallace had no answer for the swift, red Dodge and could only smile quietly as Elliott went past. Wallace appreciated the fact that the winner was going to be a veteran driver rather than one of the young whippersnappers who had gathered so many headlines this season.

Not even a caution for debris in the closing laps, brought about by a collision between Mark Martin and Ward Burton, could change the outcome of the race. Elliott streaked off when the restart came with just four laps left in the race, and Rusty had nothing for the Redhead.

Happy day! Cindy Elliott and son Chase join Bill Elliott and the entire Evernham Dodge team to celebrate being "No. 1" at The Brickyard. The winner's share of the nearly $7.5 million purse was just over $449,000.

The precious Indianapolis victory was the 43rd of Elliott's storied career, and it was incredibly popular in the garage area after the race. It seemed only fitting that one of the drivers who had helped the sport move to the plateau it now occupies would win this most prestigious race in the waning years of his career.

Matt Kenseth fought his way to third behind Wallace, while Ryan Newman charged his way to fourth ahead of Harvick and Jeff Gordon. Steve Park and Robby Gordon were ahead of Jimmie Johnson and Dale Jarrett, while Stewart faded from fourth on the final restart to 12th place after challenging for the victory throughout the race.

Brickyard 400 final race results

Fin. Pos.	Start Pos.	Car No.	Driver	Team
1	2	9	Bill Elliott	Dodge Dealers/UAW Dodge
2	35	2	Rusty Wallace	Miller Lite Ford
3	18	17	Matt Kenseth	DeWalt Power Tools Ford
4	5	12	Ryan Newman	ALLTEL Ford
5	7	29	Kevin Harvick	GM Goodwrench Service Chevrolet
6	21	24	Jeff Gordon	DuPont Chevrolet
7	6	1	Steve Park	Pennzoil Chevrolet
8	4	31	Robby Gordon	Cingular Wireless Chevrolet
9	37	48	Jimmie Johnson	Lowe's Chevrolet
10	17	88	Dale Jarrett	UPS Ford
11	40	18	Bobby Labonte	Interstate Batteries Pontiac
12	1	20	Tony Stewart	The Home Depot Pontiac
13	31	5	Terry Labonte	Kellogg's Chevrolet
14	30	36	Ken Schrader	Pedigree Pontiac
15	33	77	Dave Blaney	Jasper Engines & Transmissions Ford
16	14	15	Michael Waltrip	NAPA Chevrolet
17	41	23	Hut Stricklin	Hills Bros Coffee Dodge
18	25	28	Ricky Rudd	Havoline Ford
19	29	30	Jeff Green	America Online Chevrolet
20	10	25	Joe Nemechek	UAW-Delphi Chevrolet
21	36	07	Ted Musgrave	Sirius Satellite Radio/Kenwood Dodge
22	3	8	Dale Earnhardt Jr.	Budweiser Chevrolet
23	32	55	Bobby Hamilton	Schneider Electric/Square D Chevrolet
24	34	44	Jerry Nadeau	Georgia Pacific/Brawny Dodge
25	27	45	Kyle Petty	Sprint Dodge
26	16	43	John Andretti	Box Top for Education Dodge
27	8	40	Sterling Marlin	Coors Light Dodge
28	9	6	Mark Martin	Pfizer/Viagra Ford
29	23	99	Jeff Burton	CITGO SUPERGARD Ford
30	19	22	Ward Burton	Caterpillar Dodge
31	15	41	Jimmy Spencer	Target Dodge
32	26	98	Kenny Wallace	Stacker 2 Chevrolet
33	22	32	Ricky Craven	Tide Ford
34	20	26	Todd Bodine	Discover Card Ford
35	39	21	Elliott Sadler	Motorcraft Ford
36	13	4	Mike Skinner	Kodak Chevrolet
37	11	10	Johnny Benson	Valvoline Pontiac
38	28	7	Casey Atwood	Sirius Satellite Radio Dodge
39	12	19	Jeremy Mayfield	Dodge Dealers/UAW Dodge
40	24	09	Geoffrey Bodine	Miccosukee Indian Gaming Ford
41	38	97	Kurt Busch	Rubbermaid Ford
42	42	11	Brett Bodine	Hooters Restaurants Ford
43	43	14	Mike Wallace	Conseco Pontiac

Sirius Satellite Radio at The Glen

Ryan Newman (12) and Scott Pruett, driving the Target Dodge for Ganassi Racing, wrestle for room while rounding turn 11 at Watkins Glen International. Newman proved formidable on the road course and brought the ALLTEL Ford home in second place, while Pruett posted a strong run to sixth.

(Right) Sterling Marlin (left) hangs with a few of his more youthful competitors, Elliott Sadler, Jimmie Johnson and Dale Earnhardt Jr., while waiting to get underway at the Glen.

(Below) Pole-winner Ricky Rudd (28) jumps to the early lead in front of Michael Waltrip, who grabbed the outside of the front row in qualifying. Rudd, winner of the road-course event at Sonoma, Calif., earlier this season, stayed among the leaders to take fifth, while Waltrip posted his four career top-10 finish at the Glen in ninth.

The emotionally charged days between the Brickyard 400 and the opening of practice for the Sirius Satellite Radio-sponsored event at Watkins Glen's famed road-racing course had drained Home Depot Pontiac driver Tony Stewart.

Tony had been in the hunt for victory at The Brickyard, an event he annually put at the top of his personal and team "wish list." In the waning laps, however, he had faded from contention and his frustration showed when he marched from his car to his transporter following the event.

His physical confrontation with a photographer had ignited the headlines across the country the following day, and Stewart once again was under fire for his volatile and tempestuous outbursts. NASCAR had fined him $10,000 and put him on probation for the remainder of the season. Sponsor Home Depot had slapped an unprecedented $50,000 fine on him and had also put Stewart on probation for the remainder of the season.

A much-chagrined Stewart met with media members at The Glen, one of the most picturesque venues on the entire NASCAR Winston Cup Series tour, and Tony admitted he would be seeking professional assistance to help him manage his temper and anger. He also said he had spent considerable time watching how other drivers had dealt with their frustrations of being in position to win the Brickyard 400 but failing to do so. He noted that those other drivers, Dale Jarrett in particular, had displayed much more diplomacy in dealing with the loss.

Stewart dealt with the fines and probation during the week, and everyone in the NASCAR Winston Cup Series garage area hoped it had been the wakeup call Tony needed. There was no questioning his skill and talent behind the wheel of his orange-and-white Pontiac. The problem was how Tony dealt with things when they didn't go perfectly. All one could hope was that the move by Home Depot – the first time in NASCAR history a sponsor had stepped up to the plate and fined its driver for his actions – had delivered a meaningful message.

The Glen event annually finds some teams putting road-racing specialists in their cars in

(Above) Mark Martin (6), winner of three straight at Watkins Glen from 1993-95, gets pressure from Todd Bodine (26), driving at the track near his hometown of Chemung, N.Y. Bodine, who finished fifth here in 2001, worked past Martin to take eighth place, two spots better than the Viagra Ford driver, who moved to second in the points.

hopes of bolstering a finish, and this year was no exception. Scott Pruett found himself in a Chip Ganassi-owned Target Dodge, and P.J. Jones was enlisted to drive A.J. Foyt's Conseco Pontiac. Boris Said wheeled a Jasper Motorsports Ford and Tom Hubert was behind the wheel of Bill Davis' Hills Brothers Dodge. Joe Varde was also on hand with an entry from BACE Motorsports.

Ricky Rudd claimed his first Bud Pole of the season, earning himself a slot in the February Bud Shootout at Daytona Beach, no matter where he would be driving next season. Rudd appeared ready to be announced as the driver of a third Ganassi team entry for the 2003 season, with Texaco moving from Robert Yates Racing to the Ganassi camp. Michael Waltrip, with tutoring from road-racing specialist Ron Fellows, grabbed the outside of the front row in a surprising starting position for the NAPA Chevrolet. Waltrip has never been a good road-racing qualifier, and to find himself on the outside of the front row was a huge surprise to Michael and his team.

Stewart and red-hot Bill Elliott grabbed the second-row starting positions, and Ryan Newman and Kevin Harvick continued the surprises at the front of the field. Robby Gordon and Matt Kenseth made up the fourth row ahead of Kurt Busch and Rusty Wallace. Bobby Hamilton and Jimmie Johnson barely missed earning top-10 qualifying positions.

(Below) Sterling Marlin's Coors Dodge, which lost a motor in practice on Saturday, shows signs of more engine problems that dropped him off the pace and into 30th place by the end of the day. That result, combined with Martin's top-10 finish shaved 40 points off Marlin's lead in the standings, which stood at 53 after the race.

(Right) Robby Gordon, and accomplished road racer in his own right, pilots the Cingular Chevrolet toward the frontstretch. Gordon was very strong early in the race, taking the lead from Rudd on lap 4 and holding it for the next 21 circuits before settling in for a third-place run on the day, his first top five of the season.

(Below) Tony Stewart (20) leads the way with P.J. Jones (14) looking for an opportunity to sneak past. Jones challenged the frontrunners all day and rewarded car owner A.J. Foyt with a strong fourth place, but no one was going to deny Tony Stewart, who led more than a third of the race, including the final 19 laps.

Ricky Craven, Terry Labonte, Johnny Benson, Tom Hubert, Ken Schrader, Kenny Wallace and Joe Varde used provisionals to make The Glen's field, leaving Austin Cameron, Shane Lewis and Jimmy Spencer on the sidelines, unable to make the field. Ganassi's move to put Pruett in Spencer's No. 41 to gain car owner points worked, but Spencer, unfortunately, wasn't fast enough to make the field with the Dodge entered for him.

Point-leader Sterling Marlin had a lost weekend at The Glen, losing an engine in "happy hour" and being forced to start at the back of the field on the tricky 2.4-mile track. The rest of his weekend wasn't much better, with the Coors Dodge losing a cylinder early in the race and Marlin struggling to a 30th-place finish.

Many expected Jeff Gordon to emerge at The Glen as a challenger for victory. Since 1996, Gordon and his DuPont team have won at least one of the road-course offerings on the schedule each year, and The Glen's race marked the second and final such event for 2002.

Gordon, however, never was a player in the race and struggled home to a 22nd-place finish. Robby Gordon, Ryan Newman and Tony Stewart had the strongest cars in the field as the Glen event unwound. The trio, along with others like Rusty Wallace, Ricky Rudd, Scott Pruett, Dale Jarrett and P.J. Jones, comprised the lead pack throughout the day, and when it came down to the end, Newman was the surprise leader until

Stewart laid a kamikaze move on the rookie in the final turn on lap 72.

Once in the clear, Tony gradually built his lead, eventually building a solid, 2.5-second cushion in just seven laps. He appeared to be free and clear, headed for victory, but a pair of cautions in the final 20 laps allowed others a breath of hope. The first came when Ricky Craven ran off the track at the end of the frontstretch on lap 80, and the second came when Kenny Wallace crashed into the foam barrier lining the outside of the first turn. At the same time, Terry Labonte's Kellogg's Chevrolet blew a right-front tire and hit several safety cones, and NASCAR officials red-flagged the race to clean up the mess.

Nearly 13 minutes later, the field fired up for a one-lap sprint to the finish, and after all he had gone through during the past week, there was no

way Stewart was going to let this one get away. He accelerated a little in front of the restart line and pulled away from the surprised field to rocket around the final 2.4 miles. Some claimed he jumped the start, but most privately agreed that if it had been them at the front of the field, they would have done the same thing.

Ryan Newman finished a solid second with a superb run, while Robby Gordon fought painful ankles to heel-and-toe his way to third place. P.J. Jones gave A.J. Foyt's team its best finish of the season with a fourth place, while Ricky Rudd was fifth ahead of Scott Pruett's strong run in the Target Dodge. Jeff Burton and Todd Bodine were seventh and eighth, with Michael Waltrip ninth and Mark Martin completing the top 10.

Tony Stewart releases the champagne and likely some pent-up emotions following a tumultuous week. With his third win of the season, Stewart jumped from seventh to fourth in the standings, 104 points behind Marlin, to stake his claim as a serious contender for the championship.

Sirius Satellite Radio at The Glen final race results

Fin. Pos.	Start Pos.	Car No.	Driver	Team
1	3	20	Tony Stewart	The Home Depot Pontiac
2	5	12	Ryan Newman	ALLTEL Ford
3	7	31	Robby Gordon	Cingular Wireless Chevrolet
4	14	14	PJ Jones	Conseco Pontiac
5	1	28	Ricky Rudd	Havoline Ford
6	19	41	Scott Pruett	Target Dodge
7	25	99	Jeff Burton	CITGO SUPERGARD Ford
8	13	26	Todd Bodine	Discover Card Ford
9	2	15	Michael Waltrip	NAPA Chevrolet
10	15	6	Mark Martin	Pfizer/Viagra Ford
11	27	43	John Andretti	Cheerios/Betty Crocker Dodge
12	16	30	Jeff Green	America Online Chevrolet
13	29	67	Boris Said	Jasper Engines & Transmissions Ford
14	6	29	Kevin Harvick	GM Goodwrench Service Chevrolet
15	30	19	Jeremy Mayfield	Dodge Dealers/UAW Dodge
16	12	48	Jimmie Johnson	Lowe's Chevrolet
17	10	2	Rusty Wallace	Miller Lite Ford
18	20	77	Dave Blaney	Jasper Engines & Transmissions Ford
19	11	55	Bobby Hamilton	Schneider Electric/Square D Chevrolet
20	18	22	Ward Burton	Caterpillar Dodge
21	4	9	Bill Elliott	Dodge Dealers/UAW Dodge
22	23	24	Jeff Gordon	DuPont Chevrolet
23	24	18	Bobby Labonte	Interstate Batteries Pontiac
24	40	23	Tom Hubert	Hills Bros Coffee Dodge
25	39	10	Johnny Benson	Valvoline Pontiac
26	35	44	Jerry Nadeau	Georgia Pacific/Brawny Dodge
27	26	7	Casey Atwood	Sirius Satellite Radio Dodge
28	41	36	Ken Schrader	M&Ms Pontiac
29	34	45	Kyle Petty	Sprint Dodge
30	28	40	Sterling Marlin	Coors Light Dodge
31	38	5	Terry Labonte	Kellogg's Chevrolet
32	31	11	Brett Bodine	Hooters Restaurants Ford
33	8	17	Matt Kenseth	DeWalt Power Tools Ford
34	37	32	Ricky Craven	Tide Ford
35	21	8	Dale Earnhardt Jr.	Budweiser Chevrolet
36	42	98	Kenny Wallace	Stacker 2 Chevrolet
37	17	88	Dale Jarrett	UPS Ford
38	33	25	Joe Nemechek	UAW-Delphi Chevrolet
39	36	1	Steve Park	Pennzoil Chevrolet
40	22	4	Mike Skinner	Kodak Chevrolet
41	9	97	Kurt Busch	Rubbermaid Ford
42	43	74	Joe Varde	Staff America Chevrolet
43	32	21	Elliott Sadler	Motorcraft Ford

Michigan International Speedway

August 18, 2002

Pepsi 400 presented by Farmer Jack

Dale Jarrett (88) slips past Tony Stewart (20) on the inside at nearly 200 miles per hour on Michigan's roomy frontstretch, rocketing his way toward a hard-fought victory. Stewart followed Jarrett to the front and took second in the race.

(Above) Jeff Gordon gets a bear hug from team owner Rick Hendrick after Gordon ended his 31-race winless streak with an emotional win at Bristol. After scoring just two top 10s in the last eight races, Gordon felt this win would put his team back in the hunt as a championship contender.

(Right) Driver Mike Skinner trims tape on the front grille of his Kodak Chevrolet, looking for a little edge on the competition at Bristol.

For the top 11 drivers in the NASCAR Winston Cup Series point standings, every event had become a test of will. The point spreads between each of the drivers were so small that a good finish at a single race versus a poor performance by an adversary virtually assured a shuffle in the standings.

As teams assembled at Bristol Motor Speedway's steeply-banked cereal bowl of a half mile, Sterling Marlin had righted the ship after a pair of poor performances and posted a sixth place at Michigan. It kept the Tennessean at the top of the point ladder and gave tens of thousands of loyal Tennessee fans plenty to cheer for as Marlin arrived for the second race of the year at Thunder Valley.

Mark Martin's fifth place at Michigan allowed him to pick up a few points on Sterling, and the Arkansas native now stood just 43 points behind the Coors Light Dodge driver. Jimmie Johnson had taken home a seventh place from Michigan – a solid performance, but one that cost him a few points in his chase of both Marlin and Martin. Johnson now trailed Martin by 17 points, while Tony Stewart's battle to second place at Michigan

pushed him to within 24 points of Johnson. Jeff Gordon's winless streak reached 31 at Michigan, and his 19th-place finish put him 66 points behind Stewart and just 18 markers ahead of Ricky Rudd.

Rusty Wallace sagged to 23 points behind Rudd with his 24th-place finish at Michigan, while Bill Elliott's 22nd place allowed him to move to 45 points behind Wallace in their battle for seventh place. Matt Kenseth trailed Elliott by 59 points, while Dale Jarrett's popular Michigan victory moved him from 12th to 10th, where he was just 14 points behind Kenseth. Ryan Newman, in 11th, fell from ninth place after his 31st-place Michigan finish.

The question mark hanging over Ricky Rudd's future in NASCAR Winston Cup Series racing – the decision many felt would trigger a series of driver switches for next season – was resolved in the days between Michigan and Bristol. Rudd surprised many by making his decision to remain active as a driver and stunned even more by signing a three-year contract with the Wood Brothers and Motorcraft. Ricky's decision came after Ford and Motorcraft upped the ante with the Woods, promising more engineering and financial assistance, with Motorcraft extending its contract with the Wood Brothers through 2005.

In some ways, it made perfect sense. While Rudd was growing up, he watched David Pearson

drive the Woods' entries to victory after victory. And as a Virginian, Ricky took great pride in the Wood Brothers team and its success. Perhaps more important, the Wood Brothers have always represented the very best of the family attributes Ricky holds close to his heart, and every driver who has ever been with the Wood Brothers speaks in almost reverent tones about his experiences with the team and its personnel and management. For Rudd, admittedly in the twilight of a superb career, it was a chance to work with one of the pioneer teams in the sport, to finish his career with a Virginia team and to rejoin the folks at Motorcraft, who sponsored his efforts with Bud Moore Engineering as far back as 1985.

While Rudd, the Wood Brothers and Motorcraft were making their announcement, Morgan-McClure Racing was also making a change. The Abingdon-based team decided to cast its lot with Pontiac, switching the Kodak colors for Mike Skinner from the Chevrolet brand. Morgan-McClure became the second team to switch to Ponchos, joining Cal Wells and his Tide-sponsored entries for Ricky Craven.

Jeff Gordon may have been winless for the last 31 races, but you couldn't tell it from the results of Bud Pole qualifying. Gordon ripped off the fastest lap during qualifying to grab his third pole of the season and sent Dale Earnhardt Jr. to the outside of the front row. Michael Waltrip made it

(Above) Jimmie Johnson (48) and Mark Martin (6) slide to the apron after slamming together during a restart on lap 376. Johnson had been hit from behind by Robby Gordon and spun, collecting Martin, who was unable to avoid the Lowe's Chevrolet. Martin finished three laps down, but maintained his hold on second place in the standings, while Johnson's 34th-place finish dropped him from third to fifth in the points.

(Above) Bobby Labonte (18) and Kurt Busch (97) storm out of their pits while Matt Kenseth (17), Jeff Burton (99), Tony Stewart (20) and John Andretti (43) head back into action. With 15 cautions during the event, pit road was a very busy place all evening.

(Right) Derrike Cope (49) slides up to the second-turn wall as Ricky Rudd (28), Hut Stricklin (23), Johnny Benson (10) and Kevin Harvick (29) continue racing in the low groove. Of this group, only Benson and Harvick were running at the finish, with Harvick's fourth place giving him six top 10s in the last seven events.

two DEI Chevrolets in the first three starting positions by claiming the inside of the second row, while Rusty Wallace served notice he was also ready to end his long winless string by putting the Miller Lite Ford on the outside of the second row. Bill Elliott was in the fastest Dodge, grabbing the fifth-quickest lap of the session, while Johnny Benson was on his right. The fourth row was comprised of Ricky Craven and Kurt Busch, while yellow and black were the colors of the fifth row, with Ward Burton and Matt Kenseth lined up in the ninth and 10th starting slots.

Dave Blaney, former Bristol-winner Elliott Sadler, John Andretti, Ken Schrader, Hut Stricklin, Steve Park and Lance Hooper, in Junie Donlavey's Ford, used provisionals to make the field. That left Hermie Sadler, Carl Long, Morgan Shepherd and Tim Sauter, in Dave Marcis' Chevrolet, unable to make the field.

Bristol's night race has historically been one of the events where driver frustrations surface, and with a standing-room-only crowd and millions watching on television, this year's event would be no different. There was plenty of bumping and banging, plenty of finger pointing and heat-shield throwing and a couple of ambulance whackings tossed in. Spinning cars, burst radiators and clouds of tire smoke dotted the 500 laps, and when the annual event at Thunder Valley

finally rolled down to the final laps, the battle was between Jeff Gordon and Rusty Wallace, whose own personal winless streak was even longer than Gordon's.

Wallace flogged his Ford to the point with 18 laps to go, but one look in his mirror told him that Gordon was just as intent on winning the huge trophy that goes to the Bristol winner. Rusty hoped he could hold his line and work his way through traffic, maintaining the lead, but when he came up behind Hendrick Motorsports driver Joe Nemechek – and Joe dallied in moving out of the inside lane – Wallace knew in his heart he was beaten.

Following Nemechek killed the clean air Wallace had been enjoying and took the air off the nose of the Ford. It also allowed Gordon to close the gap, and with just two laps remaining, Gordon laid the chrome horn on Wallace's back bumper.

Jeff hit Rusty just hard enough to make Wallace momentarily bobble, but it was enough to allow Gordon to turn under the Ford and take the point. Rusty could not make up the distance in time to retaliate and Gordon rolled to his first victory of the season, ending his longest winless streak since he obtained his first victory in 1994 in his 42nd career start.

Dale Earnhardt Jr. took third ahead of Kevin Harvick and Matt Kenseth, while Kurt Busch and point-leader Sterling Marlin finished sixth and seventh. Jimmy Spencer, Bobby Labonte and Mike Wallace, in A.J. Foyt's Conseco Pontiac, completed the top 10.

(Top Left) With less than five laps remaining, Rusty Wallace (2), who took the lead for the first time on lap 482, battles in traffic while Jeff Gordon (24) closes quickly from behind.

(Middle Left) Gordon used the lapped traffic to catch Wallace and, with three to go, gives the Miller Lite driver the old "bump and run," cutting to the bottom of the track and slipping by to take the point.

(Bottom Left) After recovering from Gordon's nudge, Wallace sets out after the DuPont Chevrolet, but Gordon's car was good enough to stay out front for the final two laps and pick up the win, his first of the season.

Sharpie 500 final race results

Fin. Pos.	Start Pos.	Car No.	Driver	Team
1	1	24	Jeff Gordon	DuPont Chevrolet
2	4	2	Rusty Wallace	Miller Lite Ford
3	2	8	Dale Earnhardt Jr.	Budweiser Chevrolet
4	23	29	Kevin Harvick	GM Goodwrench Service Chevrolet
5	10	17	Matt Kenseth	DeWalt Power Tools Ford
6	8	97	Kurt Busch	Rubbermaid Ford
7	27	40	Sterling Marlin	Coors Light Dodge
8	11	41	Jimmy Spencer	Target Dodge
9	12	18	Bobby Labonte	Interstate Batteries Pontiac
10	33	14	Mike Wallace	Conseco Pontiac
11	34	55	Bobby Hamilton	Schneider Electric/Square D Chevrolet
12	6	10	Johnny Benson	Valvoline Pontiac
13	36	99	Jeff Burton	CITGO SUPERGARD Ford
14	40	36	Ken Schrader	M&Ms Pontiac
15	22	45	Kyle Petty	Sprint Dodge
16	7	32	Ricky Craven	Tide Ford
17	5	9	Bill Elliott	Dodge Dealers/UAW Dodge
18	17	7	Casey Atwood	Sirius Satellite Radio Dodge
19	39	43	John Andretti	Cheerios/Betty Crocker Dodge
20	30	31	Robby Gordon	Cingular Wireless Chevrolet
21	35	44	Jerry Nadeau	Georgia Pacific/Brawny Dodge
22	3	15	Michael Waltrip	NAPA Chevrolet
23	21	6	Mark Martin	Pfizer/Viagra Ford
24	26	20	Tony Stewart	The Home Depot Pontiac
25	13	19	Jeremy Mayfield	Dodge Dealers/UAW Dodge
26	42	1	Steve Park	Pennzoil Chevrolet
27	20	25	Joe Nemechek	UAW-Delphi Chevrolet
28	19	88	Dale Jarrett	UPS Ford
29	16	4	Mike Skinner	Kodak Chevrolet
30	24	5	Terry Labonte	Kellogg's Chevrolet
31	43	90	Lance Hooper	Lucas Oil Ford
32	28	11	Brett Bodine	Hooters Restaurants Ford
33	37	77	Dave Blaney	Jasper Engines & Transmissions Ford
34	32	48	Jimmie Johnson	Lowe's Chevrolet
35	18	30	Jeff Green	America Online Chevrolet
36	14	12	Ryan Newman	ALLTEL Ford
37	9	22	Ward Burton	Caterpillar Dodge
38	41	23	Hut Stricklin	Hills Bros Coffee Dodge
39	15	28	Ricky Rudd	Havoline Ford
40	31	27	Scott Wimmer	Hills Bros Coffee Dodge
41	29	49	Derrike Cope	MNR Productions Pontiac
42	38	21	Elliott Sadler	Motorcraft Ford
43	25	26	Todd Bodine	Discover Card Ford

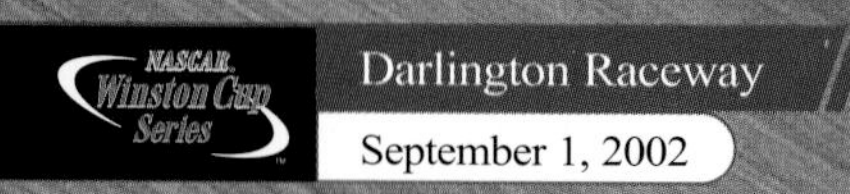

Mountain Dew Southern 500

Rusty Wallace takes the Miller Lite Ford up to the wall to challenge Bobby Labonte's Interstate Batteries Pontiac on Darlington's treacherous high banks.

GOODYEAR
Rusty Wallace
Winston Cup
True Value
Bud
Edelbrock
CLEVITE
EA SPORTS
SIMPSON
MOOG
2
Snap-on
Mazak
BOSCH
Mobil 1
LENNOX
Miller Lite
MeadWestvaco
CANNON
BATTERIES
MBNA
WIX
FILTERS

(Above Right) Team spotters take advantage of the high perch atop Darlington's press box to keep an eye on their respective drivers. At a tricky, narrow superspeedway such as Darlington, a spotter's role is especially critical to a driver's success on the track.

(Below Right) Unloading their transporter at Darlington, Sterling Marlin's team didn't have to look far to see the hauler of the DuPont team. Slowly, Jeff Gordon had been climbing the point ladder, working his way into contention for the championship and moving ever closer to the Coors Light brigade.

The long-awaited victory celebration over after a 31-race drought, Jeff Gordon and his DuPont-sponsored mates arrived at historic Darlington Raceway in search of a fifth Mountain Dew Southern 500 victory. With his bump-and-run win at Bristol the previous weekend, when he shunted Rusty Wallace from the point and then sprinted to the 59th victory of his career, Gordon proved his team had worked its way back into championship contention.

Finally, after two-thirds of the season, Gordon and his Hendrick Motorsports team were back, and as far as Gordon was concerned, there was ample time remaining in the season to mount a challenge for the championship no one had been able to put a lock on.

Sterling Marlin was taking one race at a time, maintaining the point lead he had held since the second race of the season, and his point-counting performance at Bristol was vintage Marlin. He raced his Coors Light Dodge to a rock-solid seventh-place finish at Thunder Valley and watched as three of the four closest championship pursuers fell victim to Bristol's steep banks.

Mark Martin finished 23rd and lost 52 points in his chase of Marlin for the championship. Tony Stewart, in fourth place in the standings, finished 24th and Jimmie Johnson had an even worse night under the lights. He finished 34th and fell from third to fifth in the point battle.

Of the top five, only Gordon gained points on Marlin, but the Bristol victory also moved him to within 16 points of Martin in second. Rusty Wallace's second-place finish allowed him to jump from seventh to sixth in the point standings, while Ricky Rudd fell from sixth to seventh after engine failure sidelined him and sent him reeling to a 39th-place finish. Bill Elliott, Matt Kenseth and Dale Jarrett all maintained their posi-

tions in eighth, ninth and 10th in the point standings.

Overlooked in the hoopla surrounding Gordon's first victory in nearly a year and the late-race push-and-shove were a pair of strong performances by Kevin Harvick and Mike Wallace. Harvick fought his way to his sixth top-10 finish in the last seven races in Richard Childress' GM Goodwrench Chevrolet, while Wallace posted the second top-10 finish in the last three races for A.J. Foyt's Conseco Pontiac team.

While rain delayed, and finally washed out qualifying for the Mountain Dew Southern 500 at Darlington, one of the hottest rumors of silly season flashed around the garage area. Tight-lipped about the veracity of the rumor, Rusty Wallace allowed that it was possible that the Penske team for Wallace and Ryan Newman would not be driving Ford Tauruses next season. Instead, it appeared there was more than a 50-50 chance that the team would join the Dodge Boys and field Intrepids for the coming year.

(Above) Sterling Marlin (40) and Mark Martin (6) bring the field under green to start the Mountain Dew Southern 500. Inclement weather on qualifying day forced the field to be lined up according to owner points for the start of the race.

(Left) Under the watchful eyes of NASCAR officials, team members sweep lug nuts and debris from their pit stalls after a round stops under caution, one of nine thrown during the 500-mile event.

(Top Right) Mark Martin's crew outfits the Viagra Ford with a set of fresh Goodyears and a full tank of fuel. Martin shot into the lead on lap 20, the first green-flag lap at speed, and held the point for 25 laps before settling in among the top 10 for most of the race. Finishing 11th, Martin dropped to third in the standings at the end of the day.

(Middle Right) Dale Jarrett takes his UPS Ford up near the wall, using the high groove against Jeff Burton (99) down low. Burton led 20 laps before the halfway point, but dropped from the lead pack when he slipped through a patch of oil that brought out the fifth caution of the race.

(Below Right) Jeff Gordon shows his rear bumper to Sterling Marlin (40), Ken Schrader (36) and Ryan Newman (12) – a view they would get used to before the day was done. Gordon moved into the lead for the first time on lap 240 and led all but three of the remaining 128 laps on the way to his fifth Southern 500 crown.

The qualifying rainout meant that Sterling Marlin and Mark Martin would start from the front row for the Southern 500 on the treacherous egg-shaped oval – and the gleam in Gordon's eyes was present throughout Sunday Morning. He would start the Mountain Dew Southern 500 right behind Marlin, and there are few drivers who have had success in September at Darlington like Gordon has.

Four times in his short NASCAR Winston Cup Series career, Gordon had emerged to win one of the most honored titles in the history of the sport. His four Southern 500 trophies meant he needed just one more to match the total won by Cale Yarborough.

When this year's edition of the Mountain Dew Southern 500 was completed, Gordon had that record-tying fifth trophy, his second straight win after the seemingly endless victory drought and the 60th triumph of his career.

And this one seemed to come effortlessly. Despite having a problem during a pit stop when a lug nut jammed in an air wrench, Gordon fought his way back to second and then blew past Sterling Marlin on lap 239. Once in clean air at the front of the pack, Gordon set sail and rolled to the win. No one had anything with which to challenge the DuPont Chevrolet, and Jeff led all but three of the remaining laps and barely seemed to have broken a sweat.

The race began under gray skies, and the first 19 laps of the event were under a green flag, albeit behind a pace car as NASCAR officials used heat from the exhaust pipes to finish track-drying activities. Once under green in anger, however, Marlin and Elliott clearly had the most dominant entries until Gordon emerged and rocketed past on his way to the victory.

Ryan Newman did his best to challenge Gordon at the end, but it was for naught.

Jeff Gordon receives a challenge from Bill Elliott (9) on the outside. Elliott hung with the leaders throughout the race and took third at the finish, a welcome result after three straight finishes of 17th or worse.

Newman finished more than 1.7 seconds behind, while Elliott flashed some of his early-career Darlington magic to bring his red Dodge home in third place. Marlin was a solid fourth, again taking advantage of a high point-scoring position, while Dale Jarrett finished fifth. Ward Burton made it three Dodges in the first six finishing positions when he beat Kurt Busch for the position, while Tony Stewart was eighth ahead of Jimmie Johnson and Jeff Burton. Mark Martin just missed a top-10 position, taking 11th behind his Roush Racing teammate.

Gordon's second straight victory, coupled with Martin's 11th place, moved Jeff into second place in the point standings. With his fifth Mountain Dew Southern 500 trophy safely tucked away, Gordon looked at the point standings with a smile. He was now where he wanted to be, just 91 points behind Marlin with 11 races remaining on the 2002 schedule.

Mountain Dew Southern 500 final race results

Fin. Pos.	Start Pos.	Car No.	Driver	Team
1	3	24	Jeff Gordon	DuPont Chevrolet
2	12	12	Ryan Newman	ALLTEL Ford
3	8	9	Bill Elliott	Dodge Dealers/UAW Dodge
4	1	40	Sterling Marlin	Coors Light Dodge
5	10	88	Dale Jarrett	UPS Ford
6	28	22	Ward Burton	Caterpillar Dodge
7	11	97	Kurt Busch	Rubbermaid Ford
8	4	20	Tony Stewart	The Home Depot Pontiac
9	5	48	Jimmie Johnson	Lowe's Chevrolet
10	13	99	Jeff Burton	CITGO SUPERGARD Ford
11	2	6	Mark Martin	Pfizer/Viagra Ford
12	20	30	Jeff Green	America Online Chevrolet
13	24	45	Kyle Petty	Sprint Dodge
14	16	32	Ricky Craven	Tide Ford
15	18	18	Bobby Labonte	Interstate Batteries Pontiac
16	15	8	Dale Earnhardt Jr.	Budweiser Chevrolet
17	22	31	Robby Gordon	Cingular Wireless Chevrolet
18	23	41	Jimmy Spencer	Target Dodge
19	25	21	Elliott Sadler	Motorcraft Ford
20	29	19	Jeremy Mayfield	Dodge Dealers/UAW Dodge
21	37	25	Joe Nemechek	UAW-Delphi Chevrolet
22	6	2	Rusty Wallace	Miller Lite Ford
23	26	55	Bobby Hamilton	Schneider Electric/Square D Chevrolet
24	14	15	Michael Waltrip	NAPA Chevrolet
25	34	23	Kenny Wallace	Hills Bros Coffee Dodge
26	31	36	Ken Schrader	M&M's Pontiac
27	43	07	Ted Musgrave	Kenwood/Sirius Satellite Radio Dodge
28	35	7	Casey Atwood	Sirius Satellite Radio Dodge
29	21	77	Dave Blaney	Jasper Engines & Transmissions Ford
30	7	28	Ricky Rudd	Havoline Ford
31	19	5	Terry Labonte	Kellogg's Chevrolet
32	39	14	Mike Wallace	Conseco Pontiac
33	32	26	Todd Bodine	Discover Card Ford
34	27	10	Johnny Benson	Valvoline Pontiac
35	41	74	Tony Raines	Staff America Chevrolet
36	36	1	Steve Park	Pennzoil Chevrolet
37	9	17	Matt Kenseth	DEWALT Power Tools Ford
38	33	4	Mike Skinner	Kodak Chevrolet
39	40	11	Brett Bodine	Hooters Restaurants Ford
40	17	29	Kevin Harvick	GM Goodwrench Service Chevrolet
41	38	44	Jerry Nadeau	Georgia Pacific/Brawny Dodge
42	30	43	John Andretti	Cheerios/Betty Crocker Dodge
43	42	89	Morgan Shepherd	Berlin City Ford/Red Line Oil Ford

(Right) Pre-race ceremonies centered on a patriotic theme as RIR's management sought to recognize American freedom and American heroes as the first anniversary of the terrorist attacks of 9/11 rapidly approached.

(Below) The all-rookie front row of Jimmie Johnson and Ryan Newman brings the field of 43 under the green flag to begin 400 laps at Richmond. Johnson's fourth pole of the year put him in a tie with Bill Elliott for the annual Bud Pole Award, while Newman's outside pole was his fifth front-row start of the season so far.

Any doubters who questioned if Jeff Gordon and his Hendrick Motorsports teammates were focused on making a run at the NASCAR Winston Cup Series championship had their answer after the Mountain Dew Southern 500 at Darlington. Jeff's resounding win – giving him a record-tying five Southern 500 titles – vaulted him into the runner-up position in the point standings.

As far as Gordon was concerned, season-long point-leader Sterling Marlin was now the hunted, and Gordon, less than 100 points behind, had the Tennessean squarely within his sights.

With 11 races remaining, Gordon needed to gain less than 10 points a race to claim the title. He liked his chances, but he also knew that in a point battle this close – with Mark Martin now just 34 points behind the DuPont Chevrolet, mercurial Tony Stewart just 37 behind Martin and Jimmie Johnson a mere handful of points behind Stewart – the point standings could be turned topsy-turvy at the conclusion of any of the remaining events.

Marlin and Martin, along with Stewart, Johnson and Rusty Wallace – just 63 points behind Johnson – also knew the importance of every single point in the run to the title. Racing luck would play a role in the final 11 races of the season, no doubt, and each contending driver could only hope he had more good luck than poor luck in the final stretch of races.

Wallace was licking his chops headed for Richmond. The three-quarter-mile mini-super-

Robby Gordon (31) and Mike Skinner (4) challenge each other on the inside while Todd Bodine (26) and Jerry Nadeau (44) look for position on the outside. Bodine posted a season-best performance for himself and his Haas/Carter Motorsports team with a fifth-place finish in the race, their first top five of the season.

speedway has always been one of Rusty's best tracks, and Wallace knew he was the only driver in the top 10 in the point standings who had yet to win. Penske teammate Ryan Newman was also hot to make his first visit to victory lane. He had finished second at Darlington and now stood 11th on the point ladder, just 12 points behind Matt Kenseth. Like Jimmie Johnson, there had been very few "rookie" moments for Newman this year. He ran like a seasoned veteran in almost every race and appeared ready to win for the first time in his brief NASCAR Winston Cup Series career.

Richmond's weekend continued to answer questions about the coming season. Kyle Petty and Georgia-Pacific announced the company had extended its contract with Petty Enterprises for another three years and would move over to replace Sprint on Kyle's Dodge for 2003 and beyond. Chip Ganassi ended the "where is Texaco going" question by announcing the Chevron Texaco sponsorship would be part of a third team from his shop next season, with NASCAR Busch Series driver Jamie McMurray the surprise nominee to drive for the new team. McMurray, a five-time national karting champion, had yet to win his first NBS race.

In a move that involved a pair of teams, Roush Racing and Jeff Burton announced that Paul Andrews had moved his toolbox from Steve Park's DEI Pennzoil team to the CITGO Ford driven by Burton. Frank Stoddard was relieved of his crew chief role, and all hoped the combination of Andrews and Burton would revitalize Jeff's team.

The hoopla that normally surrounds a Winston No Bull 5 event usually carries the day and sets the stage for an event, but this year's running of the Chevrolet Monte Carlo 400 was shrouded by the onrushing remembrance of the one-year anniversary of September 11.

And the folks at Richmond International Raceway did themselves proud with the planning and execution of one of the most stirring patriotic displays ever seen on the NASCAR Winston Cup Series trail. In a Stars and Stripes-bedecked spectacular, the management team incorporated every aspect of September 11, and there were few dry eyes in the huge throng of people as the all-rookie row of Jimmie Johnson and Ryan Newman led the field around the spectacular vista of grandstands.

Dave Blaney and Mark Martin were right behind Johnson and Newman on the parade laps, with Terry Labonte and Ricky Rudd comprising the third row. Todd Bodine and Mike Skinner were in the fourth row for the start of the race, with Johnny Benson and Jeff Gordon qualifying ninth and 10th. Gordon, however, went to the back of the field after crashing his Bugs Bunny Monte Carlo (part of Chevrolet's Looney Tunes promotion) during happy hour. His backup Chevrolet carried his normal DuPont colors, much to the dismay of the Looney Tunes promotion organizers.

Gordon had worked hard all season to bring his team back into title contention and thought

(Top) Dale Earnhardt Jr. (8) and Rusty Wallace (2) race together after starting the event side by side on the 12th row. They nearly finished together, but Wallace, a six-time Richmond winner, hit the wall after a tire went down late in the race. Earnhardt worked his way up to fourth to score just his second top five in the last 17 events.

(Above) Mark Martin's Viagra Ford was glued to the inside at Richmond, an advantage he uses here to slip past Dale Jarrett. Martin was the only championship contender able to take advantage of the problems suffered by Marlin and Gordon, and his sixth-place finish moved him into second place in the point standings, just nine markers out of first.

(Right) Although Matt Kenseth's DeWalt Tools Ford sits in victory lane, the right-front fender shows the trip there wasn't as easy as it looked.

he had a great chance to take over the point lead when Jeff Burton spun on the ninth lap and collected Marlin. Sterling retired to the garage with the nose pancaked on his Coors Light Dodge and had to sit and wait to see where he would be in the point standings at the end of the race after being classified 43rd.

But then Gordon bit the bullet himself. The timing chain went in his Chevrolet and he was relegated to 40th place in the final rundown. That opened the door for other challengers like Mark Martin, Rusty Wallace, Johnson and Stewart.

Ryan Newman did his best to win his first career NASCAR Winston Cup Series race, but Matt Kenseth had the answer to the Richmond puzzle in the final quarter of the race. Once past Newman, Kenseth stormed to his fourth victory of the season despite struggling early in the race with tire problems.

Rusty Wallace finally fought his way into second place and was closing on Kenseth, chopping the DeWalt Ford driver's lead with every lap, but with 11 circuits to go, Wallace had his right-front tire go flat and the ensuing pit stop dropped him to 15th place.

Stewart also fought throughout the race and

appeared headed for a rock-solid finish until, with only four laps left in the race, the rear end broke in the Home Depot Pontiac and all of Tony's hard work evaporated into a 30th-place finish.

Martin was the only challenger truly able to take advantage of the problems suffered by Jeff Gordon and Sterling Marlin. Martin took his Viagra Ford to a sixth-place finish and was doubly delighted to see his Roush Racing teammate in victory lane. When the points were totaled at the end of the evening, Martin's sixth place vaulted him past Gordon into second, where he trailed Marlin by just nine points.

Kenseth's overpowering margin of victory was

Matt Kenseth streaks under the checkered flag with a gaudy six-second margin of victory while his team members cheer the victory along pit road. With the win, Kenseth became the first four-time winner of the season.

more than six seconds at the end, while Newman notched his second straight bridesmaid's finish. Jeff Green had a superb run to third place in the AOL Chevrolet, while Dale Earnhardt Jr. took fourth. Todd Bodine's drive to fifth was the best for Travis Carter's team this season, and Ricky Rudd finished seventh behind Mark Martin. Ward Burton took eighth ahead of a strong performance by Dave Blaney, while Jeremy Mayfield completed the top 10 finishers.

Chevrolet Monte Carlo 400 final race results

Fin. Pos.	Start Pos.	Car No.	Driver	Team
1	25	17	Matt Kenseth	DeWalt Power Tools Ford
2	2	12	Ryan Newman	ALLTEL Ford
3	29	30	Jeff Green	America Online Chevrolet
4	24	8	Dale Earnhardt Jr.	Budweiser Chevrolet
5	7	26	Todd Bodine	Discover Card Ford
6	4	6	Mark Martin	Pfizer/Viagra Ford
7	6	28	Ricky Rudd	Havoline Ford
8	13	22	Ward Burton	Caterpillar Dodge
9	3	77	Dave Blaney	Jasper Engines & Transmissions Ford
10	21	19	Jeremy Mayfield	Dodge Dealers/UAW Dodge
11	38	1	Steve Park	Pennzoil Chevrolet
12	39	14	Mike Wallace	Conseco Pontiac
13	1	48	Jimmie Johnson	Lowe's Chevrolet
14	33	23	Kenny Wallace	Hills Bros Coffee Dodge
15	23	2	Rusty Wallace	Miller Lite Ford
16	19	9	Bill Elliott	Dodge Dealers/UAW Dodge
17	36	45	Kyle Petty	Sprint Dodge
18	27	29	Kevin Harvick	GM Goodwrench Service Chevrolet
19	22	97	Kurt Busch	Rubbermaid Ford
20	40	11	Brett Bodine	Hooters Restaurants Ford
21	20	32	Ricky Craven	Tide Ford
22	8	4	Mike Skinner	Kodak Chevrolet
23	43	02	Hermie Sadler	Virginia Lottery Chevrolet
24	34	7	Casey Atwood	Sirius Satellite Radio Dodge
25	28	25	Joe Nemechek	UAW-Delphi Chevrolet
26	16	36	Ken Schrader	M&M's Pontiac
27	17	44	Jerry Nadeau	Georgia Pacific/Brawny Dodge
28	11	31	Robby Gordon	Cingular Wireless Chevrolet
29	31	43	John Andretti	Cheerios/Betty Crocker Dodge
30	14	20	Tony Stewart	The Home Depot Pontiac
31	12	88	Dale Jarrett	UPS Ford
32	18	18	Bobby Labonte	Interstate Batteries Pontiac
33	37	55	Greg Biffle	Schneider Electric/Square D Chevrolet
34	35	21	Elliott Sadler	Motorcraft Ford
35	9	10	Johnny Benson	Valvoline Pontiac
36	26	15	Michael Waltrip	NAPA Chevrolet
37	42	71	Tim Sauter	Wehrs Chevrolet Chevrolet
38	41	09	Geoffrey Bodine	Miccosukee Indian Resort Ford
39	15	99	Jeff Burton	CITGO SUPERGARD Ford
40	10	24	Jeff Gordon	DuPont Chevrolet
41	5	5	Terry Labonte	Kellogg's Chevrolet
42	30	41	Jimmy Spencer	Target Dodge
43	32	40	Sterling Marlin	Coors Light Dodge

New Hampshire 300

Ryan Newman rockets through the turns on New Hampshire's 1.058-mile oval during qualifying. His track-record lap at 132.241 miles per hour gave him his third Bud Pole of the season and served notice that this weekend belonged to him.

(Above Right) Mark Martin bides his time while waiting to get underway at New Hampshire. Veteran that he is, Martin, second in points coming into the weekend, did exactly what needed to be done and moved to the top of the standings by the end of the event.

(Below Right) Johnny Benson (left) and members of his Valvoline team watch qualifying action as they wait their turn on the track. When it finally came, Benson cranked a lap faster than any but Newman's and grabbed a starting spot on the front row, his best start of the season. From there, Benson placed fourth in the race, his first top-five finish of the year.

With Sterling Marlin finishing 43rd – last – at Richmond and Jeff Gordon following Marlin to the garage area when a timing belt broke in his DuPont Chevrolet, drivers chasing the two point leaders had their chance to close the gap and turn the battle for the title into a dogfight.

And when the NASCAR Winston Cup Series teams arrived at New Hampshire International Speedway for the second time this season, the crisp September air virtually crackled with tension. Five drivers stood within 118 points of the crown with 10 races remaining on the schedule – the tightest battle among the top five drivers at this stage of the season since the current point system was initiated in 1975.

Sterling Marlin still sat in the catbird's seat, but his margin in the standings had shrunk to less then 10 points. Mark Martin – aye, yes, laddie – the same Mark Martin dismissed from the point battle earlier in the year, had mounted an extremely successful charge through the middle of the season and fought his way into second place in the standings. The Viagra Ford driver now was a mere nine points behind Marlin and, had Mark

Cars and teams line pit road, prepared for action in Sunday's main event. Rain didn't dampen the spirits of fans or competitors, as the command to start engines came about an hour after the scheduled start of the race.

finished fourth instead of sixth at Richmond, he would have unseated Marlin from the perch the Coors Light Dodge driver had held since the second race of the season.

When Jimmie Johnson set sail on his rookie NASCAR Winston Cup Series season in February, no one – not even team co-owners Rick Hendrick and Jeff Gordon – would have given two cents in a bet that Johnson would be contending for the championship with just 10 races left. With a new team, with Lowe's switching to the Hendrick camp after years with Richard Childress Racing, and with so little experience that he needed directions to get to some of the race tracks, Jimmie Johnson had merely stamped himself a true contender for the title. Here he was, late in the season, in third place in the point standings just 63 points behind Martin.

(Above) Elliott Sadler holds his Motorcraft Ford – one of several cars sporting a patriotic theme during the weekend – on the outside of Steve Park's Pennzoil Chevrolet with a pack of cars pushing them from behind in early race action.

(Left) John Andretti, Jeremy Mayfield and Ricky Rudd appear a blur to a less-than instantaneous camera shutter as they fly through New Hampshire's tight turns.

Kurt Busch (97) puts the heat on Ryan Newman (12) in their tussle for the top spot, while Jerry Nadeau (44) drifts wide to give them room to race. Newman was finally able to fend of Busch's strong challenge and held the top spot for the remaining 30 laps to seal the win.

Gordon's dismal finish at Richmond sent him back to fourth place in the point standings, but he was just 10 points behind teammate Johnson. Just 82 points out of the point lead and with back-to-back wins at Bristol and Darlington, Gordon simply could not be counted out of the looming stretch run for the championship.

But for a broken transmission with just four laps left at Richmond, Tony Stewart would have been far higher in the standings than fifth place as teams began practice for the New England 300. He finished 30th at Richmond after he appeared headed for a top-10 finish, but still found himself in the championship battle, just 36 points behind Gordon. And right behind Stewart came Rusty Wallace, still looking for his first win of the season but still capable of putting together a charge at the crown. He trailed Stewart by 28 points. Bill Elliott, in seventh place in the standings, was 38 points behind Wallace and could make some kind of a move. But for Wallace and Elliott, those moves needed to be made at New Hampshire. Neither could wait much longer if they wanted to join what was expected to be a furious battle for the championship in the closing races of the season.

Matt Kenseth's Richmond victory moved him into an eighth-place tie with Ricky Rudd, and while Kenseth's fortunes seemed to be climbing, any hope Rudd had of winning his first championship seemed to be waning. Rudd had finished seventh at Richmond, but, after the race, he was punched by one of Robert Yates' crewmen who took offense at some of Rudd's candid remarks about his lame duck situation with the Havoline team. Rudd sported a black eye at New Hampshire, and the offending Yates crew member found himself beating the bricks in search of new employment.

Ryan Newman occupied 10th place on the point ladder, boosted by consecutive second-place finishes at Darlington and Richmond. Perhaps his rookie season had not gathered all the headlines that Johnson's had, but Newman clearly had shown in his last two races that it would not be long before he found his way to victory lane for the first time in his brief NASCAR Winston Cup Series career.

Newman continued his torrid performances by claiming his third Bud Pole of the season in qualifying, besting Johnny Benson and his Valvoline Pontiac for the inside of the front row. Bobby Labonte showed signs of getting his season on track by claiming the third starting position, and on his right was Greg Biffle, filling in for the second race for Bobby Hamilton, who broke his right shoulder blade and his left wrist in a NASCAR Craftsman Truck Series event at Richmond. Mike Skinner and Kurt Busch made up the third row for the start of the New Hampshire 300, while Mark Martin and New Hampshire favorite Ricky Craven claimed the fourth row. Jeremy Mayfield and Stewart beat Petty Enterprises teammates John Andretti and Jerry Nadeau for the final top-10 starting positions, while Dale Earnhardt Jr., Elliott Sadler, Steve Park, Mike Wallace, Brett Bodine, Hermie Sadler and Morgan Shepherd all used provisionals to make the field. The only driver who failed to gain a starting spot was Carl Long.

Sunday morning, it was clear that weather was going to effect the running of the New England 300, and every driver in the field knew the chances were very good that the race would not go its entire distance. The event would, in effect, be a sprint race and every position on every lap would be hotly contested. Rain did, in fact, cause problems right from the start, with weather delaying the green flag for nearly an hour. Just 18 laps after the beginning of the event, the red flag flew again for rain, this time for the better part of two hours.

The race finally restarted and Newman was in command of the event, where he would be for the remainder of the race. His crew pitted him well throughout the afternoon, and when the final round of green-flag stops cycled through, Ryan was at the point. Johnny Benson, Ricky Craven, Tony Stewart and Kurt Busch were the drivers he would have to battle, and Busch surfaced as the best of the bunch. On lap 172, Busch did his best to unseat Newman from the point, but Ryan had what he needed in his Mobil 1 Ford and drove away from Busch.

Rain began to fall again on lap 200 and the yellow flag appeared. With the delays throughout the afternoon and with the weather radar showing little chance of the rain abating, NASCAR officials called it a day. The white flag was shown under caution on lap 206, with the race ending after 207 laps.

A very happy Ryan Newman (left) is joined by crew chief Matt Borland and Penske Racing's Don Miller (right) to celebrate Newman's first regular-season NASCAR Winston Cup Series win, coming in his 35th career start.

No one had any reason to fuss when Newman rolled into the winner's circle. He had been dominant all afternoon, leading 143 of the 207 laps and handily beating back the challenge from Busch. Busch took second ahead of Tony Stewart, while Benson had a strong run to claim fourth ahead of Bobby Labonte. Ricky Craven was a solid sixth ahead of Dale Jarrett, while Michael Waltrip claimed eighth ahead of Jimmie Johnson and Matt Kenseth.

Newman's victory was delightful, but the big news came when the points were totaled. Mark Martin finished 16th while Sterling Marlin was 21st. For the first time since the second race of the season, Marlin was out of the point lead, with Martin taking over the top rung of the ladder. He was a mere six points ahead, and behind him, the battle within the top five tightened even more.

New Hampshire 300 final race results

Fin. Pos.	Start Pos.	Car No.	Driver	Team
1	1	12	Ryan Newman	ALLTEL/Mobil 1 Ford
2	6	97	Kurt Busch	Rubbermaid Ford
3	10	20	Tony Stewart	The Home Depot Pontiac
4	2	10	Johnny Benson	Valvoline Pontiac
5	3	18	Bobby Labonte	Interstate Batteries Pontiac
6	8	32	Ricky Craven	Tide Ford
7	23	88	Dale Jarrett	UPS Ford
8	14	15	Michael Waltrip	NAPA Chevrolet
9	19	48	Jimmie Johnson	Lowe's Chevrolet
10	17	17	Matt Kenseth	DEWALT Power Tools Ford
11	37	8	Dale Earnhardt Jr.	Budweiser Chevrolet
12	18	28	Ricky Rudd	Havoline Ford
13	16	36	Ken Schrader	M&M's Pontiac
14	21	24	Jeff Gordon	DuPont Chevrolet
15	28	41	Jimmy Spencer	Target Dodge
16	7	6	Mark Martin	Pfizer/Viagra Ford
17	29	31	Robby Gordon	Cingular Wireless Chevrolet
18	30	23	Kenny Wallace	Hills Bros Coffee Dodge
19	15	2	Rusty Wallace	Miller Lite Ford
20	22	99	Jeff Burton	CITGO SUPERGARD Ford
21	24	40	Sterling Marlin	Coors Light Dodge
22	11	43	John Andretti	Cheerios/Betty Crocker Dodge
23	20	9	Bill Elliott	Dodge Dealers/UAW Dodge
24	9	19	Jeremy Mayfield	Dodge Dealers/UAW Dodge
25	25	77	Dave Blaney	Jasper Engines & Transmissions Ford
26	33	30	Jeff Green	America Online Chevrolet
27	4	55	Greg Biffle	Schneider Electric/Square D Chevrolet
28	12	44	Jerry Nadeau	Georgia Pacific/Brawny Dodge
29	39	1	Steve Park	Pennzoil Chevrolet
30	31	5	Terry Labonte	Kellogg's Chevrolet
31	40	14	Mike Wallace	Conseco Pontiac
32	34	25	Joe Nemechek	UAW-Delphi Chevrolet
33	32	29	Kevin Harvick	GM Goodwrench Service Chevrolet
34	36	7	Casey Atwood	Sirius Satellite Radio Dodge
35	38	21	Elliott Sadler	Motorcraft Ford
36	41	11	Brett Bodine	Hooters Restaurants Ford
37	42	02	Hermie Sadler	Dixie Chopper Chevrolet
38	27	22	Ward Burton	Caterpillar Dodge
39	13	45	Kyle Petty	Sprint Dodge
40	26	37	Kevin Lepage	Friendly's Ice Cream Ford
41	43	89	Morgan Shepherd	Racing With Jesus Ford
42	35	26	Todd Bodine	Discover Card Ford
43	5	4	Mike Skinner	Kodak Chevrolet

MBNA All-American Heroes 400

Jimmie Johnson's crew swarms the Lowe's Chevrolet during a stop under caution at Dover International Speedway. Johnson pitted five times under caution, and his team's fine performance on pit road put him back on the track among the leaders each time, helping to seal the victory.

(Right) Ryan Newman (left) decides to get into the act while his Penske teammate, Rusty Wallace, collects his Bud Pole Award for posting the fastest lap in qualifying, his first pole position since November 2000 at Phoenix, 66 races ago. Newman was pretty fast himself, taking fourth on the starting grid.

(Below) NASCAR history was made at Dover in the person on Hideo Fukuyama, who became the first Japanese driver to compete in a NASCAR Winston Cup Series event.

(Below Right) Fukuyama (66), who started 43rd using a provisional in a Haas/Carter Motorsports Ford, holds his own against a charging Jimmy Spencer (41) on Dover's 24-degree banks before transmission problems ended his bid.

Jimmie Johnson couldn't wait to get to Dover International Speedway for the running of the MBNA All-American Heroes 400. His spring victory on the Monster Mile put him in the unlikely position of sweeping a pair of events at one of the most physically and mentally tortuous tracks on the schedule as a rookie. But for Johnson and his Lowe's mates, it also represented the opportunity to prove to the doubters that their efforts were truly those of championship contenders.

Following the New Hampshire event, Johnson was third in the point standings, but a mere 40 points behind new NASCAR Winston Cup Series point-leader Mark Martin. His ninth-place finish at New Hampshire moved him to just 34 points behind Sterling Marlin, and although Mark Martin had taken over the point lead, Johnson finished ahead of Martin in the rundown and gained points. With a pair of wins in his pocket already, Johnson was in the position to tie Tony Stewart's record of three victories in a rookie season if he could find a way to sweep the Dover events.

On the strength of his third-place finish at New Hampshire, Tony Stewart vaulted into fourth place, and the talented driver suddenly was a major factor in the point battle as teams headed into the stretch run. The Home Depot Pontiac pilot was just 19 points behind Johnson, and it was clear from the twists and turns the point battle had taken throughout the year that anything was possible.

Jeff Gordon now held fifth place, but he was far from out of the fight for the championship. Despite his 14th-place finish at New Hampshire, Jeff was just eight points behind Stewart. Gordon was well aware that the next two races would go a long way toward determining whether he would be in the end game for this year's crown. His Dover success was fully documented, and he had won the inaugural running of the upcoming Kansas City event. Gordon believed he and his DuPont-backed team were primed for a champi-

onship run and that the trip to the title would begin at Dover.

Despite trailing Gordon by 79 points, hope still flickered within Rusty Wallace's team. Although Wallace was still mired in his winless streak and sat sixth in the standings, Rusty was less than 150 points behind Martin. Given the fact that no single driver had managed to take control of the point battle, Rusty knew he was still not out of contention for his second career NASCAR Winston Cup Series championship.

Among the rest of the top 10, Ryan Newman appeared to be the only driver capable of mounting a charge during the final races of the season. Newman's dominant victory at New Hampshire came on the heels of a pair of second-place finishes, and the rookie challenger now found himself in eighth place on the point ladder. He vaulted past Matt Kenseth and Ricky Rudd for the position and was just a single point behind seventh-place Bill Elliott. In this most bizarre of seasons, could a pair of rookies – Newman and Johnson – actually contend for the NASCAR Winston Cup Series title?

Wallace rolled to the Bud Pole during qualifying, joining the plethora of pole winners who had earned starting slots in the Bud Shootout next February at Daytona. He beat Dale Jarrett for the inside position on the front row, while Dale Earnhardt Jr. and Newman made up the second row at the conclusion of qualifying. Greg Biffle, sitting in for Bobby Hamilton in Andy Petree's Square D Chevrolet, turned in an outstanding qualifying effort to grab the inside of the third

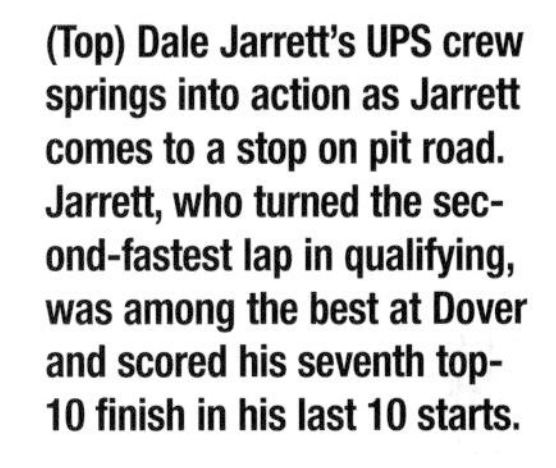

(Top) Dale Jarrett's UPS crew springs into action as Jarrett comes to a stop on pit road. Jarrett, who turned the second-fastest lap in qualifying, was among the best at Dover and scored his seventh top-10 finish in his last 10 starts.

(Above) Elliott Sadler (21) tries Steve Park (1) in the inside while the pair races for position. They would finish together at the end of the event, but several laps off the winning pace as Park's Chevrolet suffered damage after getting together with John Andretti, while Sadler fought an ill-handling Ford for most of the day.

(Left) Rusty Wallace (2) leads (in order) Jeremy Mayfield, Kenny Wallace and Steve Park under the pedestrian bridge at the second-turn exit. Wallace, a three-time Dover winner, had one of the fastest cars in the race, but a shredded tire sent him into the wall with 80 laps remaining and ended his chance to pick up the win.

Protection One 400

Rusty Wallace (2) tries the inside of Michael Waltrip (15) and Sterling Marlin on Kansas Speedway's ultra-smooth frontstretch. Wallace, looking to move into championship contention, brought his Miller Lite Ford home in third and knocked 61 points off his deficit in the standings.

(Above) Jeff Gordon claims victory after successfully defending his Protection One 400 title – and backing up his prediction made at Dover – with a strong performance that was vintage Gordon.

(Right) Sterling Marlin flashes his infectious smile prior to starting his 400-mile quest at Kansas. He had every intention of putting a halt to his recent slide in the point standings and lock up yet another top-five finish, but Lady Luck intervened in the form of an accident near the halfway point in the race.

(Below Right) Team Petty transporters roll toward the speedway at Kansas as the NASCAR Winston Cup Series makes its second visit to America's heartland. Oddly, these teams ended the race in much the same way as they arrived, with John Andretti's Cheerios Dodge finishing one spot ahead of Kyle Petty's Sprint-sponsored Intrepid.

There were mixed feelings aplenty in the garage area at Kansas Speedway as the NASCAR Winston Cup Series regulars arrived in America's heartland for the second running of the Protection One 400.

Jimmie Johnson was still on his Dover high after sweeping the season's events at the Monster Mile. The Roush Racing camp had plenty to high-five about, with Mark Martin the point leader and an outstanding showing of the Roush Ford forces at Dover. All four team drivers had finished in the top seven positions at the conclusion of the MBNA All-American Heroes 400, led by Martin's fighting second place.

Tony Stewart had raced the wheels off his Home Depot Pontiac at Dover and his fifth-place finish moved him from fourth in the point standings to third, where he now trailed Mark Martin by just 74 points.

Even Rusty Wallace had reason to grin at Kansas City. Although he had finished 15th at Dover and still had not won a race yet this year, he remained in sixth place in the standings – but more importantly was less than 200 points behind the leader. The way the point battle was going this year, Wallace believed he still had a chance if he could put together two or three strong finishes in the next few events.

While those four were feeling optimistic about their situations, there were some stone faces in the Jeff Gordon and Sterling Marlin camps. Marlin, who had lost the lead in the point battle after New Hampshire, finished 21st at Dover – his second straight 21st-place finish – and now found himself staring up at the leaders from his fourth-place rung on the ladder. Although far from out of the point battle at just 81 points behind, Sterling knew he needed to stop the bleeding at Kansas City if he wanted to contend for his first career championship.

Gordon was in worse shape. A nightmarish 37th-place finish at Dover put him 190 points behind Martin, and the Dover debacle came right at the point of the season where many had expected him to begin to take control of the battle for the championship.

Gordon came to Kansas City as the defending champion of the race, and in half-jest had told reporters at Dover he would win at Kansas City. The Dover finish, at a track where he once totally dominated the action in sponsor DuPont's backyard, now meant that Gordon and his teammates needed to make good on his joking promise if they were to be a factor in the stretch run to the title.

(Left) Jimmie Johnson (48), who qualified second for the event, tries a move on pole-winner Dale Earnhardt Jr. (8) during the race's early going. Johnson never quite got the handle right on his Lowe's Chevrolet and finished one lap down in 10th, but that was good enough to put the hot rookie driver atop the point standings after the race.

(Left, Below) Bobby Labonte's crew goes to work on the Interstate Batteries Pontiac, bearing cosmetic damage that resulted from a nine-car accident in the opening laps of the race.

The top 12 drivers in the standings were in the position to exchange places amongst themselves, with less than 30 points separating nearly every position. The closing events of the year would determine who successfully claimed a top 10 in the standings at the end of the year and who would be left by the wayside.

Dale Earnhardt Jr. claimed his second Bud Pole of the season after qualifying and found himself in the middle of a maelstrom he created when he revealed he had suffered a concussion in the April 28 California Speedway race but had continued to race through it. His disclosure that, at times, he was unable to help his crew with accurate information regarding chassis settings because of the effects of the concussion triggered a new mandate from NASCAR officials regarding driver health and safety. In the past, drivers had needed medical approval to return to competition only if they had been hospitalized. If they were released from the track's medical facility, no further checks were needed. But from now on, if track medical personnel recommend further tests, drivers will need to provide medical clearance before they can return to competition.

Rust Wallace (2) fronts a pack hugging the inside line that includes (in order) Jeff Burton, Matt Kenseth, Jimmie Johnson, Tony Stewart and Ryan Newman, with Bill Elliott's Dodge alone on the outside. Burton ran well until he was involved in an accident midway through the race. All other cars in this frame finished among the top 10.

(Above) Matt Kenseth (17) works inside Jimmy Spencer (41) on his way through the field. After starting 27th, Kenseth picked up 20 positions during the race to finish seventh, his fifth top 10 in the last six events.

(Right) Joe Nemechek (25) lurks behind the Yates Racing duo of Ricky Rudd (28) and Dale Jarrett (88) along the frontstretch. Nemechek had a fine showing at Kansas and picked up a fourth-place finish, his first top five of the season so far.

Jimmie Johnson continued his torrid rookie performance by claiming the outside of the front row, while Ryan Newman underscored his own rookie prowess by turning the third-fastest lap. Michael Waltrip had another strong qualifying performance and put the NAPA Chevrolet on the outside of the second row, while Bill Elliott and Dale Jarrett were the fastest of the "graybeards" and claimed the third row for the start of the race. Marlin and Stewart comprised the fourth row, while Martin and Gordon beat Rusty Wallace and Joe Nemechek for the final top-10 starting positions.

Jimmy Spencer, Elliott Sadler, Ken Schrader, Casey Atwood, Jerry Nadeau, Stuart Kirby (in the BAM Racing Dodge) and Morgan Shepherd all used provisionals to make the field, while Brett Bodine, Carl Long and Kirk Shelmerdine all failed to gain starting spots for the Protection One 400.

If there was any doubt that Gordon and his DuPont mates were on their game and headed for a second straight Protection One 400 trophy, the answer came on lap 148. Gordon had been a contender in the lead pack for the first half of the race, but after the eighth caution of the day, Gordon dove under leader Bill Elliott. Once in clean air at the front of the field, Jeff put the Monte Carlo in the wind and simply dominated the remainder of the race. He steamrolled the competition, and although Ryan Newman had a great afternoon, Gordon handled Newman with ease.

Jeff built a seven-second lead but watched it disappear when Johnny Benson and Jimmy Spencer tangled to bring out the 11th yellow of the afternoon with just five laps remaining. After a brief red flag to clean up the mess, the final restart came with just three laps left in the race. Any hope Newman had vanished when Gordon

ripped away from the pack by the time the field rolled through the second turn. At the finish Jeff was more than six car-lengths ahead.

The victory marked his third in the last six races, and it came at the time he was most desperate for a win to fight his way back into the point battle. Newman and Rusty Wallace gave the Penske forces a 2-3 finish, while Joe Nemechek placed a fine fourth. Bill Elliott was fifth ahead of Dale Earnhardt Jr. and Matt Kenseth, while Tony Stewart claimed eighth place ahead of Jeremy Mayfield and Jimmie Johnson.

(Above) Jeff Gordon (24) jumps ahead of the competition on the final restart with just three laps remaining, leaving second-place Ryan Newman (12) with a five car-length deficit. Hendrick Motorsports representatives Jimmie Johnson (48) and Terry Labonte (5) lead the lap-down cars on the inside.

(Left) Jeff Gordon and his DuPont teammates get the celebration underway in Kansas' victory lane. After faltering at Richmond, New Hampshire and Dover, Gordon's third win in the last six events resurrected his shot at defending his series championship.

Protection One 400 final race results

Fin. Pos.	Start Pos.	Car No.	Driver	Team
1	10	24	Jeff Gordon	DuPont Chevrolet
2	3	12	Ryan Newman	ALLTEL/Mobil 1 Ford
3	11	2	Rusty Wallace	Miller Lite Ford
4	12	25	Joe Nemechek	UAW-Delphi Chevrolet
5	5	9	Bill Elliott	Dodge Dealers/UAW Dodge
6	1	8	Dale Earnhardt Jr.	Budweiser Chevrolet
7	27	17	Matt Kenseth	DEWALT Power Tools Ford
8	8	20	Tony Stewart	The Home Depot Pontiac
9	14	19	Jeremy Mayfield	Dodge Dealers/UAW Dodge
10	2	48	Jimmie Johnson	Lowe's Chevrolet
11	26	29	Kevin Harvick	GM Goodwrench Service Chevrolet
12	18	5	Terry Labonte	Kellogg's Chevrolet
13	22	31	Robby Gordon	Cingular Wireless Chevrolet
14	21	43	John Andretti	Cheerios/Betty Crocker Dodge
15	33	45	Kyle Petty	Sprint Dodge
16	28	23	Kenny Wallace	Hills Bros Coffee Dodge
17	24	30	Jeff Green	America Online Chevrolet
18	38	21	Elliott Sadler	Motorcraft Ford
19	36	14	Mike Wallace	Conseco Pontiac
20	30	28	Ricky Rudd	Havoline Ford
21	34	77	Dave Blaney	Jasper Engines & Transmissions Ford
22	31	18	Bobby Labonte	Interstate Batteries Pontiac
23	35	10	Johnny Benson	Valvoline Pontiac
24	37	41	Jimmy Spencer	Energizer/Target Dodge
25	9	6	Mark Martin	Pfizer/Viagra Ford
26	4	15	Michael Waltrip	NAPA Chevrolet
27	41	44	Jerry Nadeau	Georgia Pacific/Brawny Dodge
28	39	36	Ken Schrader	Pedigree Pontiac
29	15	99	Jeff Burton	CITGO SUPERGARD Ford
30	17	1	Steve Park	Pennzoil Chevrolet
31	13	97	Kurt Busch	Rubbermaid Ford
32	32	4	Mike Skinner	Kodak Chevrolet
33	7	40	Sterling Marlin	Coors Light Dodge
34	16	26	Todd Bodine	Discover Card Ford
35	23	60	Jack Sprague	Haas Automation Chevrolet
36	29	55	Greg Biffle	Schneider Electric/Square D Chevrolet
37	42	49	Stuart Kirby	BAM Racing Dodge
38	20	32	Ricky Craven	Tide Ford
39	6	88	Dale Jarrett	UPS Ford
40	43	89	Morgan Shepherd	Racing With Jesus/Red Line Oil Ford
41	25	74	Tony Raines	Staff America Chevrolet
42	40	7	Casey Atwood	Sirius Satellite Radio Dodge
43	19	22	Ward Burton	Caterpillar Dodge

EA Sports 500

Ron Hornaday (55) splits Jeff Gordon (24) and Dale Earnhardt Jr. (8) with a tightly bunched pack looking to catch the draft from behind. Gordon looked poised to end Earnhardt's Talladega reign by leading on nine different occasions over the first 120 laps, but his engine expired, leaving him a bitter 42nd in the final rundown.

48
LOWE'S
48
22
BOSCH
CATERPILLAR
22
HOOTERS
Naturally Fresh
FINANCIAL
32
Tide
32
Downy
Kenmore
77
JASPER
77

(Right) The Alabama countryside has long been one of the most popular spots for fans to camp over race weekends, whether in the track's infield or on the surrounding RV parking areas.

(Middle Right) Jamie McMurray (left) gets some tips from veteran Sterling Marlin in the Talladega garage. McMurray was preparing to make his NASCAR Winston Cup Series debut in place of Marlin, who suffered a neck injury last weekend at Kansas.

(Bottom Right) Len Wood (left) and his driver, Elliott Sadler, relax between practice rounds in the Talladega garage. Both men were hoping that Sadler could transfer some of his recent prowess at Daytona (third, second and 12th in his last three starts) to it's sister tack, Talladega, where Sadler has not enjoyed a great deal of success.

Instead of taking some type of recognizable shape with just seven races remaining on the NASCAR Winston Cup Series schedule, the point battle for this year's championship became even more jumbled following the event at Kansas Speedway.

Engine failure sent point-leader Mark Martin to the garage area in the late stages at Kansas City, and the resulting 25th place on the final rundown dropped Mark to the second rung of the point ladder. Finishing 10th in the race, rookie Jimmie Johnson moved into the point lead, while Tony Stewart's eighth place left the Home Depot Pontiac driver third in the standings, but just 36 points out first place.

Jeff Gordon – the same Jeff Gordon who trailed by 190 points entering Kansas City – used his victory and Mark Martin's poor finish to move to within 109 points of the leader. Gordon's needed win in the Nation's heartland gave him plenty of reason to celebrate. As a driver, he had shown that there was still fire in his team and that the DuPont Chevrolet could still be a factor in the heated championship battle. At the same time, he took great pleasure in being co-owner of Johnson's team as the rookie moved into the point lead.

Penske South teammates Ryan Newman and Rusty Wallace, after finishing second and third at Kansas City, found themselves in the torrid hunt for the title. Wallace was just 137 points behind Johnson, while Newman was 154 out of the lead. The way things were going in the helter-skelter world of the point battle, neither driver could be counted out – stranger things had already happened.

One driver who would not be in the battle for the championship was Sterling Marlin. The Tennessean, who had appeared on the verge of his first championship just a handful of races ago, was forced to vacate his Coors Light Dodge for the remainder of the season due to a fractured vertebra suffered in his accident at Kansas City. Young Jamie McMurray, slated to drive the Texaco

Havoline Dodge for Chip Ganassi next year, would be pressed into service at Talladega. It was a difficult pill to swallow for Marlin, who had led the point standings throughout most of the season beginning with the second race of the year.

While McMurray was fitting himself into a red-and-silver uniform, Ward Burton was learning the nuances of a new crew chief. Tommy Baldwin and team owner Bill Davis had words following the Kansas City event and Baldwin found himself looking for a new place to park his toolbox. Frank Stoddard, who worked with Jeff Burton throughout the season before being relieved of his duties, signed on to work with Ward and the Caterpillar Dodge team as an interim crew chief for the remainder of the season.

The fact that NASCAR had mandated a smaller fuel tank for the EA Sports 500 at Talladega did little to keep Dale Earnhardt Jr. from being the odds-on favorite for the final restrictor-plate race of the season. Little E had won the last two Talladega races, and there was little reason to think he would not be at the front of the pack at the end of this one either. Whether it was horsepower, fuel mileage, the way the chassis handled or the way the sheetmetal was hung on the Monte Carlos, there was little question that the cars fielded by Dale Earnhardt Inc. had the restrictor-plate deal figured out. It might take Little E a while to get to the point, but once there, if he could mate up with a strong drafting partner, Earnhardt would be a factor that would have to be dealt with.

(Left) Frank Stoddard took over crew chief duties for the Caterpillar team and driver Ward Burton beginning at Talladega. Stoddard, formerly longtime crew chief for Ward's brother Jeff, helped get the program back on track after three straight poor finishes with a 10th on the Alabama superspeedway.

(Below) Dale Jarrett (88), Ward Burton (22) and Jeff Burton (99) spread their battle for position three abreast through Talladega's tri-oval, with Jeremy Mayfield (19) and Todd Bodine looking for an opening from behind. The double-numbered triumvirate finished together as well, with Ward Burton separating Jarrett in ninth and brother Jeff in 11th.

(Above) Racing four-wide on the frontstretch, Jeff Green (30), Mike Wallace (14), Ron Hornaday (55) and Ricky Rudd (28) form a moving wall of thunder at 200 miles per hour. Green and Rudd eventually bested the inside duo and captured top-five finishes in the caution-free event.

(Right) At times during the race, the front pack settled into the more traditional double-file drafting lines, with plenty of Talladega asphalt to separate the columns. Here, Dale Earnhardt Jr. leads Tony Stewart, Ken Schrader, Ryan Newman and Ward Burton on the outside, with Jeremy Mayfield, Jimmie Johnson and Jeff Gordon fronting the inside line.

Add to that, the fact that the EA Sports 500 was the final Winston No Bull 5 event of the year, and Little E had $1 million more reasons to rock and roll his way to a third straight Talladega victory.

With qualifying rained out, the field was set by car owner point standings, ensuring the enormous crowd would get to see the beginning of a battle royale at the front of the field. The assemblage got even more than that when front-row mates Jimmie Johnson and Mark Martin collided on the pace lap, sending Mark to pit road and ending any hopes he had of regaining the point lead. Johnson later went out of the race with engine failure, one of six entries with engines from Hendrick Motorsports to bite the dust at Talladega. One of those victimized by motor problems was Jeff Gordon, and his hard work to put himself back into the point battle went for naught. He was classified 42nd at the conclusion of the race, and worse, he was suddenly more than 200 points out of first place in the standings.

At the front of the pack, Little E surfaced at the point on lap 18, and then began to dominate. He ultimately led six times for 56 laps, and instead of finding fellow DEI running mate Michael Waltrip on his rear decklid, this time his drafting partner was none other than Tony Stewart.

In previous restrictor-plate races, Stewart had paired up with Little E and found his Home Depot-sponsored Pontiac ran well in Earnhardt's draft. Tony tucked in behind the Budweiser Chevrolet and the pair of cars hammered the competition. Perhaps Stewart had a chance to win, but he also considered the fact that if he made the wrong move at the wrong time, it could cost both himself and Earnhardt the chance for victory. With Mark Martin, Jimmie Johnson and

Jeff Gordon all out of the battle, Tony also knew a strong finish would push him into the point lead.

So Stewart stayed behind Earnhardt and pushed the red Chevrolet to victory, enabling Earnhardt Jr. to claim the Winston No Bull 5 check for an additional $1 million. Stewart's second place vaulted him into the point lead while Ricky Rudd fought his way to third place ahead of Kurt Busch and Jeff Green. Steve Park took sixth with his DEI Pennzoil Chevrolet, while Ryan Newman posted yet another top-10 finish with his seventh place. Michael Waltrip was eighth in his NAPA Chevrolet, putting all three DEI entries in the top eight places. Dale Jarrett and Ward Burton, working with new crew chief Frank Stoddard, completed the top 10.

Seems everything's bigger at Talladega. In victory lane, Little E's third consecutive Talladega win garnered two mega-checks from series sponsor Winston – one for Earnhardt as the Winston No Bull 5 race winner and the other for Debra Polzun of Manchester, Conn., the lucky fan paired with Earnhardt in Winston's No Bull 5 "They Win, You Win" sweepstakes. Earnhardt also found enough champagne to happily share with his teammates (below).

EA Sports 500 final race results

Fin. Pos.	Start Pos.	Car No.	Driver	Team
1	13	8	Dale Earnhardt Jr.	Budweiser Chevrolet
2	3	20	Tony Stewart	The Home Depot Pontiac
3	10	28	Ricky Rudd	Havoline Ford
4	11	97	Kurt Busch	Rubbermaid Ford
5	17	30	Jeff Green	America Online Chevrolet
6	35	1	Steve Park	Pennzoil Chevrolet
7	7	12	Ryan Newman	ALLTEL/Mobil 1 Ford
8	15	15	Michael Waltrip	NAPA Chevrolet
9	12	88	Dale Jarrett	UPS Ford
10	28	22	Ward Burton	Caterpillar Dodge
11	14	99	Jeff Burton	CITGO SUPERGARD Ford
12	20	31	Robby Gordon	Cingular Wireless Chevrolet
13	6	2	Rusty Wallace	Miller Lite Ford
14	8	17	Matt Kenseth	DeWalt Power Tools Ford
15	16	32	Ricky Craven	Tide Ford
16	22	45	Kyle Petty	Sprint Dodge
17	32	23	Scott Wimmer	Hills Bros Coffee Dodge
18	30	43	John Andretti	Cheerios/Betty Crocker Dodge
19	9	9	Bill Elliott	Dodge Dealers/UAW Dodge
20	26	19	Jeremy Mayfield	Dodge Dealers/UAW Dodge
21	24	41	Jimmy Spencer	Target Dodge
22	42	49	Stacy Compton	BAM Racing Dodge
23	33	26	Todd Bodine	Discover Card Ford
24	40	44	Jerry Nadeau	Georgia Pacific/Brawny Dodge
25	18	18	Bobby Labonte	Interstate Batteries Pontiac
26	5	40	Jamie McMurray	Coors Light Dodge
27	19	29	Kevin Harvick	GM Goodwrench Service Chevrolet
28	37	4	Mike Skinner	Kodak Chevrolet
29	41	11	Brett Bodine	Hooters Restaurants Ford
30	2	6	Mark Martin	Pfizer/Viagra Ford
31	21	77	Dave Blaney	Jasper Engines & Transmissions Ford
32	29	55	Ron Hornaday	Schneider Electric/Square D Chevrolet
33	36	33	Kenny Wallace	1-800-CALL-ATT Chevrolet
34	39	7	Casey Atwood	Sirius Satellite Radio Dodge
35	38	14	Mike Wallace	Conseco Pontiac
36	27	21	Elliott Sadler	Motorcraft Ford
37	1	48	Jimmie Johnson	Lowe's Chevrolet
38	23	5	Terry Labonte	Kellogg's Chevrolet
39	34	25	Joe Nemechek	UAW-Delphi Chevrolet
40	25	10	Johnny Benson	Valvoline Pontiac
41	31	36	Ken Schrader	M&Ms Pontiac
42	4	24	Jeff Gordon	DuPont Chevrolet
43	43	71	Jay Sauter	RealTree Chevrolet

UAW-GM Quality 500

With just a handful of laps remaining in the UAW-GM Quality 500 at Lowe's Motor Speedway, Jamie McMurray holds the Coors Light Dodge steady in the groove while Bobby Labonte mounts his challenge in the Interstate Batteries Pontiac.

LIGHT
DODGE
MOOG

(Right) Jimmie Spencer (41) and Johnny Benson (10) race in front of the frontstretch grandstands. Spencer's Target Dodge, which sported a one-off Fuji paint scheme at Lowe's, lost the engine just past the 400-mile mark.

(Below) Michael Waltrip's NAPA crew bursts over the wall for a four-tire change. Waltrip's DEI Chevrolet was not good enough to challenge for the win, but Michael was able to stay on the lead lap and just missed a top-10 finish in 11th place.

With Jimmie Johnson and Jeff Gordon both suffering engine failures in their Hendrick Motorsports Chevrolets and Mark Martin plummeting to a 30th-place finish with a flat tire at Talladega, Tony Stewart took over the NASCAR Winston Cup Series point lead for the first time in his brief career.

And as Stewart arrived at Lowe's Motor Speedway with a 72-point margin over Martin, one look around the garage area showed the effects of the results of the EA Sports 500 the previous weekend. With the exception of second-place Martin, every driver in the top 10 had changed places following the Alabama race.

Jimmie Johnson now found himself 10 points behind Martin and 82 points behind in his quest to win the NASCAR Winston Cup Series championship in his rookie year. And Ryan Newman, the other sensational rookie, vaulted all the way from seventh to fourth place following his sixth straight top-10 finish, trailing Johnson by 55 points.

Rusty Wallace was just 10 points behind his Penske South teammate in fifth place, a total of 147 points away from the lead, while Matt Kenseth and Jeff Gordon were tied for sixth place, 54 points behind Wallace. Rusty would have been in fourth place in the standings, breathing down Jimmie Johnson's neck, except he was docked 25 championship points when his Miller Lite Ford was found with an unapproved spoiler.

Bill Elliott moved from ninth to eighth place, 28 points behind the tie for sixth, and Ricky Rudd rode his third-place Talladega finish to ninth, 17 points behind Elliott. Sterling Marlin, unable to compete for the remainder of the year, slid to 10th in the standings.

With six races remaining on the schedule, some garage watchers were putting Stewart in the driver's seat in the point battle. The inability of others to mount a race-to-race challenge for the title coupled with Stewart's late-season consistency was one factor, and some were quick to point out that Joe Gibbs Racing had plenty of experience in the run to the title, having won the crown with Bobby Labonte just two years ago. The lessons learned in the cauldron of the stretch run would be the basis of Stewart's bid for his first crown.

While teams were preparing for the UAW-GM Quality 500, Roger Penske, Rusty Wallace and Ryan Newman confirmed to media members they would, indeed, switch from Ford to Dodge for the 2003 season. A Ford team since 1994, the decision to join the Dodge Boys was a difficult one and came after the team built and aero-tested a Dodge Intrepid and the Penske motor department built engines and found what they would do on the dynamometer. Penske's DaimlerChrysler dealerships and other business dealings with the company also played a part in the decision.

Heavy weather plagued the Lowe's Motor Speedway weekend, with qualifying rained out for

the second straight race and teams forced to start the event based on points. That put Stewart on the pole with Martin alongside, while Johnson and Newman lined up in the second row.

Rain also affected the running of the UAW-GM Quality 500, with the race delayed for three hours before taking the green and yellow flags to start the event. From the beginning, Johnson underscored his determination to win at his sponsor's speedway, battling at the front of the pack with the hot-running Roush Racing duo of Matt Kenseth and Kurt Busch. Few in attendance gave much thought to young Jamie McMurray, starting only his second NASCAR Winston Cup Series race in place of the injured Sterling Marlin.

It wasn't until McMurray remained on the

(Above Left) Rusty Wallace's crew pits the Miller Lite Ford under green. Quick stops and a strong car kept Wallace near the front for the entire distance and resulted in a fifth-place finish, keeping Rusty's championship hopes alive.

(Above Right) Wallace's Penske teammate, rookie Ryan Newman (12), battles in tight quarters with sophomore driver Kurt Busch. With his eighth place in the race, Newman stretched his record of consistency to 12 top fives and 16 top 10s in his last 21 starts. Wallace and Newman, currently fifth and fourth in the points, respectively, announced during the weekend they would be switching to Dodges for the 2003 season.

(Left) The field fans out along the backstretch at Lowe's Motor Speedway after a restart, with Kevin Harvick (29) and Dave Blaney (77) dropping to the inside to make it three wide heading toward turn three. Blaney had a strong run to 10th place, his fourth top 10 of the season.

(Right) Crews sweep pit road after the final round of green-flag stops with about 35 laps remaining in the race. With the start of the race delayed by rain, the lights at Lowe's Motor Speedway came on, allowing the entire 500-mile distance to be run for the estimated crowd of 100,000.

(Below) Jamie McMurray (40) clears traffic with teammates Bobby Labonte (18) and Tony Stewart (20) trying to close from behind. McMurray held his own, kept the Pontiacs at bay and drove his Dodge all the way to victory lane in a performance almost Jamie, himself, could not believe.

track during the fourth caution, brought out when Ricky Rudd whacked the wall, that fans realized the substitute Coors Light Dodge driver had a car capable of leading the pack. Totally focused on the job at hand and receiving encouragement on the radio from crew chief Tony Glover, McMurray fought off a challenge from Bobby Labonte and then held the point while the field scrambled behind him.

McMurray was in front of a 10-car accident triggered by Todd Bodine, and after the wreckage was cleared, the event ran green until the end. McMurray found himself at the front after the green-flag pit stops cycled through, and then the nervousness set in.

He had not won a NASCAR Craftsman Truck Series event, nor had he been to victory lane in two years on the NASCAR Busch Series tour. Now, here he was, in front of the pack on a track he considered to be one of his worst, and in position, if he could just keep it all together, to win at the NASCAR Winston Cup Series level in only his second start.

Bobby Labonte was in his mirror, and Tony Stewart was closing on the two leaders. As the laps wound down, McMurray held his line, kept his focus and, when Labonte's run came in the final laps, Jamie had just enough Dodge – and just enough focus – to keep Labonte at bay.

Labonte was forced to settle for second, three

Jamie McMurray celebrates his first big-league win with former Miss Winston Ceilo Garcia. McMurray's unexpected victory came in just his second NASCAR Winston Cup Series start, making him the earliest winner since Johnny Rutherford won in his first appearance in February 1963 at Daytona.

car-lengths behind, while Stewart served notice he was a bona fide point leader by taking a rock-solid third. Jeff Gordon was fourth, but it appeared his return to form was too little, too late in the point battle. Rusty Wallace took fifth with another strong performance from the Miller Lite Ford driver, and Jimmie Johnson finished sixth, keeping his championship hopes flickering.

Jeff Burton was seventh ahead of Ryan Newman, who notched his seventh-straight top-10 finish. Dale Earnhardt Jr. was ninth, while Dave Blaney posted a solid run in the Jasper Motorsports Ford to grab 10th place ahead of Michael Waltrip.

UAW-GM Quality 500 final race results

Fin. Pos.	Start Pos.	Car No.	Driver	Team
1	5	40	Jamie McMurray	Coors Light Dodge
2	18	18	Bobby Labonte	Interstate Batteries Pontiac
3	1	20	Tony Stewart	The Home Depot Pontiac
4	8	24	Jeff Gordon	DuPont Chevrolet
5	6	2	Rusty Wallace	Miller Lite Ford
6	3	48	Jimmie Johnson	Lowe's Chevrolet
7	14	99	Jeff Burton	CITGO SUPERGARD Ford
8	4	12	Ryan Newman	ALLTEL Ford
9	13	8	Dale Earnhardt Jr.	Budweiser Chevrolet
10	21	77	Dave Blaney	Jasper Engines & Transmissions Ford
11	15	15	Michael Waltrip	NAPA Chevrolet
12	11	97	Kurt Busch	Rubbermaid/Sharpie Ford
13	39	44	Jerry Nadeau	Georgia Pacific/Brawny Dodge
14	12	88	Dale Jarrett	UPS Ford
15	34	1	Steve Park	Pennzoil Chevrolet
16	2	6	Mark Martin	Pfizer/Viagra Ford
17	37	14	Mike Wallace	Conseco Pontiac
18	26	10	Johnny Benson	Valvoline Pontiac
19	28	21	Elliott Sadler	Motorcraft Ford
20	22	45	Kyle Petty	Sprint Dodge
21	24	5	Terry Labonte	Kellogg's Chevrolet
22	20	29	Kevin Harvick	GM Goodwrench Service Chevrolet
23	30	43	John Andretti	Pillsbury Grands Dodge
24	36	4	Mike Skinner	Kodak Chevrolet
25	31	23	Kenny Wallace	Hills Bros Coffee Dodge
26	40	11	Brett Bodine	Hooters Restaurants Ford
27	29	55	Bobby Hamilton	Schneider Electric/Square D Chevrolet
28	25	19	Jeremy Mayfield	Dodge Dealers/UAW Dodge
29	17	30	Jeff Green	America Online Chevrolet
30	38	7	Casey Atwood	Sirius Satellite Radio Dodge
31	32	36	Ken Schrader	M&Ms Pontiac
32	23	41	Jimmy Spencer	Fuji Film/Target Dodge
33	27	22	Ward Burton	Caterpillar Dodge
34	7	17	Matt Kenseth	DeWalt Power Tools Ford
35	9	9	Bill Elliott	Dodge Dealers/UAW Dodge
36	16	32	Ricky Craven	Tide Ford
37	33	26	Todd Bodine	Discover Card Ford
38	19	31	Robby Gordon	Cingular Wireless Chevrolet
39	10	28	Ricky Rudd	Havoline Ford
40	35	25	Joe Nemechek	UAW-Delphi Chevrolet
41	43	02	Hermie Sadler	M&W Windows Chevrolet
42	42	49	Stacy Compton	BAM Racing Dodge
43	41	90	Jason Hedlesky	Lucas Oil Ford

Old Dominion 500

Dale Earnhardt Jr. (8) uses the outside groove to work around Robby Gordon (31) and John Andretti (43) on Martinsville's tight half mile. The Budweiser Chevrolet had several close calls during the race, but Earnhardt kept the damage to a minimum and drove to a well-earned fourth-place finish.

(Above) Crew members line up outside the Goodyear center to wait for new Eagles to be mounted on their teams' wheels. The harder tire compound used this season adapted well to the changes in the track surface, a combination that allowed two good racing grooves and provided for a very competitive race.

(Above Right) Ward Burton holds his Caterpillar Dodge on the inside in front of Ricky Rudd's Havoline Ford, with Jeff Burton (99), Jimmie Johnson, (48) and Tony Stewart (20) vying for positions on the outside. Ward Burton took the lap-leader bonus by leading 145 laps in the first half of the race before settling for a fifth-place finish.

(Below Right) The Hills Bros Dodge, driven by Geoffrey Bodine at Martinsville, receives attention on the brake system prior to the race. Brake management is one of the most important factors for success at Martinsville.

After the Talladega and Charlotte races, it was beginning to appear that Mark Martin's bid for his first NASCAR Winston Cup Series title was star-crossed. His engine problems at Talladega coupled with the pace-lap collision with Jimmie Johnson that sent Mark to pit road and an eventual 30th-place finish, combined with a less-than-stellar 16th place at Charlotte, dropped him to third in the standings as teams headed for Martinsville Speedway and the final short-track race of the year.

Not only was Martin in third place, but he also had dropped to 122 points behind table-leading Tony Stewart. Martin knew he wasn't out of the running yet, but things had to change quickly if he were to mount any kind of run in the final handful of races of the year.

After taking the lead in the point standings following the Talladega event, Stewart solidified his margin by taking the Home Depot Pontiac to third place at Charlotte. Jimmie Johnson and his Lowe's Chevrolet stayed in the hunt in the battle of home improvement sponsors by finishing sixth at Lowe's Motor Speedway. Johnson, in the midst of a spectacular rookie season, trailed Stewart by 97 points after the 31st race of the season.

Ryan Newman maintained his fourth-place slot on the point ladder with an eighth-place finish at LMS, while Penske teammate Rusty Wallace fought to fifth place and moved to within 17 points of Newman. Jeff Gordon – fourth at LMS – broke out of a tie for sixth place with Matt Kenseth, while Bill Elliott, Kurt Busch and Ricky Rudd completed the top 10 in the point standings.

Teams arrived at Martinsville's flat half-mile oval to find the track's management team had opted to grind down some of the concrete in the turns at the ends of the paper clip-shaped track. The plan was to provide for better racing and it worked like a charm, but the ensuing fuss from drivers centered more on the fact they felt they should have been consulted. Jeff Burton might

have hit the nail on the head when he said that the track officials could have talked with a half-dozen drivers and received a half-dozen different opinions. Perhaps that's why Martinsville president Clay Campbell just went ahead and had the work done.

Among the drivers who had little trouble adjusting to the changes in the surface was rookie Ryan Newman, who merely went out and turned the fastest lap during qualifying, claiming his fourth Bud Pole of the year and moving into a tie with Bill Elliott and Jimmie Johnson for the most poles so far in the 2002 season.

Jeff Gordon claimed the outside of the front row, with Bill Elliott and Ward Burton making it an all-Dodge second row ahead of Rusty Wallace and Joe Nemechek. Johnson was on the inside of the fourth row for the start of the Old Dominion 500, while Hermie Sadler had a great run in his privateer Chevrolet to grab the eighth-fastest lap of the session. Mike Skinner and Dale Earnhardt Jr. completed the top 10 qualifiers.

(Above) Bill Elliott (9) crunches down on Mark Martin (6) in their fight for position behind Johnny Benson (10). Elliott, who qualified with the third-fastest lap, was in and out of the top 10 during the day until contact with the frontstretch wall ended his effort. Martin was able to avoid serious problems to capture a top-10 finish.

(Left) Ricky Rudd's crewmates fall to work on the Havoline Ford under one of the event's 12 cautions. A cut tire in the opening laps dropped Rudd two laps off the pace, but the team recovered well and Rudd drove an inspired race to regain his laps and come away with a fine third-place effort.

(Right) Jeff Gordon (24) drifts high to avoid contact with Dave Blaney (77), who battles side by side with Mark Martin (6). Blaney led 18 laps in the early going before eventually falling a lap off the pace, while Gordon, who started second, was eliminated from winning contention after getting knocked into the wall.

Michael Waltrip, Kyle Petty, Elliott Sadler, John Andretti and Hideo Fukuyama all used provisionals to make the field, as did Steve Grissom and Geoffrey Bodine. Grissom was pressed into service to drive the Georgia Pacific Dodge after Jerry Nadeau was injured racing go-karts the day before practice opened. Bodine was behind the wheel of the Hills Bros Dodge entry owned by Bill Davis.

Five drivers – Brian Rose, Carl Long, Morgan Shepherd, Ryan McGlynn and Kirk Shelmerdine – all failed to make the field and were forced to watch the race unfold from the sidelines.

Martinsville's close quarters has always spelled slam-bang action for fans and a frustrating afternoon of rubbing sheet metal for drivers. Pushing and gouging has always been a hallmark of Martinsville's racing – there is no room for much of anything else. It's a slugfest that always leaves some drivers red-faced and displeased with the actions of others when the race is over, and, usually, only the victor emerges with a smile. For everyone else, it's simply an afternoon of grinding and bumping and trying to salvage the best possible finish after 500 difficult laps.

The Old Dominion 500 was another exciting chapter in the history of Martinsville, and the work done by Clay Campbell and his troops bore spectacular fruit for the fans. The track suddenly was a two-groove short track, and drivers were able to slash their way forward without having to put the chrome horn to the car in front.

(Below) Kurt Busch (97) and Johnny Benson (10) stage a side-by-side duel for the lead with the laps winding down in the race. Bush, who took the lead for the first time with 112 laps left, was able to fend off Benson's challenge and hold the point for all but one of the remaining laps.

Virginians were disappointed when Ricky Rudd headed for pit road early in the event with a flat tire, losing two laps in the process. And then they rose cheering as Rudd began fighting his way back from the deficit, eventually regaining the lead lap and battling all the way to a simply sensational third-place finish.

Stewart fans cheered when Tony rocketed his way from the 31st starting position to the lead, but then had their hopes dashed when Stewart was sandwiched between Dale Jarrett and Dale Earnhardt Jr., falling to an eventual 11th-place finish. Jeff Gordon fans moaned when they saw the DuPont Chevrolet driver's title hopes vanish after a wall-banging incident. Little E had more than one contretemps, and Bill Elliott's powerful run ended just 75 laps from the end of the race when he whacked the frontstretch wall.

Race winner Kurt Busch high-fives team members in victory lane after scoring his second win of the season. His victory was well earned; Busch started 36th as the last driver to qualify on speed and then had to overcome a spin near the 200-lap mark before finally dominating the last 100 circuits on the way to the win.

The huge throng cheered the loudest – and longest – however, when Kurt Busch made Martinsville history by coming from the farthest back in the field that any driver has ever done to emerge victorious at the fabled half mile. Busch started 36th, and after a pit stop during the 10th caution of the race put him in position to challenge, the youngster fought his way to the front and dominated the final 100 laps of the race.

Johnny Benson emerged as the most serious challenger at the end of the race, and although Benson had the chance to play spin and win in the final laps, the Michigan native decided that when he won his first career NASCAR Winston Cup Series race, he wanted it to be a clean victory. He drove as hard as he could in the Valvoline Pontiac, but never got into Busch's Rubbermaid Ford. Kurt didn't put a wheel wrong and drove to his second victory of the year, while Benson had to be content with finishing second.

Despite all the beating and banging, Little E finished fourth behind Rudd's scintillating drive, while Ward Burton was fifth ahead of Jimmie Johnson. Ricky Craven took seventh place ahead of Dale Jarrett, while Rusty Wallace was ninth. Mark Martin finished 10th just ahead of point-leader Tony Stewart.

Old Dominion 500 final race results

Fin. Pos.	Start Pos.	Car No.	Driver	Team
1	36	97	Kurt Busch	Rubbermaid/Sharpie Ford
2	11	10	Johnny Benson	Valvoline Pontiac
3	18	28	Ricky Rudd	Havoline Ford
4	10	8	Dale Earnhardt Jr.	Budweiser Chevrolet
5	4	22	Ward Burton	Caterpillar Dodge
6	7	48	Jimmie Johnson	Lowe's Chevrolet
7	14	32	Ricky Craven	Tide Ford
8	15	88	Dale Jarrett	UPS Ford
9	5	2	Rusty Wallace	Miller Lite Ford
10	20	6	Mark Martin	Pfizer/Viagra Ford
11	31	20	Tony Stewart	The Home Depot Pontiac
12	29	18	Bobby Labonte	Interstate Batteries Pontiac
13	40	43	John Andretti	Cheerios/Betty Crocker Dodge
14	27	40	Mike Bliss	Coors Light Dodge
15	1	12	Ryan Newman	ALLTEL Ford
16	16	1	Steve Park	Pennzoil Chevrolet
17	35	99	Jeff Burton	CITGO SUPERGARD Ford
18	37	15	Michael Waltrip	NAPA Chevrolet
19	17	17	Matt Kenseth	DeWalt Power Tools Ford
20	30	77	Dave Blaney	Jasper Engines & Transmissions Ford
21	22	7	Casey Atwood	Sirius Satellite Radio Dodge
22	34	5	Terry Labonte	Kellogg's Chevrolet
23	12	31	Robby Gordon	Cingular Wireless Chevrolet
24	21	41	Jimmy Spencer	Target Dodge
25	23	55	Bobby Hamilton	Schneider Electric/Square D Chevrolet
26	25	36	Ken Schrader	M&Ms Pontiac
27	26	14	Mike Wallace	Conseco Pontiac
28	24	19	Jeremy Mayfield	Dodge Dealers/UAW Dodge
29	19	07	Ted Musgrave	Sirius Satellite Radio/Kenwood Dodge
30	32	26	Todd Bodine	Discover Card Ford
31	13	29	Kevin Harvick	GM Goodwrench Service Chevrolet
32	28	30	Jeff Green	America Online Chevrolet
33	9	4	Mike Skinner	Kodak Chevrolet
34	39	21	Elliott Sadler	Motorcraft Ford
35	8	02	Hermie Sadler	Virginia Lottery Chevrolet
36	2	24	Jeff Gordon	DuPont Chevrolet
37	38	45	Kyle Petty	Sprint Dodge
38	33	11	Brett Bodine	Hooters Restaurants Ford
39	41	23	Geoffrey Bodine	Hills Bros Coffee Dodge
40	42	44	Steve Grissom	Georgia Pacific/Brawny Dodge
41	6	25	Joe Nemechek	UAW-Delphi Chevrolet
42	3	9	Bill Elliott	Dodge Dealers/UAW Dodge
43	43	66	Hideo Fukuyama	World Berries Ford

NAPA 500

Team members join their driver, Mark Martin (in director's chair), while waiting out a rain delay at Atlanta. Martin, third in points entering the weekend, grabbed an eighth place in the NAPA 500, but dropped 23 points to leader Tony Stewart, who finished fourth.

VIAGRA
GRA
citrate) tablets
EBB
EAGLE

(Above) Kurt Bush congratulates teammates as he emerges from his car in Atlanta's victory lane after capturing his third win of the season. Outstanding work by his crew on pit road, particularly during the final round of green-flag stops, helped Busch gain the track position needed to seal the win.

(Right) With track drying nearly complete, drivers and crew members make final preparations to return to action after a red flag for rain that lasted 2 hours, 26 minutes.

With just four races remaining in the chase for the 2002 NASCAR Winston Cup Series championship, five drivers remained in contention for the crown as the tour moved to Atlanta Motor Speedway. Of the five, few would have given two of them any chance to contend for the title at the beginning of the season.

Jimmie Johnson and Ryan Newman were considered talents of the future when they began their rookie seasons at Daytona last February. Granted, both were with well-funded and well-equipped teams, but both were – after all – rookies. In some cases, they needed directions to find some of the tracks they would race on during the course of the season.

Who, then, could have given either much of a chance that they would be in the battle for the title with just four races remaining in the season? Yet they were, with Johnson wheeling his Lowe's Chevrolet with elan, entering Atlanta just 82 points behind leader Tony Stewart.

And Ryan Newman had driven his ALLTEL Ford with great brio during the season, belying his rookie status. After finishing 15th at Martinsville, Newman was fifth in the point standings. His chance to claim the title was still glimmering – he was less than 180 points behind – but he would have to put together an incredible string of finishes in the final four races. Still, to be within 200 points of the leader with four to go was a great tribute to both Newman and his Penske team.

Veterans Mark Martin and 1989 NASCAR Winston Cup Series Champion Rusty Wallace were still in the hunt, as well. Wallace – still winless for the season – finished ninth at Martinsville and moved past Newman into fourth place in the standings. Rusty simply refused to count himself out of the championship battle. His experience told him that anything could happen in the four remaining races – a flat tire at the wrong time, being in the middle of someone else's mess, an engine failure, a bungled stop on pit road. Wallace knew any number of things could change the complexion of the title chase, and he had been around long enough to see others chase down a championship from further back in the pack than he was.

Like Wallace, Martin knew the chase wasn't over until everyone had been eliminated and there was just one driver standing at the top of

the hill. Mark finished 10th at Martinsville and remained in third place. He now trailed Stewart by 123 and was keenly aware that he needed just a little help to get close enough to breathe down the neck of the point leader.

In the first half of the season, few counted Tony Stewart as a bona fide championship contender. During his brief NASCAR Winston Cup Series career, inconsistency had marked the first half of his seasons, and although he always seemed to close with a rush, many discounted his efforts because he was in a Pontiac. Fords, Dodges and Chevrolets had garnered the headlines during the season. Stewart and his Joe Gibbs team had steadily chipped away with solid finishes in the middle of the year, and in the season's final third, they had truly come to the fore.

Stewart appeared headed for another top-five finish at Martinsville before he was sandwiched between Dale Jarrett and Dale Earnhardt Jr. He ultimately fought to an 11th-place finish and lost points to Jimmie Johnson, but with events at Atlanta, Rockingham, Phoenix and Homestead remaining on the tour, he knew he had a real chance to claim his first title.

Tony Stewart (20) and Jimmie Johnson (48) pace the field as drivers prepare to get underway in the NAPA 500. For the third time in the last four events, car owner points determined the starting lineup after rain washed out qualifying.

(Left) Kevin Harvick ponders a difficult sophomore season during a rare moment of relative seclusion in the Atlanta garage. Harvick captured his first victory at this track early last season in just his third career start, a win that launched a brilliant rookie campaign.

That put the leaders in the point standings in the front of the pack, and it also meant that eight drivers were unable to take a crack at making the NAPA 500 field. Those who lost out because of the inclement weather were Geoffrey Bodine in a Phoenix Racing Ford, Frank Kimmel in his own Ford, Scott Wimmer in a Bill Davis Dodge entry, Greg Biffle in a Roush Racing Ford, Buckshot Jones and Kerry Earnhardt in a pair of Michael Waltrip Racing Chevrolets, Ron Hornaday in a Hendrick Motorsports Chevrolet and Jack Sprague in a Haas Motorsports Chevrolet.

Like qualifying, race day at Ed Clark's superb facility was hampered by rain. Just 26 laps into the NAPA 500 the cars were brought to pit road as rain brought out the second caution flag and the race was stopped for nearly two and a half hours. Finally restarted at 3:25 p.m., the field worked its way around the track to finish drying the 1.5-mile oval until the green flew again on lap 46. During those caution laps, Tony Stewart was one of many who made pit stops, but a loose lug nut on the left-front wheel sent him plummeting to 32nd place.

Stewart began slashing his way through the field when the green flew, and by lap 54, he had picked up 15 spots in eight laps and continued to work his way toward the front. In the meantime, Jeff Gordon and Joe Nemechek were battling Kurt Busch for the lead, and just after half-distance Stewart had streaked all the way to the front.

(Above) Underway again after the delay, the drivers descend on their pits for tires and adjustments before resuming the race at speed. Tony Stewart, pitted in the first stall at the near end of pit road, had to come hack around to tighten loose lug nuts, which dropped him far back in the field at the restart.

Stewart found himself on the inside of the front row for the start of the NAPA 500 in the hometown of his sponsor, The Home Depot. It wasn't because he turned the fastest lap of the qualifying session, but rather because once again Bud Pole qualifying was rained out.

(Right) Dale Jarrett's UPS Ford gets hustled through the garage on its way to the starting grid. Jarrett, who started 11th based on car owner points, soldiered his way toward the front and picked up a third place at the finish, moving him into ninth in the late-season point standings.

He fought his way past Nemechek on lap 188 and immediately drew away while Dale Earnhardt Jr. fought his way past Busch to take third place.

The race turned in the next 10 laps. During green-flag stops, Kurt Busch emerged from pit road the leader, and when the field cycled around, Busch was in command and in search of becoming just the third driver this year to win back-to-back races.

The work done on pit road by the Rubbermaid team paid off. Once in clean air, Busch set off in search of his third victory of the season, and although Joe Nemechek made a strong effort, he could not handle the black Ford Taurus. When rain brought out the fifth caution flag of the day on lap 242, NASCAR officials made the decision to end the race on lap 248.

Busch won his third race of the season, with Nemechek a disappointed second. Dale Jarrett's UPS team worked throughout the day to improve his brown-and-white Taurus and Jarrett emerged third at the finish. Stewart was fourth after battling his way forward throughout the day, while Jamie McMurray continued his torrid performances in Sterling Marlin's Coors Light Dodge, taking seventh behind Little E and Jeff Gordon. Mark Martin was eighth, Matt Kenseth ninth and Ryan Newman took 10th.

Joe Nemechek (25) mounts his challenge on Kurt Busch (97) in the late stages of the event, but to no avail. Busch led a total of 84 laps, including the last 43, while Nemechek was his strongest competition over the final 100 circuits and took home a season-best second-place finish.

NAPA 500 final race results

Fin. Pos.	Start Pos.	Car No.	Driver	Team
1	8	97	Kurt Busch	Rubbermaid/Sharpie Ford
2	36	25	Joe Nemechek	UAW-Delphi Chevrolet
3	11	88	Dale Jarrett	UPS Ford
4	1	20	Tony Stewart	The Home Depot Pontiac
5	13	8	Dale Earnhardt Jr.	Budweiser Chevrolet
6	7	24	Jeff Gordon	DuPont Chevrolet
7	4	40	Jamie McMurray	Coors Light Dodge
8	3	6	Mark Martin	Pfizer/Viagra Ford
9	9	17	Matt Kenseth	DeWalt Power Tools Ford
10	6	12	Ryan Newman	ALLTEL Ford
11	15	15	Michael Waltrip	NAPA Chevrolet
12	14	99	Jeff Burton	CITGO SUPERGARD Ford
13	17	18	Bobby Labonte	Interstate Batteries Pontiac
14	22	45	Kyle Petty	Sprint Dodge
15	33	1	Steve Park	Pennzoil Chevrolet
16	27	22	Ward Burton	Caterpillar Dodge
17	5	2	Rusty Wallace	Miller Lite Ford
18	28	21	Elliott Sadler	Motorcraft Ford
19	19	77	Dave Blaney	Jasper Engines & Transmissions Ford
20	20	31	Robby Gordon	Cingular Wireless Chevrolet
21	16	32	Ricky Craven	Tide Ford
22	2	48	Jimmie Johnson	Lowe's Chevrolet
23	25	10	Johnny Benson	Valvoline Pontiac
24	18	30	Jeff Green	America Online Chevrolet
25	23	5	Terry Labonte	Kellogg's Chevrolet
26	35	4	Mike Skinner	Kodak Chevrolet
27	26	19	Jeremy Mayfield	Dodge Dealers/UAW Dodge
28	39	44	Ted Musgrave	Georgia Pacific/Brawny Dodge
29	42	74	Tony Raines	Staff America Chevrolet
30	24	41	Jimmy Spencer	Target Dodge
31	37	14	Mike Wallace	Conseco Pontiac
32	10	28	Ricky Rudd	Havoline Ford
33	12	9	Bill Elliott	Dodge Dealers/UAW Dodge
34	40	11	Brett Bodine	Hooters Restaurants Ford
35	29	55	Bobby Hamilton	Schneider Electric/Square D Chevrolet
36	32	23	Kenny Wallace	Hills Bros Coffee Dodge
37	41	49	Derrike Cope	BAM Racing Dodge
38	38	7	Casey Atwood	Sirius Satellite Radio Dodge
39	43	59	Carl Long	Check-to-Cash Dodge
40	21	29	Kevin Harvick	GM Goodwrench Service Chevrolet
41	34	26	Todd Bodine	Discover Card Ford
42	31	36	Ken Schrader	M&Ms Pontiac
43	30	43	John Andretti	Cheerios/Betty Crocker Dodge

(Above) A crowd estimated at 50,000 looks on at North Carolina Speedway as the final chapters of the 2002 NASCAR Winston Cup Series championship unfold on a beautiful autumn afternoon.

(Right) Jamie McMurray, who qualified a sparkling second, leads Bill Elliott (9) and Jeremy Mayfield (19) in a Dodge trio at Rockingham. Although it was McMurray's fourth career start, this was the first time the Coors Light driver qualified on speed as the fields in his three previous races were set by points due to rain.

And then there were three. Atlanta's rain-splattered results left the battle for the NASCAR Winston Cup Series championship up for grabs among three drivers. Ryan Newman, Rusty Wallace and Atlanta-winner Kurt Busch didn't want to hear that little piece of news, but for all intents and purposes the long struggle for supremacy had worked its way down to just three drivers.

Tony Stewart maintained his lead after Atlanta. The Home Depot Pontiac driver had worked his way to a hard-fought fourth place at the conclusion of the race, and that finish, coupled with Jimmie Johnson's self-induced twin spins and Mark Martin's eighth place, allowed Tony to pad his lead while Martin and Johnson swapped places on the point ladder.

Now, with just three races left in the long season, Stewart had a seemingly-safe 146-point margin over Martin, while Johnson was four points behind the Viagra Ford driver.

For Newman, 10th place at Atlanta did no good in cutting into Stewart's margin, and Rusty Wallace's 17th place in the rain-shortened event

didn't help his cause either. Kurt Busch may have won and moved from seventh to sixth place on the point ladder, but he was 297 behind Stewart and had no hope of fighting his way into contention with just three races left.

Jeff Gordon, who, at one point in the stretch run, looked as though he was leading a rush at a fifth career title, fell to seventh place in the standings, despite finishing sixth at Atlanta. He was now more than 300 points off the pace and locked in a furious battle with Busch and Wallace in hopes of claiming the final slot in the top five at year's end.

Matt Kenseth, Dale Jarrett and Ricky Rudd completed the top 10, while Dale Earnhardt Jr. was 46 points behind Rudd with three races remaining on the schedule and appeared determined to battle his way into the top 10.

The "silly season" was in full swing at Rockingham. Mike "Fatback" McSwain, Ricky Rudd's crew chief at Robert Yates Racing, was released by RYR and within hours was unpacking his tool box at Joe Gibbs Racing, where he was slated to take over as head wrench for Bobby Labonte with the promotion of Jimmy Makar to team manager.

While Fatback and Bobby were learning to communicate, Todd Bodine was taking a long hard look at what was available for the coming season. Discover Card had informed team owners Carl Haas and Travis Carter its sponsorship would not be extended to 2003 and Todd, on probation after the multi-car accident at Charlotte, was unclear in regard to what he would be driving next season.

Todd wasn't the only one on tenterhooks. Rumors swirled around Casey Atwood and Jimmy Spencer, and both drivers merely could state they were driving their cars that weekend and expected to be driving them the next weekend at Phoenix. It appeared Atwood had team co-owner Ray Evernham's confidence and Spencer said he believed he was set in the Target Dodge for the coming season. Only time would tell.

Ryan Newman again set the pace during qualifying, amazingly nailing down his fifth Bud Pole of the season. And while Newman grabbed the inside of the front row, Jamie McMurray continued his startling performances as Sterling Marlin's substitute, putting the Coors Light Dodge on the outside of the front row. Todd Bodine and Mike Skinner gave their teams plenty to crow about by

Point leaders Tony Stewart (20) and Mark Martin (6) find each other on the race track ahead of Mike Wallace (14) and Hank Parker Jr. (91), who was making his NASCAR Winston Cup Series debut driving a Dodge for car owner Jim Smith. Stewart, fighting an ill-handling car throughout the day, fought gamely to 14th place at the end and maintained a comfortable margin of Martin in the standings.

(Below) Kevin Harvick's GM Goodwrench Chevrolet fronts Ricky Craven's Tide Ford and Bobby Labonte's Interstate Pontiac. Craven and Labonte worked past Harvick and scored top-10 finishes with Labonte seventh and Craven ninth.

(Bottom) Jeff Burton (99) slides past Bill Elliott (9) on his way to a fourth-place finish, the first top five for the CITGO Ford in the last 11 events. Elliott ran well, but a failed water pump ended his day with fewer than 100 laps to go.

(Bottom Right) On a roll of late, Kurt Busch (97) leads Ryan Newman (12) while trying for three consecutive wins. Busch looked like he might just do it, too, until teammate Mark Martin and Johnny Benson overtook him in the late stages of the race.

notching the second-row starting positions, while Martin and Jeff Green were fifth and sixth fastest. Kurt Busch, on a back-to-back victory high, qualified seventh, a tick faster than Rusty Wallace. Robby Gordon and Bill Elliott nailed down the final top-10 starting positions, beating Bobby Labonte and Ken Schrader for those spots.

Dale Jarrett, Terry Labonte, Bobby Hamilton, Steve Park, Mike Wallace, Casey Atwood and Brett Bodine used provisionals to start the race, leaving Tony Raines, Tim Sauter, Carl Long, Ron Hornaday and Hideo Fukuyama on the sidelines for the Pop Secret Microwave Popcorn 400.

Almost from the opening laps, it was clear to tens of thousands in the stands and millions watching on television that Tony Stewart was struggling. By lap 70, Tony had faded to 32nd, and at the front of the field it was just as clear that Mark Martin was giving this race everything he had in hopes of narrowing the point difference. Stewart went on to struggle throughout the afternoon and, with great determination, finally fought his way to a decent 14th-place finish.

Martin was in the battle for the victory throughout the afternoon and led the field off pit road during the final caution period of the afternoon on lap 293. Mark led until lap 340 when Roush Racing teammate Kurt Busch caught him and passed the Viagra Ford for the lead. Nine laps later, Johnny Benson caught and passed Martin and then set his sights on Busch.

On lap 360, Busch and Benson made a sandwich of Jimmy Spencer as they lapped him, and after a six-lap battle Benson emerged the leader with his Valvoline Pontiac. Two laps later, Martin went past Busch and began stalking Benson. For nearly 20 laps, Martin tried to find a way past Benson but was unable to get the right line to pass the Michigan native. Martin was forced to settle for second ahead of Busch and Jeff Burton. Jeff Gordon took fifth ahead of Mike Skinner, and Bobby Labonte was seventh in his first outing with crew chief McSwain. Matt Kenseth, Ricky Craven and Jeff Green completed the top 10.

Benson's first career victory in 226 NASCAR Winston Cup Series starts was a joyous one. A second-generation driver, he became the 18th different winner of the season. Ironically, it was the first time Valvoline had been to victory lane since the company sponsored Mark Martin in 2000.

(Above) Johnny Benson (10) and Mark Martin (6) battle side by side for the lead with the laps winding down at Rockingham. Benson finally got past Martin and took the point for the first time in the race with 28 laps remaining and held on the capture the popular win.

Benson had the chance to win at Martinsville two weeks earlier, but he refused to put the chrome horn to Kurt Busch in the final laps. Johnny didn't want to win that way, and with Mark Martin behind him in the final laps at Rockingham, he knew the battle for victory would be a clean one.

Benson's win came after he had twice been forced to vacate the Valvoline Pontiac earlier this season with rib injuries from accidents. No one was more pleased to notch his first career victory after a season of great pain and difficulty.

(Left) In the winner's circle, Benson and crew chief James Ince (left) congratulate each other on a job well done. Together since the beginning of the 2000 season, the pair had knocked on the door to victory lane on several occasions before finally tasting sweet success.

Pop Secret Microwave Popcorn 400 final race results

Fin. Pos.	Start Pos.	Car No.	Driver	Team
1	26	10	Johnny Benson	Valvoline Pontiac
2	5	6	Mark Martin	Pfizer/Viagra Ford
3	7	97	Kurt Busch	Rubbermaid Ford
4	29	99	Jeff Burton	CITGO Ford
5	18	24	Jeff Gordon	DuPont Chevrolet
6	4	4	Mike Skinner	Kodak Chevrolet
7	11	18	Bobby Labonte	Interstate Batteries Pontiac
8	19	17	Matt Kenseth	DEWALT Power Tools Ford
9	23	32	Ricky Craven	Tide Ford
10	6	30	Jeff Green	America Online Chevrolet
11	9	31	Robby Gordon	Cingular Wireless Chevrolet
12	37	88	Dale Jarrett	UPS Ford
13	16	23	Kenny Wallace	Hills Bros Coffee Dodge
14	24	20	Tony Stewart	The Home Depot Pontiac
15	2	40	Jamie McMurray	Coors Light Dodge
16	27	21	Elliott Sadler	Motorcraft Ford
17	30	77	Dave Blaney	Jasper Engines & Transmissions Ford
18	35	43	John Andretti	Pop Secret Microwave Popcorn Dodge
19	36	15	Michael Waltrip	NAPA Chevrolet
20	20	28	Ricky Rudd	Havoline Ford
21	17	19	Jeremy Mayfield	Dodge Dealers/UAW Dodge
22	12	36	Ken Schrader	M&M's Pontiac
23	1	12	Ryan Newman	ALLTEL/Mobil 1 Ford
24	40	1	Steve Park	Pennzoil Chevrolet
25	13	44	Greg Biffle	Georgia Pacific/Brawny Dodge
26	32	29	Kevin Harvick	GM Goodwrench Service Chevrolet
27	8	2	Rusty Wallace	Miller Lite Ford
28	21	25	Joe Nemechek	UAW-Delphi Chevrolet
29	42	7	Casey Atwood	Sirius Satellite Radio Dodge
30	14	45	Kyle Petty	Sprint Dodge
31	15	41	Jimmy Spencer	Target Dodge
32	38	5	Terry Labonte	Kellogg's Chevrolet
33	25	91	Hank Parker Jr.	USG Dodge
34	22	8	Dale Earnhardt Jr.	Budweiser Chevrolet
35	28	60	Jack Sprague	Haas Automation Chevrolet
36	43	11	Brett Bodine	Hooters Restaurants Ford
37	31	48	Jimmie Johnson	Lowe's Chevrolet
38	39	55	Bobby Hamilton	Schneider Electric/Square D Chevrolet
39	10	9	Bill Elliott	Dodge Dealers/UAW Dodge
40	34	22	Ward Burton	Caterpillar Dodge
41	33	02	Hermie Sadler	MW Windows Chevrolet
42	3	26	Todd Bodine	Discover Card Ford
43	41	14	Mike Wallace	Conseco Pontiac

Checker Auto Parts 500 presented by Pennzoil

Fans line the backstretch at beautiful Phoenix International raceway for the penultimate event of the 2002 NASCAR Winston Cup Series season.

(Below) Ryan Newman (12) set the pace in qualifying with a lap at 132.655 miles per hour to gain his sixth Bud Pole of the year and lock up the annual Bud Pole Award for the 2002 season. His fast lap didn't translate into the race however, as Newman went a lap down and finished 18th.

(Below Right) Point-leader Tony Stewart wears a confident smile at Phoenix while he waits to get underway in the 312-lap event. He had reason to be confident – in three career starts at PIR, Stewart won in 1999, finished 14th in 2000 and fifth last year.

Mark Martin drove the wheels off his Viagra Ford at Rockingham, leading the most laps and then waging a furious battle near the end before coming up just short of passing eventual winner Johnny Benson. He gave it everything he had in his black-and-blue Taurus and, along the way, chopped Tony Stewart's lead by 59 points.

Martin's gritty performance moved him within 87 markers of Stewart with a pair of races left on the schedule – at least until the post-race technical inspection at The Rock. NASCAR inspectors found the left-front spring in the Taurus measured 4 3/8 coils instead of the prescribed 4 1/2 – and for want of an eighth of a coil, Martin was docked 25 championship points. That put him 112 behind as teams arrived in the Valley of the Sun for the next-to-last NASCAR Winston Cup Series race of the season.

As if that wasn't enough, Stewart has always run well at Phoenix International Raceway and at Homestead, the site of the season finale. There couldn't be two worse tracks on the tour for Martin to try to make up his deficit.

But Martin, a true racer's racer, would give it his best effort.

Benson's popular victory in the North Carolina Sandhills overshadowed an outstanding performance by the entire Roush Racing effort. Martin was second, while Kurt Busch continued his torrid performances (eight top 10s in the last 11 races) with a fighting third place, and Jeff Burton looked like he was finally untracked, finishing fourth. Matt Kenseth took eighth, putting all four Roush cars in the top eight finishing positions.

The battle for the NASCAR Winston Cup Series title, which just two races ago had included five drivers, was now down to just two – Martin and

Stewart. Jimmie Johnson's hopes ended with a wheel hub problem at Rockingham, and Johnson now found himself more than 200 points behind. Busch's third place moved him past Rusty Wallace into fifth in the standings, a result of his late-sea-

(Left) Johnny Benson, fresh off his win at Rockingham, and Jeremy Mayfield (19) streak under the pedestrian bridge in turn four, which also serves as a good perch for photographers.

(Below) Dave Blaney (77) challenges Jimmy Spencer (41) and his Target Dodge, the car Blaney was rumored to be a candidate to drive next season. After qualifying fifth for the race, Blaney scored a season-best seventh-place finish in the Jasper Ford.

son surge, while Wallace fell into a virtual dead-heat with Jeff Gordon in their personal battle for sixth. A single point separated the two. Kenseth, Dale Jarrett and Ricky Rudd completed the top 10 in the standings, while Dale Earnhardt Jr. was 11th, 88 points behind Rudd.

For several drivers, the chances to win this season were dwindling. Jeff Burton, the only Roush driver yet to win this year, was delighted to head for Phoenix where he was the two-time defending champion of the event. Rusty Wallace, mired in a 60-race winless streak, was grimly determined to win a race before the year was over. With his 16-year string of winning at least one race each season at stake, Wallace was steely-eyed in his quest for a victory.

The rumors that had swirled around Jimmy Spencer and Casey Atwood at Rockingham proved to be true by the time teams arrived at Phoenix. Ray Evernham had dissolved his partnership with Jim Smith and the Ultra/Evernham effort, and Atwood found himself without a ride at Phoenix. Under contract to Evernham through 2003, Casey would be in a research and development Dodge for Evernham at Homestead, but he had been replaced by Smith with Jason Leffler for Phoenix. Spencer was hot under the collar of his Target driver's suit after receiving word that his

(Right) After a disappointing 29th-fastest effort in qualifying, Rusty Wallace (2) battles through the pack in his bid to pick up a win before the 2002 season draws to an end. With a fast car and good pit strategy, Wallace passed everyone but Kenseth and wound up second at the end.

(Below) Jimmie Johnson (48), Jeff Burton (99) and Dale Jarrett (88) hug the bottom through the third and fourth turns with Kevin Harvick (29) and Ken Schrader (36) on the outside. Among the group, Dale Jarrett fared best with a top-10 finish, while two-time defending race champion Burton fell to 12th.

services would not be required in the coming season at the Chip Ganassi stable. What infuriated Spencer was that he had been assured he would be retained, then was cut loose with a phone call.

One place Spencer would not drive in 2003 was with the MB2 Motorsports effort. The team announced at Phoenix it had obtained sponsorship from the U.S. Army for 27 races in 2003 and that Jerry Nadeau would drive the new black-and-gold cars. It also appeared that a pair of top-five finishes in the last six races had brought Joe Nemechek into favor at Hendrick Motorsports and Joe would be retained for the coming season.

Ryan Newman was once again the Bud Pole winner during qualifying and locked up his sixth pole of the season, setting a new NASCAR mark by a rookie candidate and erasing Davey Allison's 1987 record of five. It also clinched the 2002 season's Bud Pole Award for Newman. John Andretti claimed the outside of the front row, while Dale Earnhardt Jr. and Jeff Gordon earned second-row starting positions. Dave Blaney, rumored to be Jimmy Spencer's replacement in the Target Dodge, took the inside of the third row with his Jasper Motorsports Ford, while Kenny Wallace was sixth fastest ahead of Mark Martin

and Joe Nemechek. Robby Gordon and Spencer rounded out the top 10 on the starting grid.

Using provisionals to make the field were Jimmie Johnson, Michael Waltrip, Jeff Green, Bobby Hamilton, Mike Wallace, Derrike Cope and Tony Raines. Among those not making the field were Brett Bodine and Ted Musgrave.

With a packed house on hand to watch the festivities, point-leader Stewart and his Home Depot Pontiac started 16th as he began his quest to ice the championship. Martin was just as determined to chop into the point lead, but the race was destined to reward neither contender with victory.

Rusty Wallace did his best to score his first win of the season, using a two-tire stop in the final portion of the race in hopes of gaining track position and the clean air at the front of the pack. His gamble failed, however, when Matt Kenseth used the same two-tire strategy and beat the field off pit road to take the lead on lap 261 of the 312-lap race.

Once in the clean air, Kenseth's DeWalt Ford turned into a rocket ship, and no one had the answer for the yellow-and-black Taurus. Kenseth rolled to his fifth victory of the season, beating Wallace by more than 1.3 seconds. Jeff Gordon took third place and Martin fought to fourth ahead of Little E and Kurt Busch. Dave Blaney underscored his talent with a strong seventh place in the Jasper Ford, while Tony Stewart cut his losses well with an eighth place. Dale Jarrett and Elliott Sadler completed the top 10, with Sadler ahead of Kenny Wallace and Jeff Burton at the conclusion of the race.

(Top) Steve Park (1), who started 32nd, follows 28th-place starter Matt Kenseth (17) in early-race action. Like Wallace, Kenseth used pit strategy and a well-handling race car to get to the front where he led the final 52 laps on his way to the win.

(Above) The DeWalt team lets the bubbly fly as the victory celebration gets underway in Phoenix. With their fifth win of the year, Kenseth's team assured themselves of having the most wins of the 2002 NASCAR Winston Cup Series campaign.

Checker Auto Parts 500 presented by Pennzoil final race results

Fin. Pos.	Start Pos.	Car No.	Driver	Team
1	28	17	Matt Kenseth	DEWALT Power Tools Ford
2	29	2	Rusty Wallace	Miller Lite Ford
3	4	24	Jeff Gordon	DuPont Chevrolet
4	7	6	Mark Martin	Pfizer/Viagra Ford
5	3	8	Dale Earnhardt Jr.	Budweiser Chevrolet
6	13	97	Kurt Busch	Rubbermaid/StainShield Ford
7	5	77	Dave Blaney	Jasper Engines & Transmissions Ford
8	16	20	Tony Stewart	The Home Depot Pontiac
9	27	88	Dale Jarrett	UPS Ford
10	15	21	Elliott Sadler	Motorcraft Ford
11	6	23	Kenny Wallace	Hills Bros Coffee Dodge
12	20	99	Jeff Burton	CITGO SUPERGARD Ford
13	24	28	Ricky Rudd	Havoline Ford
14	2	43	John Andretti	Cheerios/Betty Crocker Dodge
15	37	48	Jimmie Johnson	Lowe's Chevrolet
16	23	10	Johnny Benson	Valvoline Pontiac
17	25	29	Kevin Harvick	GM Goodwrench Service Chevrolet
18	1	12	Ryan Newman	ALLTEL/Mobil 1 Ford
19	26	22	Ward Burton	Caterpillar Dodge
20	38	15	Michael Waltrip	NAPA Chevrolet
21	32	1	Steve Park	Pennzoil Chevrolet
22	30	26	Todd Bodine	Discover Card Ford
23	10	41	Jimmy Spencer	Target Dodge
24	34	4	Mike Skinner	Kodak Chevrolet
25	11	19	Jeremy Mayfield	Dodge Dealers/UAW Dodge
26	31	5	Terry Labonte	Kellogg's Chevrolet
27	9	31	Robby Gordon	Cingular Wireless Chevrolet
28	41	14	Mike Wallace	Conseco Pontiac
29	40	55	Bobby Hamilton	Schneider Electric/Square D Chevrolet
30	14	9	Bill Elliott	Dodge Dealers/UAW Dodge
31	36	7	Jason Leffler	Sirius Satellite Radio Dodge
32	18	45	Kyle Petty	Sprint Dodge
33	8	25	Joe Nemechek	UAW-Delphi Chevrolet
34	35	32	Ricky Craven	Tide Ford
35	39	30	Jeff Green	America Online Chevrolet
36	22	83	Ron Hornaday	RacingUSA.com Chevrolet
37	21	36	Ken Schrader	Pedigree Pontiac
38	42	49	Derrike Cope	BAM Racing Dodge
39	33	18	Bobby Labonte	Interstate Batteries Pontiac
40	12	40	Jamie McMurray	Coors Light Dodge
41	17	44	Christian Fittipaldi	Georgia Pacific/Brawny Dodge
42	19	27	Scott Wimmer	Seimens Dodge
43	43	74	Tony Raines	Staff America Chevrolet

Ford 400

The Home Depot team erupts in celebration on pit road at Homestead-Miami Speedway as their driver, Tony Stewart, clinches the 2002 NASCAR Winston Cup Series championship.

(Below) With photographers all around, Tony Stewart and crewman Jeff Chandler relax on pit road before the festivities begin. Stewart had reason to be confident: In three starts at Homestead-Miami Speedway, Stewart had two wins, in 1999 and 2000, and led the most laps in last year's event.

(Below Right) The tension before the Ford 400 must have been great on Mark Martin, who qualified a disappointing 34th. But veteran that he is, Martin still found reason to have a good laugh before getting underway in the race. Martin raced well but ended his season as the runner-up for the fourth time in his NASCAR Winston Cup Series career.

And so it all came down to the end game. For the first time since 1997, the NASCAR Winston Cup Series championship would be decided in the final race of the season, and Tony Stewart brought his 87-point lead to South Florida.

He was not home free by any means – anything could happen, and the way the entire 2002 season had gone, the chances were good something might happen. But Stewart, in command of the point ladder since the EA Sports 500 at Talladega, would be able to watch where Mark Martin was running during the Ford 400 and race accordingly.

Stewart was clear in his objectives as he headed for the 1.5-mile Homestead-Miami Speedway. He took his best car – the Home Depot Pontiac he had debuted at Chicagoland and the same chassis that had produced top-10 results in six of the seven races it had run. It was the same Pontiac that sat on the pole and led 43 laps at Indianapolis. He would drive to win if he could, but if not, then he would do his best to protect his point lead.

Martin, on the other hand, faced a double uphill battle. He had fought back with a fourth place at Phoenix, which narrowed the point gap entering the final race of the season. Still, 87 points was a huge pile to try to erase at a track where Stewart owned a pair of victories. Martin also knew Roush Racing's appeal of the 25 points taken from him for having the non-approved spring in the left front of his Ford at Rockingham probably would not be successful. If the points were reinstated, his job would be easier at Homestead, but if not, the deficit might be just too much to overcome.

While Mark and Tony would battle for the championship, Homestead's Ford 400 meant a great deal to those battling for third through seventh places in the point standings. Kurt Busch held third headed into the finale, but was just eight points ahead of Jimmie Johnson and Rusty Wallace, tied for fourth in the standings. Jeff Gordon was a single point behind the tie, while Ryan Newman trailed Gordon by just 14 points. A total of 23 points separated the five drivers after 35 races.

Rusty Wallace headed to Homestead determined to take his Miller Lite Ford to victory lane. He had been close to visiting the winner's circle several times during the season and now found himself with just a single race left to enable him to extend his 16-year streak of winning at least one race.

Kurt Busch, perhaps the hottest driver on the tour in the last 10 races, put together a superb run to claim his first Bud Pole of the season and secure entry to the Bud Shootout at Daytona Beach in February. Dale Earnhardt Jr. joined Busch on the

front row for the Ford 400, while Jimmy Spencer, in his last outing with Chip Ganassi's team, put the Target Ford on the inside of the second row. Joe Nemechek qualified fourth fastest, just a tick faster than Greg Biffle, driving Petty Enterprises' Georgia Pacific Dodge. Stewart qualified sixth fastest, with Jeff Burton, Kenny Wallace, Ricky Rudd and Bill Elliott completing the top 10 for the Ford 400.

Martin struggled in qualifying, drawing a slot that put him on the track during the hottest time of the qualifying session. His lap was only good for 34th on the starting grid. Jeff Gordon, Jeff Green, Robby Gordon, Johnny Benson, Mike Skinner, Todd Bodine and Derrike Cope used provisionals for the event. Left on the sidelines were Hermie Sadler, Brett and Geoffrey Bodine, Tony Raines, Carl Long, Boris Said, David Green and Mark Harmon.

After rain washed the track Saturday evening, drivers were greeted by a "green" surface when they took the green flag for the Ford 400. All eyes were on Martin and Stewart as the two drivers fought for the championship in the battle that had begun in February up the Florida coast in Daytona Beach.

In clean air, Joe Nemechek had one of the

(Above) A critical moment in the race came here, on the restart at lap 205, with Dale Jarrett (88) leading Joe Nemechek (25) and Kurt Busch (97). Tony Stewart (20) had already fallen a lap down, but he charged past Jarrett after the restart and regained position on the lead lap, where he remained until the finish.

(Left) Joe Nemechek (25) races with Kurt Busch (97) in one of their duels for the lead. Nemechek had an outstanding run to second place after leading the most laps in the race driving the No. 25 Chevrolet he'll drive next season.

(Below Left) Jack Sprague (left) chats with Jeff Gordon and Kevin Harvick (right) during pre-race ceremonies. Sprague, scheduled to run for rookie honors in 2003, was making his third start of the season driving a Chevrolet for Haas CNC Racing.

(Right) Pole winner Kurt Busch (97) led the race on three different occasions before having to deal with Ryan Newman (12), who grabbed the point for 28 laps in the late going. Busch worked past the 2002 Rookie of the Year with 11 to go and held on for the win.

(Below Right) Jack Roush congratulates his driver in victory lane after the 24-year-old took his fourth win of the season and nailed down third place in the final point standings, joining Roush teammates Martin (second) and Kenseth (eighth) in the final top 10.

(Below) Mark Martin (6) and Roush teammate Jeff Burton (99) look for room on the inside to squeeze past Geoffrey Bodine (26), with Ted Musgrave (07) following in the Ultra Motorsports Dodge. Burton and Martin stayed close to each other and finished together, with Burton taking third ahead of Martin in fourth.

best cars during the afternoon, leading at will during the middle portion of the Ford 400. Stewart fought an ill-handling Home Depot Pontiac during two green-flag runs that saw him drop off the lead lap, while Martin doggedly fought his way forward from his 34th starting position.

Stewart regained the lead lap with a timely caution late in the race and then battled his way to an 18th-place finish, ensuring his first NASCAR Winston Cup Series championship. Martin did all he could, grimly driving the wheels off his Viagra Taurus, but could only manage fourth place at the conclusion of the race. It brought him to within

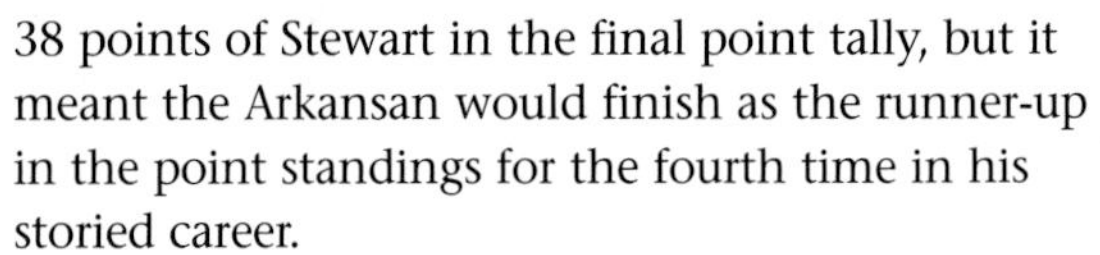

38 points of Stewart in the final point tally, but it meant the Arkansan would finish as the runner-up in the point standings for the fourth time in his storied career.

While Stewart and Martin were having their private battle for the championship, Kurt Busch found a way past Ryan Newman with 11 laps left in the race, and, once at the point, Busch rolled to his third victory in the last five races. His performance in the specially painted "Little Tykes" Ford ensured his third-place finish in the point standings, while Nemechek continued his torrid late-season performances by finishing second. Jeff Burton finished third, giving Roush Racing a 1-3-4 finish at Homestead-Miami Speedway. Jeff Gordon finished fifth behind Martin, moving to fourth place in the final standings, while Newman faded to sixth place. Bill Elliott took seventh place ahead

(Left) Surprisingly, the Home Depot Pontiac began the race handling poorly, which dropped Tony Stewart back into traffic and down one lap. But the team made adjustments to the car over the first 200 laps and that, combined with a couple of timely cautions, let Stewart climb to 18th – good enough to allow him to take his place on the Champion's Podium (below left).

(Above) It didn't take long for Stewart to begin his duties as the new champ as he was swarmed by reporters after the event – something he'll get used to before the 2003 season is out.

of Jimmie Johnson and Elliott Sadler, while Bobby Hamilton was 10th in his final outing with Andy Petree's Chevrolet.

Rookies Jimmie Johnson and Ryan Newman finished fifth and sixth in the final standings, with Newman named the Rookie of the Year immediately after the race. Rusty Wallace took seventh in the standings and saw his 16-year string end, while Matt Kenseth, Dale Jarrett and Ricky Rudd completed the top 10 in the point standings after the 36-race season.

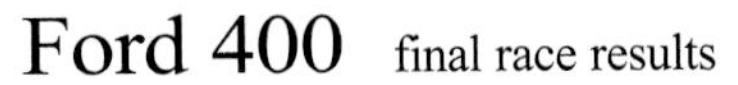

Ford 400 final race results

Fin. Pos.	Start Pos.	Car No.	Driver	Team
1	1	97	Kurt Busch	Little Tykes/Rubbermaid Ford
2	4	25	Joe Nemechek	UAW-Delphi Chevrolet
3	7	99	Jeff Burton	CITGO Ford
4	34	6	Mark Martin	Pfizer/Viagra Ford
5	37	24	Jeff Gordon	DuPont Chevrolet
6	15	12	Ryan Newman	ALLTEL/Mobil 1 Ford
7	10	9	Bill Elliott	Dodge Dealers/UAW Dodge
8	16	48	Jimmie Johnson	Lowe's Chevrolet
9	24	21	Elliott Sadler	Motorcraft Ford
10	17	55	Bobby Hamilton	Schneider Electric/Square D Chevrolet
11	20	14	Mike Wallace	Conseco Pontiac
12	26	22	Ward Burton	Caterpillar Dodge
13	40	10	Johnny Benson	Valvoline Pontiac
14	18	2	Rusty Wallace	Miller Lite Ford
15	19	88	Dale Jarrett	UPS Ford
16	28	07	Ted Musgrave	Sirius Satellite Radio/Kenwood Dodge
17	23	1	Steve Park	Pennzoil Chevrolet
18	6	20	Tony Stewart	The Home Depot Pontiac
19	9	28	Ricky Rudd	Havoline Ford
20	36	29	Kevin Harvick	GM Goodwrench Service Chevrolet
21	2	8	Dale Earnhardt Jr.	Budweiser Chevrolet
22	14	40	Jamie McMurray	Coors Light Dodge
23	8	23	Kenny Wallace	Hills Bros Coffee Dodge
24	27	32	Ricky Craven	Tide Ford
25	5	44	Greg Biffle	Georgia Pacific/Brawny Dodge
26	39	31	Robby Gordon	Cingular Wireless Chevrolet
27	22	36	Ken Schrader	M&M's Pontiac
28	30	5	Terry Labonte	Kellogg's Chevrolet
29	35	18	Bobby Labonte	Interstate Batteries Pontiac
30	32	60	Jack Sprague	NetZero/Haas Automation Chevrolet
31	33	45	Kyle Petty	Sprint Dodge
32	42	26	Geoffrey Bodine	Discover Card Ford
33	31	19	Jeremy Mayfield	Dodge Dealers/UAW Dodge
34	43	49	Derrike Cope	BAM Racing Dodge
35	29	7	Jason Leffler	Sirius Satellite Radio Dodge
36	41	4	Mike Skinner	Kodak Chevrolet
37	12	91	Casey Atwood	Mountain Dew Dodge
38	38	30	Jeff Green	America Online Chevrolet
39	21	43	John Andretti	Chex by Petty Dodge
40	13	17	Matt Kenseth	DEWALT Power Tools Ford
41	11	15	Michael Waltrip	NAPA Chevrolet
42	3	41	Jimmy Spencer	Target Dodge
43	25	77	Dave Blaney	Jasper Engines & Transmissions Ford

Reflections 2002
NASCAR
Winston Cup
Series
Bud

OFFICIAL
NASCAR
Winston Cup
Series

(Right) When fans arrived in Sonoma, Calif., for the Dodge/Save Mart 350, many were surprised to find the name of the speedway had changed overnight to Infineon Raceway, joining Lowe's Motor Speedway as the only two venues to contract naming rights from corporate sponsors – so far.

(Below) Speedweeks 2002 marked the end of an era when Dave Marcis hung up his helmet after competing in his 33rd Daytona 500 (right). After 882 starts, mostly in his own cars, Marcis remains active in the sport and, during the year, could be seen talkin' racin' with the likes of Richard Petty, with whom he competed for more than 30 years.

Joe Nemechek rode the emotional roller coaster in 2002, but came away smiling as the season drew to a close. Contracted to drive the No. 26 Fords for Haas/Carter Motorsports at the beginning of the year, Joe could only watch as sponsorship money from Kmart dried up just as the season began. After seven starts for the financially-strapped team, Joe then filled in for injured Johnny Benson in one event before taking the wheel of the No. 25 Chevrolet at Hendrick Motorsports. With a fourth place at Kansas and a second at Atlanta as the season wound down, Hendrick signed Nemechek to remain with the team in 2003.

Stacy Compton (14) and Elliott Sadler (21) found each other competing for room at Martinsville in April, and example of the rubbing and paint swapping that was commonplace on the ultra-competitive short tracks. After competing in 18 events, Compton found himself looking for a ride when owner A.J. Foyt released him from his duties. Sadler, on the other hand, shocked some with his mid-season announcement that he intended to leave the Wood Brothers at year's end, sparking the unofficial beginning of silly season.

Motorcraft
QUALITY PARTS
Ford Motor Company
21
Goodwrench
Snap-on
SYLVANIA
OREO
29
REALTREE
76

(Top) At California Speedway, Jimmie Johnson got a little lesson from Rick Hendrick in how to celebrate a NASCAR Winston Cup Series victory. By this, the 10th race of the season and the 13th start of his young career, Johnson had many garage watchers wide-eyed with two Bud Poles and seven top-seven finishes to start a brilliant rookie campaign.

(Middle) Bobby Labonte was all smiles at Martinsville in April after scoring his first career win on a short track. Uncharacteristically inconsistent in the first eight events of the season, Bobby felt this win would get his Interstate team back on track for a run at a second championship.

(Bottom) Brothers Todd (left) and Brett Bodine were caught chatting at Pocono in June. After starting the season still looking for sponsorship on his Fords, Brett got together with Hooters at Atlanta in March, a deal that quickly developed into a season-long package for the independent team. Todd also began the year sans sponsorship after Kmart left, and Todd missed nine events before Haas/Carter Motorsports inked a deal with Discover Card that continued for the rest of the season.

(Above) Ryan Newman gets belted up in the Darlington garage for the fifth race of the season. By then, he had already qualified on the front row twice and would start third here. By the end of the year, his qualifying prowess resulted in a rookie-record six Bud Poles and the annual Bud Pole Award.

(Far Left) The 2002 season was somewhat of a coming out party for sophomore driver Kurt Busch. After picking up his initial NASCAR Winston Cup Series win at Bristol in March, Busch put together back-to-back wins at Martinsville and Atlanta in October and finished the season among the top five in the point standings.

(Left) Bill Elliott felt like a million dollars after driving to the win in the Brickyard 400 in one of the biggest victories of his career. Elliott had broken into victory lane a week earlier at Pocono and felt as though his Dodge team was building steam toward a title run.

(Right) The Caterpillar Dodge crew whooped it up at Daytona after Ward Burton scored the win for team owner Bill Davis and crew chief Tommy Baldwin in the season-opening Daytona 500. Burton scored a second win at New Hampshire in July and was signed to a contract extension before the year was out.

(Below Right) At Rockingham in early November, Johnny Benson added his name to the first-time winners' list, joining Kurt Busch, Jimmie Johnson, Ryan Newman and Jamie McMurray in that category for the season. Benson's team had shown its strength on several occasions over the past few years, and this win was extremely popular among fans and competitors alike.

(Below) Richard Childress watched his three teams all year long, but the success he expected seemed elusive for the most part. Kevin Harvick picked up a win at Chicagoland, which accounted for the only victory at RCR in an uncharacteristically off year.

(Above) Matt Kenseth and crew chief Robbie Reiser (left) had their entire package in good working order throughout the season. Their first win came in the second race of the year at Rockingham, which sent Kenseth into a few celebratory spins (above right) – a scene worth repeating on four other occasions during the year as the DeWalt team scored a series-leading five victories.

(Left) Team owners Rick Hendrick (left) and Roger Penske each were given plenty of reasons to smile by young and old alike in 2002. Their "young" drivers, Jimmie Johnson and Ryan Newman, enjoyed great success in their torrid battle for rookie honors, while their "old" drivers, Jeff Gordon and Rusty Wallace, spent mid-season in contention for the title. In the end, all four drivers landed squarely among the top 10 in the final point standings.

The turning point in Tony Stewart's season came here, at Watkins Glen in August. A season so far marked by inconsistency had culminated the week before when a frustrated Stewart had an altercation with a photographer after a 12th-place run at Indianapolis. The highly-publicized incident drew the ire of NASCAR and team sponsor Home Depot, and Tony responded the way he knew best – by winning. His emotional victory at The Glen vaulted him from seventh to fourth in the standings, and from there, Stewart was brilliant for the rest of the season.

MOOG
CHASSIS PARTS
CLEVITE
WIX
FILTERS
76
Edelbrock
MBNA
3M
Bud
24

(Right) Veteran drivers and longtime friends Ken Schrader (left) and Terry Labonte enjoy a couple of laughs before getting down to Sunday business. Schrader's season was highlighted by an outside pole at Rockingham, while Labonte showed he could still scald a road course with a third place at Sonoma, California.

(Below Right) History was made in 2002 when Hideo Fukuyama (left) became the first Japanese driver to compete in the NASCAR Winston Cup Series. Fukuyama drove at Dover in September and at Martinsville in October, wheeling a Ford fielded by Travis Carter (right).

Autographs 2002

UMI Publications, Inc. publishes The Official NASCAR Preview and Press Guide.
For subscription information, call 1-704-374-0420 or visit our web site at www.umipub.com.